D1766833

Engaging with Student Voice in Research,
Education and Community

Nicole Mockler • Susan Groundwater-Smith

Engaging with Student Voice in Research, Education and Community

Beyond Legitimation and Guardianship

 Springer

Nicole Mockler
University of Newcastle
Ourimbah
New South Wales
Australia

Susan Groundwater-Smith
University of Sydney
Sydney
New South Wales
Australia

ISBN 978-3-319-01984-0   ISBN 978-3-319-01985-7 (eBook)
DOI 10.1007/978-3-319-01985-7
Springer Cham Heidelberg New York Dordrecht London

Library of Congress Control Number: 2014951519

© Springer International Publishing Switzerland 2015
This work is subject to copyright. All rights are reserved by the Publisher, whether the whole or part of the material is concerned, specifically the rights of translation, reprinting, reuse of illustrations, recitation, broadcasting, reproduction on microfilms or in any other physical way, and transmission or information storage and retrieval, electronic adaptation, computer software, or by similar or dissimilar methodology now known or hereafter developed. Exempted from this legal reservation are brief excerpts in connection with reviews or scholarly analysis or material supplied specifically for the purpose of being entered and executed on a computer system, for exclusive use by the purchaser of the work. Duplication of this publication or parts thereof is permitted only under the provisions of the Copyright Law of the Publisher's location, in its current version, and permission for use must always be obtained from Springer. Permissions for use may be obtained through RightsLink at the Copyright Clearance Center. Violations are liable to prosecution under the respective Copyright Law.
The use of general descriptive names, registered names, trademarks, service marks, etc. in this publication does not imply, even in the absence of a specific statement, that such names are exempt from the relevant protective laws and regulations and therefore free for general use.
While the advice and information in this book are believed to be true and accurate at the date of publication, neither the authors nor the editors nor the publisher can accept any legal responsibility for any errors or omissions that may be made. The publisher makes no warranty, express or implied, with respect to the material contained herein.

Printed on acid-free paper

Springer is part of Springer Science+Business Media (www.springer.com)

Contents

Part I
The Field Today

In this opening section, we map the contemporary 'field' of student voice and explore current social and policy contexts with regard to the use of student voice. In constructing this 'mapping', we are acutely aware of the long and rich history of student voice work, internationally: ideas about the importance of students engaging as active agents and participants in their learning go back to the multiple works of John Dewey in the early Twentieth century, whose ideas are very closely connected to the basis of contemporary approaches to student voice. Our concern in this section is to contextualise our discussion of student voice work theoretically, politically and in terms of key contemporary conceptualisations of 'student voice'.

We explore the participation of children and young people in research, developing a theoretical case for the creation of authentic, dialogic conditions that transcend consulting children and young people for the purposes of human capital development. We argue for the primacy of the more profound and robust question of education for citizenship and democracy. We use critical social theory as reflected in the work of Habermas and draw upon issues of dialogue, power and participation to identify challenging practices in educational institutions, constituting young people as agents within their communities.

In Chap. 3, we build on this theoretical foundation to consider the contemporary social and policy context of student voice work. Against a backdrop of the current push for compliance entrenched in neoliberal approaches to education, we argue that student voice work, understood in the context of democratic education, can offer an avenue for resistance. It is a participative process providing schools and teachers with a framework for action and practice that might be employed to 'push back' against the narrow and impoverished view of education encapsulated in the compliance agenda.

Finally, we explore the rationale for democratic student agency as it exists in the field of student voice work, problematising in the process the widely-adopted and seldom questioned principle of 'student empowerment' as a tenet of student voice. Furthermore, drawing links between student voice work and participatory action research or practitioner inquiry, we explore and trouble the framework of evidence-based practice as it has been employed within education and the place of student voice work in this context. We work with alternative approaches to student voice, arguing that a more appropriate rationale for this work lies in the building of democratic practices and student agency within schools and other educational institutions.

Chapter 1
Introduction: Beyond Legitimation and Guardianship

'Student voice', its articulation and integration into decision-making processes in schools and other educational and youth-focused institutions has become increasingly popular in recent years. Under the guise of 'evidence based practice', processes of gathering and using data from school and university students and other young people have been integrated into quality assurance regimes across a wide variety of contexts including schools and universities.

In this book we seek to interrupt the student voice juggernaut, asking what we regard as important questions about the use of student voice. Far from arguing *against* the importance of seeking to listen to, understand and respond to the concerns, perceptions and perspectives of young people, we aim to render problematic both the discourse of 'empowerment' surrounding the notion of consulting young people as well as the instrumentalist drive to utilise the voices of students and other young people as part of the 'what works' (Atkinson 2000; Biesta 2007; Mockler 2011) agenda.

We are mindful that research, be it with children and young people, or with others participating in one social act or another is always political. Santos (2012, p. 114), in writing of participatory action research writes that it is essentially so:

> since it entails human beings coming together, aiming to help identify and bring about suitable and meaningful forms of organisation—the *polis* through which members of communities—the polity can achieve their common goals.

This holds particularly so when considering the positioning of children and young people in relation to power and authority. Even with goodwill and determination it is difficult to dispute the discussion by Arnot and Reay (2007) that young people's voices are created by the relations in which they find themselves rather than in circumstances that are needed for change and reform.

Nonetheless, the case for consulting children and young people has been recognised, even sanctified by the United Nations.

© Springer International Publishing Switzerland 2015
N. Mockler, S. Groundwater-Smith, *Engaging with Student Voice in Research, Education and Community*, DOI 10.1007/978-3-319-01985-7_1

The Case for Consulting Young People

The United Nations Convention on the Rights of the Child, endorsed by the UN General Assembly in 1989, sets out the civil, cultural, economic, political and social rights of people under the age of 18 in its 54 articles and two optional protocols. The four core principles underpinning the Convention are as follows:

- non-discrimination;
- devotion to the best interests of the child;
- the right to life, survival and development; and
- respect for the views of the child.

The Convention is comprehensive and entitles children to a broad range of rights including, *inter alia,* the right:

- to express views in all decisions that affect them and the opportunity to be heard in any court or administrative proceedings;
- to freedom of expression and the right to seek, receive and impart information of all kinds;
- to have their best interests treated as a primary consideration in all actions concerning them, including decision relation to their care and protection;
- to free education available on the basis of their capacity; and
- to enjoy the highest attainable standard of health and an adequate standard of living.

In particular, Article 12 indicates that:

> States Parties shall assure to the child who is capable of forming his or her own views the right to express those views freely in all matters affecting the child, the views of the child being given due weight in accordance with the age and maturity of the child. (United Nations 1989)

In this way the Convention recognises that children have particular needs and vulnerabilities which require special protection beyond the rights to which adults are entitled. Further, it establishes four principles to guide the interpretation of the Convention and assist countries in implementing their obligations these being: (i) non-discrimination; (ii) that the best interests of the child must be a primary consideration in all decisions concerning children; (iii) the right to survival; and iv) the development and respect for the views of the child. Thus these rights outline the minimum standards necessary to ensure the wellbeing of children—including the right to an adequate standard of living, the right to health care, the right to education, the right to family life, the right to protection from violence, and the right to participate in one's culture.

The UN Convention on the Rights of the Child (UNCRC) is the most widely ratified human rights instrument in history (Payne 2009), with all but two of the 194 member countries of the United Nations (Somalia and the United States of America) having ratified the Convention to date (UNICEF 2012). However, while it may be said that significant advances have been made in providing organizational means for children's views to be heard through such mechanisms as Children's Commissioners and Ombudsmen, further sustaining and developing opportunities for young people to be fully engaged in those social agencies that govern their lives remains a challenge. The actualizing of these mechanisms cannot be said to have permeated more generally into services such as schooling, health and justice in ways that enable children and young people to be genuinely participative in processes of decision-making about issues of importance to them.

As a driver the UNCRC clearly gives legitimacy to consulting children and young people in diverse contexts, however, it is also the case that there is not a strong tradition of children's rights contributing to meaningful decision making regarding issues of significance and importance to them (Wisby 2011).

In this book, we aim to explore the expressive, referential, interactional, and social implications of seeking and listening to the voices of young people, within educational and cultural settings, both through the enactment of participatory research and also through the privileging of student voice in the everyday practices of these institutions. Our stance is such that we recognise not only the desirability of doing so, but the necessity of engaging with young people in ongoing and authentic dialogue if we are to realise the democratic, pedagogical and social aims of education in the twenty first century.

We recognise that following this call does not constitute an easy path: in many ways this kind of engagement is countercultural in times when, as we shall discuss below, instrumentalist discourses are powerful and intransigent; furthermore, the multifaceted ethical considerations embedded in this work can also add to the complexity of its enactment within educational and other communities. Nonetheless, we believe that the enterprise is more than worth the opportunity cost required for a more authentic inclusion of the contribution of children and young people who are often left at the margins of social enterprise.

In the remainder of this introductory chapter, we explore three concepts key to the notion of seeking and listening to student voice, namely the context of 'evidence based practice' as enacted within education and other social service fields over the past decades; the role of student voice in the development of 'person-centred learning communities'; and the different levels of student voice engagement in educational communities and the implications of these. Each of these key concepts will be further expanded in subsequent chapters within the book. We conclude this introductory chapter with an overview of the remainder of the book.

Subverting the Dominant Paradigm: Evidence Based Practice and 'What Works'

The notion of evidence based practice in education has grown steadily since the 1990s, when David Hargreaves invoked medical-style evidence-based practice as a 'way forward' for the teaching profession (1996) in a drive to uncover and implement 'what works' (Hargreaves 1997). Here, as elsewhere (Groundwater-Smith et al. 2013), we wish to render problematic the very notion of evidence-based practice in education, arguing, along with others (e.g. Biesta 2007; Elliott 2001), that the narrow notions of 'evidence' inevitably embedded and enacted within a highly positivistic frame serve schools, teachers and the education enterprise very poorly indeed, despite serving compliance agendas perfectly well.

Our understanding of the notion of evidence in educational settings is informed by the Stenhousian notion of 'research based teaching' (Stenhouse 1983), which, interestingly, considering the focus of this book, is dually focused on issues of pedagogy and research. As John Elliott writes:

> For Stenhouse, *research-based teaching* is an implication of a theory of education that places induction into knowledge structures at its centre, and then characterises them as *objects for speculative thought*. This theory of education implies a logical framework for a teaching and learning process. At the centre of this framework is a pedagogical aim.... (Elliott 2001, p. 81)

Within Stenhouse's notion of research based teaching, evidence (broadly defined), teacher professional judgement, and the inquiry process itself form the basis for both teacher and, in turn, student learning. For Stenhouse, inquiry and teaching and learning are inseparable in the context of classroom practice, and here we find two key questions and concepts to which we shall return over the course of this book.

First, our advocacy of and belief in the importance of systematically gathering, listening to and integrating student voice into decision making processes, from the voices of those beginning their schooling through to those of students engaged in tertiary learning, relies on a particularly broad understanding of what 'evidence' is and how we believe it should be used. We are not advocating here an instrumentalist or compliance-driven model of 'student feedback', but rather a rich and complex process whereby teachers, students and others engaged in the education process work together to ask about, explain and listen to each others' perspectives. Such evidence is to be treated in a way more 'forensic' than 'adversarial' reaching toward what Michael Fielding (2011) has termed 'intergenerational learning as lived democracy', enacted within a context of democratic fellowship.

Second, we believe that the issue of privileging student voice in the context of practitioner inquiry raises many questions and implications for educational practice. Ethical and democratic classroom practice, we believe, engages students consistently in discussion of the processes and practices of learning, supports their metacognitive capacities and their capacity to make good decisions about their learning, and builds trust and respect between students and teachers. We do not believe that the use of 'student voice' within school or university communities should be confined to the peripherals of schooling, such as canteen menus and school uniforms, but rather that working authentically with student voice necessitates and ongoing pedagogical dialogue played out in classrooms on a consistent basis. For these are the communicative contexts within which exchanges may be fractured and fragmented or developed as coherent dialogic conditions for powerful and meaningful learning.

Educational Institutions as 'Person-Centred Learning Communities'

Fielding (2008) uses philosopher John Macmurray's distinction between functional and personal relations to explore the differences between schools as 'high performance learning organisations' and 'person-centred learning communities'. Fielding's conclusion is that 'high performance learning organisations' tend to privilege functional relations, "those that are overwhelmingly instrumental in their intention and expression and are defined by their purposes" (p. 61), using personal relations, those that "we enter into … with others because it is through them that we can be and become ourselves" (*ibid.*) for the sake of these. On the other hand, 'person-centred learning communities' tend to utilise the functional for the sake of developing the personal. The difference is a subtle but important one, described by Fielding thus:

> In essence we are talking about one mode which says 'Have a nice day' as part of a human relations mantra, and another mode which is genuinely welcoming and engaging of us; one mode which uses extra time for tutorials to jack up test scores, and another that places personal encounter through dialogue at the very heart of its daily educational processes and intentions; one in which the new sanctioning of creativity and personalisation is primarily the servant of the same narrow standards agenda, and another in which creativity and the engagement with young people as persons is the harbinger of a much richer, more demanding fulfilment of education for and in a democratic society. They are worlds apart; their felt realties are utterly at odds with each other. And yet, it is not always clear which frame is dominant, whose purposes are being served, whether we are the victims of those whose interests are quite other than those we would applaud, or whether we are part of something which is likely to turn out to be fulfilling and worthy of our support. In sum, it is not clear whether personalisation is a seductive re-articulation of corporate insinuation or a genuinely different orientation to what we do and how we might do it. (2008, p. 63)

In short, this is the difference between two sets of schools or organisations that claim to put 'relationships' at the heart of their enterprise. On the one hand, we see those organisations that privilege the instrumental, perhaps having taken on what Peter Taubman has called the "melancholic embrace" of audit (2009, p. 150), associated with the production of what Power (2003) has drawn as "the auditee":

> The auditee is undoubtedly a complex being: simultaneously devious and depressed; she is skilled at games of compliance but exhausted and cynical about them too; she is nervous about the empty certificates of comfort that get produced but she also colludes in amplifying audit mandates in local settings; she fears the mediocrity of the auditors at the same time as she regrets their powerlessness to discipline the "really bad guys"; she loathes the time wasted in rituals of inspection but accepts that this is probably what "we deserve"; she sees the competent and excellent suffer as they attempt to deal with the demands of quality assurance at the same time as the incompetent and idle manage to escape its worst excesses; she hears the rhetoric of excellence in official documents but lives a reality of decline; she takes notes after meetings with colleagues "just in case" and has more filing cabinets now than she did a few years ago; she knows the past was far from being a golden age but despairs of the iron cage of auditing; she knows public accountability and stakeholder dialogue are good things but wonders why, after all her years of training, she is not trusted as an expert anymore. (2003, p. 199–200)

On the other hand, we see schools and organisations where the seductive powers of audit and instrumentalism have not been so strong, where trust typically permeates and audit cultures, inescapable as they may be in the contemporary age, are seen more as a necessary evil than as a raison d'etre.

The strength of audit cultures within higher education and other public institutions can often obscure the voices of children and young people, simultaneously emphasising the importance of 'feedback' while at the same time failing to foster the authentic and ongoing discussions about learning that are the hallmarks of real learning communities. One of our intentions in this book is to explore the impact of audit upon educational institutions and understand the ways in which cultures of audit undermine real community, particularly in relation to student voice.

The authentic and consistent integration of student voice is both a marker of and an obligation for schools that aim to function as person centred learning communities. We believe strongly that the 'community' dimension implies an ongoing dialogue on the part of all community members, an understanding that different individuals play different roles within the community, but also, a willingness to be open and respectful of the voices of those who might otherwise wield less power despite having at least as much invested in the educative process as others.

Beyond Legitimation and Guardianship: Not All 'Student Voice' is Equal

As alluded to in the sections above, a variety of different approaches to and 'uses' of student voice can be identified: some supporting the development of generative learning communities and others feeding more instrumentalist agendas. This can be said to hold for students at all levels of the educational provision, from early childhood to tertiary engagement. For example, the rise of audit cultures in universities, closely linked to the commodification of higher education and the positioning of students as 'consumers' of a product, has led to a widespread adoption of 'student voice' as a marketing tool. In situations such as this, it could be argued that feedback from students is wielded as something of a blunt instrument and used in a purely transactional manner, generally not reaching what we would consider to constitute authentic engagement. In a similar manner in the UK the requirement of the British Education Act 2002 has placed a duty on schools and local authorities to consult young people about decisions affecting them, thus the Office for Standards in Education, Children's Services and Skills (OFSTED) requires the systematic collection of the views of children and young people, but whether these are ultimately employed as celebratory accounts or authentic critiques of practice may be seen as a moot point. In a contrary way it has also been possible to use (or mis-use) the voices of young people to impose impossible conditions on educational institutions. Stronach's poignant account of the demise of Summer hill points to little attention being paid to the views of those who would be most affected by the changing of the school's ethos (2002).

Michael Fielding (2011) has elaborated a hierarchy of interaction between adults and young people in educational contexts. The typology, entitled *Patterns of partnership: How adults listen to and learn with students in schools*, comprises the following:

1. Students as data source—in which staff utilise information about student progress and well-being
2. Students as active respondents—in which staff invite student dialogue and discussion to deepen learning/professional decisions
3. Students as co-enquirers—in which staff take a lead role with high-profile, active student support
4. Students as knowledge creators—in which students take lead roles with active staff support
5. Students as joint authors—in which students and staff decide on a joint course of action together
6. Intergenerational learning as participatory democracy—in which there is a shared commitment to/responsibility for the common good (Fielding 2011, p. 67)

While Fielding conceptualises the forms of interaction as manifesting differing power relations, he is clear that all types of engagement, from teachers utilising test scores to make judgements about the best course of action for individual students (i.e. 'students as data source') to situations in which students and teachers work together to plan learning experiences (i.e. 'intergenerational learning as participatory democracy') constitute authentic engagement. Over the years, we have been involved with many school and institutional contexts where staff and students have engaged at all six levels, often in a sequential or semi-sequential process, where, for example, teachers find that 'mining' student results to inform teacher decision-making opens the door to seeking out more active dialogue with students regarding their learning, which in turn opens the door to working alongside students in the course of inquiry, and so on. The case studies presented in Part II of this book explore a range of ways in which adults working in schools, cultural institutions and universities can and do engage young people and the conditions and dispositions that foster authentic engagement.

The Structure of this Book

This book is presented in three parts, focusing variously upon the mapping of the field and current policy and social contexts; case study examples from a variety of different contexts; and finally, philosophical and practical perspectives on how to engage with student voice in research, classroom and other institutional contexts, such that ongoing and authentic dialogue with students becomes not only part of 'what we do' in educational communities but indeed shapes 'who we are'.

Chapter 2 develops the theoretical case for the creation of authentic, dialogic conditions that transcend consulting children and young people for the purposes of human capital development, and recaptures the more profound question of education for citizenship. Here, we use as reference points critical social theory as reflected in the work of, among others, Habermas, and Bourdieu.

Chapter 3 takes up the key issues raised in this introductory chapter and the theoretical foundations chapter, and explores the tension between the current push for compliance and approaches to education and inclusion that seek to legitimately enfranchise young people. We explore more fully the impact of compliance and audit on educational and other public institutions and highlight the ways in which these can be counterproductive to the kinds of democratic practices we are arguing for.

In *Chap. 4*, we explore the rationale for democratic student agency and problematise the widely-adopted notion of 'student empowerment' and the framework of evidence-based practice as it has been employed within education. In this chapter we work with the 'ladder of participation' to consider what it means for the involvement of children and young people in research and inquiry as well as the implications for classroom practice and pedagogy of young people's active engagement in dialogue and decision making about their education.

Chapter 5 marks the beginning of Part 2, in which we outline three cases located in Australia, but clearly having a wider application, as narratives of practice, designed to elicit principles of practice which will be further explored in Part 3. The case embedded in Chap. 5 elaborates the experience of a comprehensive government co-educational high school that has, for four years invited mainly Year nine students to investigate the school they would like, the learning they would like, the student that they would like to be and what they would like to learn.

The case embedded in *Chap. 6* relates to cooperating with learner services offered by cultural institutions outside the classroom. The case study will draw on our experiences working with organisations such as The Australian Museum, the NSW State Library and Taronga Zoo Education to examine the ways in which student voice contributes to 'audience research' in these contexts and the part young people can and do play in shaping the pedagogical intent and practice of organisations such as these.

In *Chap. 7*, we explore the development of sustainable and collaborative partnerships (including those with health, recreation and environmental agencies). By moving beyond school education to consider the ways in which the voices of children and young people can make a meaningful contribution to services designed for them in such varied contexts as juvenile justice and town planning we explore ways in which new models of participation might be built.

In *Chap. 8*, the context of higher education is explored. Here we examine and critique the trend to collect student feedback through student satisfaction with teaching and learning and resource management as a measure of 'service quality' typically using 'one-off' inventories. We explore the implications of these approaches using our participatory lens.

Part 3, encompassing Chaps. 9 to 12, explores philosophical and practical perspectives on engaging with student voice across different educational and community contexts. In *Chap. 9*, we explore an assembly of methods for engaging students in participatory inquiry, including surveys, observations, interviews (individual and group), using visual processes and social media. Here we aim to provide a rationale for the use of different methods in participatory research with young people, and argue for the use of different strategies and approaches at different stages.

Chapter 10 explores the emerging ethical issues in researching with children and young people as the practice has burgeoned and evolved. While originally the concern was to minimise harm, we argue that a more nuanced understanding of power relations is required, such that the goals of ethical praxis and those embedded in the United Nations Declaration on the Rights of the Child, are honoured.

Chapter 11 focuses on the links between pedagogical reform and student voice, and the implications of the authentic embedding of student voice in educational cultures for pedagogical practice. Here we highlight the links between inquiry and pedagogy, and explore the kinds of pedagogical practices that align with the democratic values embedded in authentic learning communities and those that might hinder or undermine participatory and democratic practice.

Finally, in *Chap. 12* we develop a 'charter for reform'. We argue for a critical alignment of epistemology, principles and practices, and suggest ways in which practitioners and leaders in schools, universities and other institutions might work to bring about this alignment to the benefit of their students and communities more broadly.

Contemporary expressions of 'student voice work' are often limited to the use of students as data source: most generally, it is used to legitimate decisions taken by adults within the community and to position the most powerful members of the community as guardians of the status quo while at the same time paying lip service to democratic practices. Our argument in this book is that if schools and other institutions are to function as places where human beings and human community flourish, a different vision must be employed. In short, we must push student voice work 'beyond legitimation and guardianship' (Fielding and Moss 2011). While we do not claim to have all the answers as to what this vision might look like and how it might function in the myriad of educational and other communities that might wish to take it up, we do wish that our writing and the many examples that we have selected can act as provocations for those who would desire to do things differently. Indeed, we would argue, such an approach runs counter to our ongoing critique of 'what works', and rather moves towards multiple and various possibilities that can lead to authentic transformations in practice.

Chapter 2
Theorising the Participation of Children and Young People in Research

In this discussion, in which we identify the conditions under which the participation of children and young people in research and inquiry can be theoretically understood, we are mindful that while the emphasis is upon students in schools we also argue that they can also apply to students in higher education, albeit somewhat differently. Certainly such students may well be mature and not come under the United Nations Convention of the Rights of the Child (aged 0–18 years) but their relative status within the structure of universities and colleges remains similar. This will become evident later, in the section of this book that draws upon examples from the field. We also will be considering the participative conditions for children and young people in research and inquiry in relation to their wider engagement in the community.

Creating Authentic Dialogic Conditions

Before more fully exploring the case for the creation of authentic, dialogic conditions for engaging with children and young people about events and policies that govern their lives through research and inquiry we turn to one of social psychology's notorious experiments that can be perceived as a touchstone for the ways in which various research enterprises have exploited and deceived young people in the past. We do this both to demonstrate the distance that has been travelled, and the need for continuing vigilance regarding what may seem more benign processes but ones that continue to require our attention if we are to move beyond legitimation and guardianship.

Inside the Robbers Cave

Over fifty years ago a well-regarded social psychologist, Muzafer Sherif, brought two groups of eleven and twelve year old boys to a summer camp in a small national

© Springer International Publishing Switzerland 2015

N. Mockler, S. Groundwater-Smith, *Engaging with Student Voice in Research, Education and Community,* DOI 10.1007/978-3-319-01985-7_2

park in Oklahoma. The experiment was designed such that the boys' behaviour could be studied, analysed and discussed in the context of cold war discourses regarding war, difference, prejudice and discrimination. The boys had been carefully selected from middle class families to take part in, for what seemed to them, an exciting three weeks of outdoor activity (Sherif et al. 1988). Researchers, doubling as counsellors divided the boys into two social groups and constructed circumstances where they would come into conflict with one another. Initially, each group did not know of the other group's existence. The object of the study was to observe how the boys dealt with friction that had resulted, for example, from the unfair distribution of prizes during various competitions between the two groups. Then, later, the objective shifted to how the groups reduced the conflict that had been constructed when faced with the achievement of tasks that required intergroup cooperation (Sidanius and Pratto 1999).

In a recent Australian Broadcasting Corporation program, *Hindsight,* Gina Perry, a well regarded psychologist and investigator of the Milgram experiments[1] (Perry 2012) created an episode that featured interviews with, among others, some of the boys who had participated in the experiment—boys who were now mature men (ABC radio 2013). A number expressed dismay at the ways in which they had been misled and portrayed. As one put it:

> I don't remember it as a bad experience, viscerally. It's in retrospect reading these transcripts, I ask myself, 'who are these bastards?'... These men taking notes and pictures of kids struggling over a tug of war? It's not a bad thing, but it was the wrong thing to do morally (3 min prior to the conclusion of the broadcast)

Although memories were now fading the participants maintained that their own recollections of their experiences could have been related in a very different voice. The study collected only the observations of the investigators, whose beliefs and desires for a particular outcome were seen to shape their observations. Staff appeared to "play to the script" and to "push things along in line with the hypothesis".

In an interview, re-played in the broadcast, Sharif was asked whether he saw any ethical problem with an experiment that was designed to deceive those who took part, his answer was "No, not at all." It has since been pointed out that codes of practice for organisations such as the American Psychological Association (APA) are not grounded in moral philosophy (Kimmel 2007). However, our argument throughout this book is that engaging in participative research with children and young people **is** a moral enterprise that has at its heart a democratic impulse.

We turn, then, to consider more fully the case for authentic dialogic conditions for working with children and young people in inquiry settings under the broad category of 'student voice'.

---

[1] The Milgram experiments were a series of social psychology experiments designed to measure the ways in which participants were willing to obey a person with authority who required them to perform a series of electric shocks in conflict with their conscience. Perry believed that just as these experiments were coercive and unethical, so too were the Sherif experiments with young people.

Authentic Dialogic Conditions for Working with Children and Young People

Engaging in dialogue, in conversation, in interaction with one another is a fundamental human activity and one that is ordinarily taken for granted. But the conditions for taking part in such activity will significantly moderate who can say what, when and how. We may well argue that the conditions that ordinarily prevail in educational practices may not always allow for "conversation", in that the moderators relate closely to issues of power and authority. Thus in theorising the participation of children and young people in inquiry that requires reciprocity and respect and which embodies concepts of active citizenship as opposed to a purpose of human capital development, it is essential to examine the prevailing conditions, and, in particular the ways in which the exercise of power plays out in education settings. Kazepides (2012, p. 914) talks of education as dialogue that is undoubtedly normative, ideally being in every sense caring, engaging and inseparable from the demands of reason. He sees reasoning as embodying the principles of freedom, truth telling and respect for others. This position stands in contrast to Smyth & McInerney's view regarding those for whom mainstream schooling has failed when they write such young people "are the most salient witnesses of what occurs in schools and classrooms, yet at the same time they are the most marginalized and excluded" (Smyth and McInerney 2012, p. 3) a matter to which we return in Chap. 7.

The Dialogic Process

Initially the issues that we wish to discuss here arise from understandings of Habermasian concepts of the dialogic process, or as Linklater (2005) has characterised them, "dialogic politics". Linklater refers us to the matter as to whether engaging in dialogue is a civilising process based upon the rights of the speaker to be heard under circumstances that are fair to all. This resonates to the conditions that Habermas (1974, 1984) first articulated when he wrote of the "ideal speech situation" (ISS) where he identified four conditions for authentic dialogue: that no one who is capable of making a relevant contribution has been excluded; that all participants have an equal voice; that they are free to speak to their opinions without deceiving others or themselves; and, that there is no coercion built into the processes or procedures of the discourse. This can be said to contribute to a well conducted 'language game' (McCarthy 1976, p. xiii–xiv).

The employment of the word 'ideal' should enable us to understand that Habermas did not see such interaction as a normal feature of human communication. Indeed it is counterfactual and what we must be alert to is the distortion to the communicative possibilities that arise as we struggle for understanding one another. The ISS is an aspiration and can become the basis by which we can recognise asymmetry or mismatches. The most systematically distorting feature for Habermas (1984, p. 332) is the extent of the participants' desire to succeed in socially competitive situations versus the desire to reach understanding. "Such communication patholo-gies can be conceived of as the result of a confusion between actions oriented to reaching understanding and actions oriented to success".

Linklater sees that this tussle establishes "a need for permanent openness to dia-logue" as social structures grow, wither or change. While he does not specifically consider schools in his exegesis, it is within these contexts that much of our discus-sion is grounded as we ask ourselves 'how within such structures it is possible to maintain an openness to dialogue without it becoming a power struggle?'

To reiterate, the position taken by Habermas, his discussion of the ISS both in his early and later work, rests on the claim that individuals have the right to be con-sulted about decisions that affect them and to be protected from both intended and unintended forms of harm. This position challenges the ways in which barriers are constructed that prevent full participation in the discourses and decisions that arise from them by less privileged and less powerful groups, in the case of our discussion, children and young people. Thus, Linklater rightly sees the need for a core com-mitment to discourse ethics, that all human beings have a right to participate in the communities to which they belong and that their freedoms grow from non-coercive communication. Clearly, then, the process is one that is political and being political must take account of the ways in which power is exercised in the relationships be-tween children, young people, and the adults with whom they engage, in particular in school settings.

Devine (2002, p. 303) insists that a theory of power is central to any discussion of children's rights in having a voice and being heard. Her discussion is grounded in a discourse of citizenship and the centrality of participation that challenge tra-ditional patterns of association: children with adults, adults with children; students with teachers, teachers with students.

Theorising Issues of Power and Active Citizenship

Power and citizenship as understood by Devine and characterised in terms of iden-tity and belonging is built upon a concept of the development of social capital, that is the social glue that holds individuals, functioning in social institutions such as schools and universities together. Of course the concept has a far wider reach, but for our purposes building social capital in schools, in particular, means creating bonds and bridges that will contribute to and sustain group norms as a form of active citizenship. In the main, these norms are those that are determined by the school's own structure. Although we also admit the caveat that in general school structures are directed to mainstream students, but we argue should also be concerned with those of marginalised and minority groups. As McMurray and Niens (2012, p. 214) have observed participatory processes that aim to promote social capital as citizen-ship need to be well planned and structured to enable young people to work effec-tively together. But they also note the insidious effect of the lack of transparency when social capital is treated unproblematically as if the term and its meaning is agreed by all who participate and all have an equal share.

It is for this reason that examining the nature of power and its manifestation in schools, and indeed in universities, is critical to theorising matters of participation.

Power Cannot be Gifted as a Product, but Understood as a Process

Good hearted though the intentions may be in terms of enabling children and young people to have a voice in their schooling, and in a broader sense, their education, there are structural features that ensure that the distribution of power is unequal. Students may be afforded a voice, but they cannot be 'empowered' as though power is a gift that can be bestowed. As we have already observed, students have a right to be heard; however, there is a persistent perception that those who establish forums for students to engage in meaningful dialogue see themselves doing so as an act of generosity. This issue is of such significance that it will be further discussed in Chap. 4 where we consider manifestations of power in relation to current formulations of evidence based practice—a nostrum of great appeal to those who govern.

While we take issue with Taylor and Robinson (2009, p. 169) in their assertion that Habermasian models of dialogue "posit communication processes as transparent and unproblematic" nonetheless, their stance that takes the matter of power as central to more adequately theorising issues around student voice, leads us to a more critical understanding. They take a clear position when they assert "student voice is a normative project and has its basis in ethical and moral practice which aims to give students the right of democratic participation in school processes" (p. 161). They go on to argue that the relation of voice to power has not received sufficient theoretical attention.

If we see power as a tangible *product* it may then be constructed as some sort of commodity to be transacted and even shared piece by piece. Those who claim that they are 'empowering' students may unwittingly be attempting to diffuse dissent by co-opting their voice. In effect, they may be wishing to enable the less powerful to be treated with respect and consideration and to embolden them to have a capacity to make significant decisions regarding their engagement and wellbeing and ultimately to contribute to the improvement of educational practice, but their intention is to enhance the reputation of the school, or indeed the university or college, rather than the agency of the students. Taylor and Robinson point out that much of the enactment of "student voice" policies has been directed to school improvement around the "present performance-dominated climate" (p. 163) and that students' contributions have been coopted to produce surface compliance. This view could be seen as merely palliative, ensuring an adjustment to norms and conditions inherent in the organisation of educational practices.

However, if we conceive power as an often intangible *process* then access to power becomes a critical and thorny issue. This requires an examination of the underlying structures that determine the distribution and underlying assumptions of the power matrices; that is there is a need to render them visible. When students enter into learning institutions, be they schools, universities or colleges, they are confronted by management practices that have grown over many generations and which may seem to them to be immutable.

Fox (2005) in his examination of the difference between rights and power imbalances argues that robust theories of power need to take account of both power as product and power as process. The Rights of the Child as discussed in our opening chapter may be recognised institutionally but the differentials that exist in such major social settings as cited above may mean that children and young people are not able to claim them. Lundy (2007, p. 933) requires four elements to be satisfied as necessary for the implementation of Article 12 of the UNCRC:

- Space: Children must be given the opportunity to express a view
- Voice: Children must be facilitated to express their views
- Audience: The view must be listened to.
- Influence: The view must be acted upon, as appropriate.

These elements are necessarily influenced by the micro-processes of any given school or place where children and young people are to be engaged in participatory inquiry and research. Furthermore, even with goodwill in many school settings, it is the adults who will decide: when students will meet; where they will meet; how long their meeting may last; and, to what purpose their meeting is conducted (l'Anson 2011). Time and space questions are often treated as unproblematic because they lie at the very heart of the ways in which institutions such as schools are managed. Of all the matters that children and young people can control the timetable is inviolable, particularly in most secondary schools and large universities with their organisation of blocks of learning time and room allocations.

It could be said that the tyranny of the timetable is part and parcel of a custodial regime within school systems where students are required to attend. The parallels between schools and prisons are not as unlikely as they first appear; boredom, fear and powerlessness are but a part of a mix where there are groups that are unequal in terms of power, status and resources. Even the primary school with its greater flexibility is not free from such constraints. Devine (2002, p. 310–311) reported children's comments on the lack of consultation regarding the management of their time

I'd like to be able to choose more… 'cos every day we do the same thing and it gets boring… and if you want to do say PE she wants to do maths or something… she sticks to the same routine all the time. (Boy in fifth class, Hillview)

Sometimes it feels a bit like being a robot… like as if the teacher is in the middle of the room with a great big remote control and you have to be able to do everything she says or you will get into trouble. (Girl in second class, Churchfield)

Just as the provision of time and space is a manifestation of the exercise of power, so too is the matter of 'voice'. In his challenging piece regarding how we position young people as 'learner', 'student' and 'speaker' Biesta (2010) draws our attention, most poignantly, to the last of these. Writing in the context of emancipatory education and invoking the work of Jacques Ranciere, Biesta argues that positioning the student as 'speaker' provides us with a different starting point; one that places power sharing at the commencement of education and not as its end point. It is not merely a matter of those who have the power recognising their students and allowing them to speak, but rather that they should avoid effacing emancipation by valorising instruction—that is telling students what they may speak of.

> The question here is not about who has the ability or capacity to speak—which would at the same time suggest that there are some who are disabled or incapacitated in the domain of speech. The question of who can speak is, in a sense, about who is allowed to speak. But the 'in a sense' is important here, as we shouldn't read 'being allowed' in terms of the master who claims the power to decide whether his learners are allowed to open their mouth or not. (Biesta 2010, p. 545)

This is not only a matter for schools. For example, in our universities, the typical organisation of the curriculum into lectures and tutorials positions the students, with little negotiating power, failing to allow them to become 'speakers'. Hil (2012) refers to the practices of what he calls "production-line teaching" (pp. 101–130) arguing that the university experience has been "de-intellectualised". Teaching-related activities have been standardised, with set templates for course outlines with rigid learning objectives giving students (and indeed lecturers) little agency. Students may be given some opportunities to provide feedback, but only in the terms determined by tick-a-box course evaluations in the form of student experience surveys. Students may be seen, sitting in their serried ranks in lecture theatres, but they are not recognised as being other than respondents to questions determined by others. We take this matter up more fully in Chap. 8.

For Fitzgerald, Graham, Smith and Taylor (2010, p. 295) recognition lies at the heart of participation. The struggle is a one *over* recognition, not only in terms of affirming the young people, but also in recognising how they might contribute:

> Nevertheless, the young people identified limited opportunities for participation and were strongly of the view their 'participation' is experienced as superficial and constrained: About the only thing the SRC [Student Representative Council] did was raise money for Daffodil Day[2]. SRCs are … a popularity contest … it's not necessarily who'll do the best job…

The preposition 'over' is a critical one here. Fitzgerald et al see that more often the discussion is limited to a struggle *for* recognition that eschews a dialogic approach. Seemingly, more often than not, the recognition is accorded by an agent with the power, the school teacher, the university academic, in contrast to when intersubjective norms of recognition are established with each recognising and affirming the other.

As we have noted, listening to and giving due weight to the perspectives and insights of children and young people has been touted as a requirement of the United Nations Rights of the Child. But too often their actual participation in various forms of decision making, research and inquiry is nominal and tokenistic. There is a desire to consult, but only on the terms of the powerful adults who may well mediate who takes part in any systematic process of consulting, research and inquiry. This leads us to consider who may be included and conversely, who is excluded.

---

[2] 'Daffodil Day' is the Australian Cancer Council's largest national fundraising even in which most of the nation's schools participate.

The Politics of Inclusion and Exclusion as a Manifestation of Power

How tempting it is to select those children and young people who will dance to a tune that has already been chosen—that is those students who will be the good ambassadors for the school or institution within a burgeoning culture of neo-liberal economic orthodoxy that markets places for learning as it might the high street shops. While Rudduck and Flutter (2004, p. 137) argued how important it is that the views of a diverse range of students should be sought and that "participation is not just afforded to the articulate and literate" much depends upon what is at stake. In England and Wales, what has been at stake in the past has been very high indeed as consulting students was a central part of Ofsted inspections. For a number of years the managerial hand of Ofsted has played a significant part in insisting that children and young people be consulted; although with little reference to their capacities to undertake research and inquiry. We cite the practice here, as a case. This is in spite of its demise in the new framework for school inspections that removes all pressure on schools to involve their students in self evaluation on the grounds that good schools do this anyway.

The Case of the influence of Ofsted in England and Wales

Until very recently in England and Wales the Office for Standards in Education (Ofsted) required schools to demonstrate effective consultation with students. In spite of the injunction that the schools should work with students from varying backgrounds and abilities, the reports from the office suggest that in only exceptional instances was this the case.

According to 'The Evaluation Schedule for Schools' January 2010 (Teaching Times 2010), Inspectors should evaluate:

- the extent to which pupils, including those from different groups, take on responsibilities and play a part in the school and wider community
- the extent to which pupils, including those from different groups, engage in decision-making or consultation about issues which affect the quality of their learning and well-being
- the impact of the pupils' contribution to the school and wider community.

The Guidance Inspectors were asked to take account of the extent to which the school engaged with, among other things:

- the proportion of pupils from different groups who take on positions of responsibility and leadership in school and in the wider community, such as leadership and volunteering activities promoted through the school
- the proportion of pupils from different groups who participate in activities which contribute to the quality of life in, and sustainable development of, the school and wider community

- the quality of the work of the school council or other arrangements which enable pupils to contribute to, and influence, decisions made about life in school and the wider community
- how well pupils participate in activities, such as surveys and discussion, which encourage them to express their views and ideas about the school and wider communities
- the extent to which pupils are involved in working with teachers and other staff in planning and making decisions about their learning and well-being

Antidote News (2010) reported, in the face of Ofsted inspections, that schools should be an environment where students have an authentic voice and engage in real dialogue with adults. The organisation's program cites the research of Fielding and Kirby (2009) on student led reviews where they emphasise the importance of developing, among other things:

- the wider school culture and day to day relationships between young people, pupils and staff, staff and staff, staff and parents
- that are respectful, caring of and attentive to each other. Positive relationships across the school community make it more possible for students and parents to feel able to communicate what they think within reviews.
- the organisational structures of the school to support the kinds of conversations that develop the skills, and encourage the dispositions and attitudes required to enable young people to lead the review with confidence and enthusiasm.
- the formal opportunities for pupil involvement in the life of the school that extends beyond committees and representational bodies which inevitably involve a small handful of motivated students to include multiple occasions and opportunities for a wide range of pupils. It is unlikely that students could meaningfully contribute to their reviews if they were not also supported to have a voice within other school contexts.
- the pupils' experience of the curriculum—ie the daily opportunities for learning inside and outside the classroom—includes many and varied ongoing occasions in which they can choose what, where, when, how and with whom they learn. Students are specifically supported to become skilled in reflecting on their learning (eg using assessment for learning) and this is seen as important for them to be able to participate in reviews.
- the focus is on establishing learning conversations with students, rather than perceiving their ideas and views as challenging, in order to develop their capacity for learning. In the words of one teacher "students' new ideas are not a form of criticism." Thus, Students become intrinsically, rather than extrinsically, motivated in their learning.
- Involving students meaningfully within their review means encouraging a genuine belief in its value and an understanding of how to engage young people respectfully. But how do schools support staff to listen to students, without letting their presuppositions about the child get in the way, and without being overbearing or condescending? This takes time and leadership.

Thus, under this regime, school-wide enabling conditions were established, leadership and support staff were committed, students were appropriately supported and there was to be an ethos of shared responsibility. This can only lead us to wonder why such a powerful tool has been abandoned.

Following the scrapping of the requirement to engage students in providing testimony regarding the school's policies and practices as valued input into the inspectorial process, a number of concerns have been expressed. As the National Union of Teachers put it:

> Most importantly, inspection will still be punitive and high-stakes for schools, teachers and head teachers, rather than developmental and supportive. While teachers understand the need for accountability, school evaluation is at its most effective when school communities understand its purpose and relevance. Sadly, the new inspection arrangements are likely to increase the perception that schools need to put on a performance for the inspectors.

Who is Participative and why?

In spite of the admonition to solicit the views and experiences of a diverse range of children and young people it is the case that those most likely to unsettle practice and induce a sense of discomfort are also those who are least likely to be consulted and engaged in inquiry and research (McIntyre et al. 2005).

Members of established bodies such as Student Representative Councils (SRCs) are more often called upon than those who hold divergent and challenging views. Devine (2002) argued, for example, that the power imbalance in the staff–student relationships was particularly evident within a primary school when the class teacher's choice of student researchers was based on accepting only those she considered possessed the specific, desirable characteristics she wanted the researchers to possess. The process of choosing such individuals and rejecting others resonates with work by McIntyre et al. (2005, p. 155) who questions whether participation in student voice work results in a "dividing practice", where confident, articulate students are divided from those who "don't fit the dominant discourse and academic aspirations of their school". Similarly, Fielding (2001) in an early demonstration of his work engaging young people as radical agents of change pointed out that "the value of student perceptions in contemporary high stakes contexts consists largely in their capacity to alert schools to shortcomings of their current performance and possible ways of addressing the deficiencies" (p. 123). That is, in most instances, their engagement is satisfying an entirely instrumental, performative interest.

A decade later Fielding (2011) advances the notion of participation, taking it from 'student voice' to a 'lived democracy' that produces intergenerational learning between all who are participating in the educational enterprise. This view is echoed by Thornberg (2010) who acknowledges that in order to create deliberate democratic meetings with authentic student participation in school settings, the traditional student control discourse has to be replaced with a deliberative democratic discourse—one that contributes to active citizenship as discussed above Thus, if students are to have a genuine voice in school regarding the right to participate in decisions affecting them, staff need to learn to put their own views to one side and engage in a more democratic dialogue with students, without attempting to control their voices and actions. This returns us then to our notion of the participation of children and young people, including tertiary students in consultation, research and inquiry, as the formation of a dialogic community.

Conclusion

This chapter has drawn upon issues of dialogue, power and participation. It has identified challenging practices within the complex social world of schools, and from time to time, universities and colleges. It places children and young people as agents who may be constrained by historical and organisational conditions. We are reminded by Fielding and Moss (2011, p. 151) that "if schools and other social institutions are to prefigure radically different futures, they will need to do more than embrace consultative or participatory processes". As we progress through this book we shall argue for a future that faces down some of the current inhibiting discourses generated by an audit society. To do this our theories need to be robust and defensible, remembering that:

> Theory isn't abstract; it isn't words on a page; it … it isn't … aesthetically pleasing patterns of ideas and evidence. Theory is concrete. It is distilled practice. Above all, theory is felt, in the veins, in the muscles, in the seat on your forehead. In that sense, it's moral … and binding. It's the essential connective imperative between past and future. (Griffiths 1974, quoted in Gibson 1985, p. 64)

Chapter 3
Democratic Education in an Age of Compliance

Having explored and theorised the participation of children and young people in the research enterprise, arguing for the development of a number of dialogic conditions that might give rise to participation within schools and other institutions, we turn now to explore the context of education in the early twenty-first century. The rise of neoliberal agendas in education, represented in the Global Education Reform Movement (Sahlberg 2011), has seen an associated rise in cultures of compliance and audit in education. Reminded by Rowlands and Rawolle (2013), however, that "neoliberalism is not a theory of everything" (p. 260), let us be clear about what we mean when we refer to the 'neoliberal' turn. Robert McChesney's definition employed by Michael Apple in *Education the 'Right' Way* (2006) resonates with us:

> Neoliberal initiatives are characterised as free market policies that encourage private enterprise and consumer choice, reward personal responsibility and entrepreneurial initiative, and undermine the dead hand of incompetent, bureaucratic and parasitic government, that can never do good even if well intentioned, which it rarely is. (1999, p. 7)

Furthermore, Raewyn Connell has extended these ideas:

> Neoliberalism broadly means the agenda of economic and social transformation under the sign of the free market. It also means the institutional arrangements to implement this project that have been installed, step by step, in every society under neoliberal control. (2013, p. 100)

Neoliberalism, then, might be seen as a collection of philosophies and strategies that privilege the market and, in the context of education, have led to the increasing marketisation of education at all levels (Apple 2011; Connell 2013; Marginson 1997). Within this, compliance and audit cultures (Power 1999) might be seen as technologies of neoliberalism, some of the 'institutional arrangements' to which Connell refers.

This chapter will explore the tension between the current push for compliance and approaches to education and inclusion that seek to legitimately enfranchise young people. We will examine the impact of compliance and audit on educational systems and institutions, and highlight the ways in which these can be counterproductive to the kinds of democratic or transformative educational practices we advocate. The chapter begins with an examination of the compliance agenda in

© Springer International Publishing Switzerland 2015

N. Mockler, S. Groundwater-Smith, *Engaging with Student Voice in Research, Education and Community,* DOI 10.1007/978-3-319-01985-7_3

education, looking specifically at the technicisation of teaching and teacher professional learning through regimes of standards and accountability; the standardised testing agenda; and the 'harmonisation' of curricular and pedagogical practice that is underway in some jurisdictions. Next, we explore the very concept of 'democratic education', asking what this concept means given the constraints of our time and the context of compliance, linking explicitly to student agency and education for active citizenship, and suggesting implications for teaching practices. Finally, we examine how far notions of democratic and transformative education constitute 'uncomfortable bedfellows' with compliance and audit agendas, suggesting spaces where effective 'pushback' might take place, particularly in relation to teacher education (both pre-service and in-service) and classroom practice. We argue that it is possible for the project of democratic and transformative education to succeed despite the tyranny of compliance that characterises contemporary education.

Education in an Age of Compliance

On a global, or at least western scale, education in the current age is dominated by the twin ideologies of accountability and standardisation deeply entrenched in what Sahlberg has referred to as "the viral spread of GERM (the global education reform movement)" (2011, p. 99). In a Bourdieuian sense, what might be observed in the spread of these twin and complementary ideologies is a weakening of the autonomy of the field of education as the logics of practice of the field of economics come to bear on the educational realm (Lingard et al. 2005), similar to the colonisation of other fields by economics at the same time (Bourdieu 2003). The commonsense wisdom of standardisation and accountability has come to pervade education in a myriad of ways, from the positioning and regulation of teachers' work as 'public property' to the exaltation of standardised test results as a proxy for educational quality.

While much has been written on the impact of these trajectories on schools and education systems (see, for example, Biesta 2009; Stobart 2008; Taubman 2009), here we aim to give merely a brief overview, providing a background snapshot and context to our discussion of democratic education, by way of furthering the central argument of this book. Four of the primary tenets through which the standardisation and accountability agendas have come to manifest in education relate to curriculum, assessment, pedagogy and the nature of teachers' work, each of which simultaneously feeds into and is reflected in the global 'what works' (Atkinson 2000; Biesta 2007, 2010b; Mockler 2011b) agenda.

'Teacher-Proofing' the Classroom: Standardising the Curriculum

The growth of national curricula initiatives in the west over the past 20 years highlights the growing importance of what Karseth and Sivesind have called "the recurrent question pertaining to curricula: what knowledge is of most worth for the millennial citizen?" (2011, p. 58). Yates and Grumet (2011) write of curriculum as responsive to the social and political context of its time, an idea salient in Australia at the time of writing, where the incoming conservative Government has recently vowed to revise the newly developed and recently-implemented national History curriculum, on the grounds that "[conservative] prime ministers had been airbrushed out in a rewrite of history" (Owen 2013).

Parallel to the growth in a variety of fundamentalisms in response to the uncertainty of the 'information age', curriculum in many parts of the world has become increasingly prescribed, articulating in great detail the content knowledge that students are 'assured' to learn regardless of their context or circumstance. In NSW, over the course of the past two decades, syllabus documents have transformed from aspirational scaffolds for student learning within which teachers were required to apply professional judgement and decision-making, to great lists of 'dot points' designed to, in the words of the President of the then NSW Board of Studies "provide teachers with greater clarity" (Alegounarias 2011) in their curriculum planning. In the past, teacher professional judgement was expected and indeed required to fill the conceptual gap between curriculum as object and curriculum as action (Grundy 1987, 1998), otherwise understood as the difference between curriculum as intention and curriculum as reality (Stenhouse 1975) or the space "between hope and happening" (Lundgren 1983). In this new era, much of the "guaranteed and viable" (Marzano 2003a, b; Marzano et al. 2001) curriculum of the twenty-first century leaves little room for prioritisation, local decision making or any other kind of judgement or creativity in the part of teachers.

This notion that curriculum can and should be 'teacher proofed' fails to recognise the essential humanity of education, the idea that "education is first and foremost the interaction between teachers, adults and children" (Ravitch, in Scribner 2013), a phenomenon pointed to by Raewyn Connell when she writes: "To say that education involves nurture is important. Education involves encounter between persons, and that encounter involves care" (2013, p. 104). In classroom contexts, care is necessarily enacted through the provision of learning experiences that recognise and value students' differences, and we understand this provision to be critical to improving educational outcomes for all students, particularly those students who may be marginalised (Hayes et al. 2006, p. 67 ff.) by virtue of their circumstances.

Pedagogy, however, is the primary vehicle for the enactment of the curriculum in classrooms (Ladwig 2009), and as a principal site for the exercise of teacher professional judgement, it has also been subject to moves toward standardisation in recent years.

Teaching to the Script: Standardising Pedagogy

Despite substantial evidence around the value of critical and authentic approaches to pedagogy developed in Australia and elsewhere over the past two decades, (see, for example, Hayes 2003; Hayes et al. 2006; Ladwig 2009; Ladwig et al. 2007;

Lingard et al. 2006; Munns 2007; Munns et al. 2013; Newmann et al. 1996) increasingly educators are under pressure to standardise their pedagogical practice. The valuing of scripted lessons, designed once again to 'teacher proof' education by limiting the scope for teacher autonomy and professional judgement, is a key tenet of these moves.

In the US, the provision of 'scripted lessons' as part of the Common Core curriculum, reflects a key strategy of long-standing programs such as *Success for All*, *Direct Instruction* and *Open Court*. As argued by a New York-based secondary school English teacher in the *Washington Post*, the scripting of lessons within the Common Core is based upon a number of, we would say, misplaced assumptions:

- That anyone who can read a lesson aloud to a class can teach just as well as experienced teachers;
- That teaching is simply the transference of information from one person to another;
- That students should not be trusted to direct any of their own learning;
- That testing is the best measure of learning.

Put together, this presents a narrow and shallow view of teaching and learning (Chaffee 2012).

In England, the allegiance of the current Education Secretary and his Department to the 'what works' agenda (Atkinson 2000; Biesta 2007, 2010b), which places emphasis on conventional notions of 'evidence-based practice', privileges that which can be packaged and 'implemented' across a variety of school contexts over local and contextualised pedagogical practice. The provision of "planning exemplifications" at different stages of the national curriculum, devised ostensibly to support teachers' curriculum design efforts but which coincidentally also contain a range of scripted 'exemplars' indicates a preference here for standardisation over free-range teacher professional judgement.

In Australia, the incoming Minister for Education has indicated his preference for "Direct Instruction", a pre-packaged program involving scripted lessons, and the intention to 'roll out' such an approach to all disadvantaged students, based on the alleged success of the Program in remote indigenous community schools in the far north of the country.

Decoupling teachers from the capacity to make informed and tailored pedagogical decisions with particular reference to their students and classroom contexts is dangerous ground. Embedded in these attempts is an impoverished view of education that assumes that learning is transmitted or 'delivered', that all students respond in identical ways to teaching and learning strategies, and that 'good education' can be replicated by anybody, anywhere.

Measuring What Matters: Standardising Assessment

Much has been written in the past decade on standardised testing regimes, both national and international, and their impact on the ecologies of education and schooling (see, for example, Biesta 2010a; Lingard 2010; Lingard and Sellar 2013; Sellar and Lingard 2013; Stobart 2008; Taubman 2009, 2011). The most pervasive example of what Gita Steiner-Khamsi has termed 'policy borrowing and lending' (Steiner-Khamsi 2004), standardised testing has become in many cases not only a proxy for educational quality of a variety of kinds, but also a catalyst for a significant narrowing of the curriculum in a range of national and state contexts (Lipman 2004; Thompson 2012; Thompson and Cook 2012).

Biesta (2010a) reminds us of the difference between measuring what we value and valuing what we measure in education, arguing that the rise of 'measurement cultures' has had a broad impact at both macro (education policy) and a micro (classroom practice) level, changing the shape of what is valued in classrooms, schools and communities. Indeed, when the essentially blunt instrument of test scores is used as a proxy for everything from teacher quality, student proficiency, and school viability to national prowess, we are indeed witnessing a situation where "means become ends in themselves so that targets and indicators of quality become mistaken for quality itself" (Biesta 2010a, p. 13).

The publication of test scores, as happens under the OfSTED system in the UK and via the MySchool.edu.au website in Australia, and the use of school data to inform the closing of 'failing' schools or public ranking of teachers such as occurs in the US, attaches far higher stakes to assessment for schools and teachers than for students themselves. Furthermore, the use of international data such as that generated via PISA or TIMSS testing to create national anxiety around the effectiveness of schooling (such as that which has recently led Australia to build the intention to be in the 'top 5 by 2025' into legislation) (Australian Education Act 2013), or to create a national mandate for the kinds of approaches to curriculum, pedagogy and assessment that will maximise test scores at the expense of actual education, is highly problematic.

'Teacher Quality': Standardising Teachers' Work

The 'teacher quality' agenda, the final trans-national trajectory of neoliberal education policy, has seen the spread of professional standards over much of the western world in the past two decades. As one of us has argued elsewhere (Mockler 2011a, 2013), the shift from teach*ing* quality to teach*er* quality over that timeframe is a subtle but significant one. In the first place, the teacher quality agenda generally pays naught but lip-service to the professional learning needs of teachers and the role of professional learning in the ongoing formation and mediation of professional identities. Second, embedded into the teacher quality agenda is an understanding of "good teaching as *embodied* rather than *practised*" (Gore et al. 2004, p. 5, my emphasis), and "the promulgation of heroic narratives of exemplary teachers" (Taubman 2009, p. 12), which together mitigate against authentically addressing issues of teach*ing* quality in ways that might be generative for teachers and consequently, students.

We do not claim that teaching standards are intrinsically bad. As Sachs and Mockler have argued (2012), there is a range of purposes and foci for standards, from those aimed at regulation and measurement to those with a more developmental edge. What professional teaching standards tend to share in common, however, is essentially a hollow, technicised depiction of teachers' work that assumes that good teaching can be neatly catalogued and categorised. Regardless of whether standards are more or less prescriptive or expansive, intrinsically they value the standardisation of practice, the idea that various elements of teaching practice can be decontextualized and judged as either 'good' or 'bad', neatly 'ticked off' a list and used as 'evidence' of enhanced practice.

Our primary problem with this is first that teaching is always contextual, with "the teacher's practice evolv[ing] in response to the learner's development and needs" (Connell 2013, p. 104). To posit that good teaching practice exists and can be quantified in a vacuum, decontextualized from students, is a nonsense. Second, teaching standards in their very nature present as the simple answer to the relentlessly complex problem of educational practice. To suggest to teachers that the 'secret' to improving (and we use the word advisedly) practice lies in 'meeting' or demonstrating professional standards denies the reality that the search for improvement in teaching practice relies on a deep understanding of context, well-honed and utilised professional judgement, and endless engagement in professional dialogue and discourse based on the problematisation of practice. Professional standards are a very poor substitute for any of these.

Education Under Audit: Winners and Losers in the Marketplace

The standardisation of curriculum, pedagogy, assessment and teaching practice are tools of the neoliberal education agenda under the auspices of audit and accountability. Here the market reigns supreme, for "...accountability redefines relationships in economic terms. As a result, the accountability becomes a *formal* relationship where "quality", the most empty and abused word of the past decade, becomes confined to processes and procedures, rather than relating to content and aims" (Biesta 2010a, p. 69). Furthermore, market forces in education, predicated upon the supremacy of choice and competition, entrench inequity while never recognising that dictums of choice and competition were largely responsible for the creation or at least carriage of the very inequities they seek to address (Ravitch 2013, p. 33).

Educational historian Diane Ravitch reminds us that the key players in educational reform, particularly in the US but increasingly elsewhere, are corporate, with a consequential orientation toward marketization:

> ...the idea of turning the schools into a market is something that's been foisted on us by people like Bill Gates and the Walton family of Wal-Mart and Michael Bloomberg. These are all people who have made billions of dollars because they're very good at the market. Then we have a group called Democrats for Education Reform—these are Wall Street hedge fund managers. They believe in the market, that's what they do every day. They're in the market, so it works for them and they think it's going to work for everybody, but what

the market never does is to create equality of educational opportunity. It creates winners and losers and that happens in schools—there are winners and losers, but that's not the purpose of schooling. (Ravitch, in Scribner 2013)

Meanwhile, Stephen Ball's recent work on policy and advocacy networks (2012) reminds us that the issue of who gains from the increasing standardisation of education is an interesting one. Pearson and the Gates Foundation have recently partnered in the US in curriculum support for 'delivering' the Common Core Standards (Gewertz 2011), and in recent years in Australia the administration of NAPLAN testing has been contracted to Pearson, which also publishes copious materials supporting curriculum implementation, student performance on standardised tests and teacher professional development (Hogan 2013). Education is not merely a 'public good', but also a multi-million dollar business, with the key policy players no longer confined to 'the usual suspects' (Ball 2012).

While the technologies of the neoliberal education agenda are alive and well, they do not tell the whole story of education in the early twenty-first century. Spaces for resistance exist, and one of out interests lies in exploring the notion of 'democratic education' as one such space: a way of transcending the mandate of compliance to support a more expansive vision of education, young people and society more broadly. Taking student voice 'beyond legitimation and guardianship' relies on such a vision, and it is to exactly what we mean by 'democratic education' that we now turn.

Democratic Education: Beyond 'Accountability' to 'Responsibility'

The very idea of democratic education is not new. John Dewey's approach to education, encapsulated in works such as *The School and Society* (1899) and *Democracy and Education* (1916) had at its heart a vision of the school and the educative process itself as a modelling and induction ground for democratic principles and practices. Written relatively early in his career and consistent with his later works on education and democracy, Dewey's *Pedagogic Creed* laid out these ideas at length across its five articles:

> I believe that the only true education comes through the stimulation of the child's powers by the demands of the social situations in which he finds himself. Through these demands he is stimulated to act as a member of a unity, to emerge from his original narrowness of action and feeling and to conceive of himself from the standpoint of the welfare of the group to which he belongs. Through the responses which others make to his own activities he comes to know what these mean in social terms. The value which they have is reflected back into them. (Dewey 1897, p. 77)

More recently, Apple and Beane, in their work *Democratic Schools* (1995), argued that "…democratic schools, like democracy itself, do not happen by chance. They result from explicit attempts by educators to put in place arrangements and opportunities that will bring democracy to life… These arrangements and opportunities involve two lines of work. One is to create democratic structures and processes by which life in the school is carried out. The other is to create a curriculum that will give young people democratic experiences" (Apple and Beane 1995, p. 6). Our discussion in this book is for the most part confined to the first of these—the development of democratic structures and processes, across schools and other educational institutions, by which student voice might be authentically engaged with and valued within the community. It is also our belief, however, that without curricular and pedagogical experiences—returning to the notion above that pedagogy is the key technology through which the curriculum is enacted—that model and provide experience of democracy in the classroom, that those structures and processes remain ineffective and inauthentic. Students spend the vast majority of their school time in classrooms, and in school environments where the valuing of student voice is confined to the meta-structures of the school, in other words, 'checked at the door' of most classrooms, the net effect is that little more than lip service is paid to ideas of democracy and student voice.

Biesta (2010a) draws on Onora O'Neill's Reith Lectures (O'Neill 2002) to explore the dynamic of accountability in relation to democracy, arguing that the narrow accountabilities that have become entrenched in education by virtue of the GERM in fact function as "an apolitical and antidemocratic strategy that redefines all significant relationships in economic terms, and hence conceives of them as formal rather than substantial relationships" (Biesta 2010a, p. 59). His argument, after O'Neills, is that these new forms of accountability render teachers more accountable to the various regulators than to the public, or the communities of students, practitioners and parents they serve.

O'Neill expresses a doubt that "the present revolution in accountability will make us all trustworthier" (p. 57), arguing that what is required is a different revolution, one that takes us toward "intelligent accountability", and which focuses on good governance and the building of social trust, both personal and institutional. Biesta drives this further, exploring the links between accountability and responsibility, and drawing on the work of Levinas and Bauman in the argument that "a moral relationship *is* a relationship of *responsibility*. What distinguishes a moral relationship from a contractual relationship is that responsibility is *not* reciprocal" (Biesta 2010a, p. 63), and that the current regimes of accountability education pose a significant threat to responsibility. This is reminiscent of Pasi Sahlberg's recent observation that "accountability is what is left once responsibility has been subtracted" (Sahlberg, in Partanen 2011).

So exactly what is democratic education in an age of compliance? Given the constraints and pressures of accountability and compliance, and the desire, on our part, to advance an agenda for education that is both intelligently accountable but also recognises, and indeed, places at its centre, the responsibility implicit in the kind of moral relationship encompassed in education, we suggest here five key tenets of democratic education in an age of compliance. These tenets should not be regarded as all-encompassing, but for the purpose of our discussion of student voice and a concern for the embedding of student voice within a democratic approach to education, we argue that they are key tenets for teachers, school leaders and those who support their work, such as teacher educators, to consider.

Risk Taking and Trust

Many of the technologies of audit and accountability are focused on mitigating risk. Indeed, in an era of 'risk management', 'risk' has become somewhat synonymous with 'threat', and the elimination of risk has become desirable. In terms of democratic education, however, we find the idea of minimisation, mitigation or elimination of risk problematic for two reasons. First, risk is the flip-side of trust. As Barbara Misztal writes in her work *Trust in Modern Societies*, "trust always involves an element of risk resulting from our inability to monitor others' behaviour, from our inability to have a complete knowledge of other people's motivations and, generally, from the contingency of social reality" (1996, p. 18). Environments devoid of risk are necessarily also devoid of trust, and high levels of trust, we argue, is a necessary component of a democratic education system: trust between students and their peers, students and teachers, teachers and teachers, and teachers and parents. High levels of trust, it seems, do not come about by coincidence in the contemporary school, but rely on a willingness on the part of members of the community to take risks in their relationships with each other, understanding, in Misztal's words, that the "contingency of social reality" means that nothing is in fact certain.

Second, in the context of teaching and learning, risk minimisation is hardly desirable. Only through taking appropriate risks (with appropriate scaffolds and supports available to 'catch' them should they 'fall') do young people learn to push their own boundaries, to try new experiences and develop more sophisticated understandings of themselves as learners. When schools remove or limit opportunities for students to take risks, they necessarily also limit the available scope for learning. Democratic education provides at every turn opportunities for young people to, individually and in concert with others, 'try out' and 'try on' different identities, approaches to learning, and ways of being in the world. Risk taking (and the support of trusted others, both students and teachers) is critical to the enabling of these opportunities.

Rights, Responsibilities and Citizenship

Schools that employ democratic approaches to education operate as environments where students can explore and develop their capacities to engage as citizens. Truly democratic schools are those where teachers and students alike have a strong sense of their own role and contribution within the community, and where expectations and responsibilities are both transparent and shared. In terms of student voice, Michael Fielding has called this "intergenerational learning as lived democracy" (2011, p. 72 ff.), suggesting that in these contexts, there exists not one set of rules for teachers and another for students, but rather, that the 'rules' of community are shared and engaged with in different ways by different community members.

Responsibility for learning, therefore, is conceptualised as jointly shared by teacher and student, where the teacher's role lies in the construction of the framework and environment for learning for (and with) the student, and the support of the student as they engage in the learning environment and framework, while the student's role lies in the demonstration of their learning over the course of the learning process and at the conclusion. Classrooms where the responsibility for learning is conceived of in this way are those where, over time, young people learn to exercise and understand the meaning of rights and responsibilities in action, as they navigate citizenship within the school and classroom context.

Decision Making and Consequences

Connected to shared responsibility within the school community, as well as to the exercise of risk taking in learning, is the notion that young people, through their schooling experience, learn to become decision makers and to understand the consequences of the decisions they make. This can only occur in communities where young people's voices are sought out and valued, and in classrooms where students are supported to make real decisions about their learning and provided the kind of guidance that helps them to become wise decision makers in regard to their own learning.

An understanding of and willingness to 'live' with the consequences of decisions is an important disposition for democratic schools to develop in young people, for it is only through anticipating and accepting consequences that true responsibility for learning is achieved. In environments where the responsibility for learning is construed as primarily that of the teacher, where decisions made by students are rare or generally inconsequential ("will I create a travel brochure or a poster?"), the opportunity for students to understand the consequences of their decisions for their learning and development is significantly curtailed. Wise decisions about learning made by young people with a strong sense of themselves as learners feed into dispositions regarding participation and responsibility that are amongst the aims of democratic education.

Student Agency and Power

Linked with notions of democratic participation, as well as to the ideas regarding responsibility and decision making discussed above, one of the central tenets of democratic education is the exercise of student agency and a level of transparency regarding the 'power dynamic' of the school. 'Student agency', of course, comes in many forms, but here we are referring to the kinds of authentic student agency where students are extended an active voice not only in matters of little consequence to them, but where teachers and students act as agent-partners in the construction and habitation of the school.

In the context of teaching and learning, this might be seen to manifest in a curriculum more negotiated than 'rolled out'; in consideration being given to students' background knowledge and prior experience in the construction of learning and assessment tasks; in the establishment of processes that lead to the authentic differentiation of the curriculum, not merely along the lines of 'ability' or 'learning preference', but holistically taking each student into account in the negotiation of appropriate learning pathways at each point along the way.

Furthermore, while it would be both naïve and foolish to suggest that the power dynamic entrenched in the very structure of the classroom could or should be overturned, with respect to the issue of power, we suggest that democratic schools are those where the dynamic of power is explicitly acknowledged, and where the exercise of power by all members of the community is encouraged and understood within the context of roles and responsibilities. Within the ideals of democratic education, power is acknowledged and wielded wisely and fairly.

Transformation Over Transmission

The final tenet relates to the very purpose of education and the role of schools and teachers in the building of knowledge and understanding. Democratic education seeks personal as well as societal transformation, and to this end emphasis is placed on the development of critical and inquiring dispositions and the building of cultural capital on a variety of levels. Rather than notions of 'delivery' that sit within a more traditional transmissive model of education, democratic education is informed by notions of students as active knowledge creators; the importance of information and critical literacy; and the joint role of teachers and students as architects of the learning environment.

Within a transformative approach to teaching and learning, students exercise agency and decision making, negotiate and take responsibility for their learning and navigate considerable risks in order to make gains in their learning. Implicit in this is the idea that students will have a strong voice in their learning, wherein they are able and indeed, expected to engage in a joint enterprise with their teachers as different-but-equal partners in the construction of their learning.

Democratic Education in an Age of Compliance: Uncomfortable Bedfellows?

Clearly these tenets of democratic education share many points of tension with the accountability and standardisation agenda outlined in the first half of this chapter. While aspects of democratic education or 'education for democracy' are often embedded in the aspirational education policy documents produced by governments to frame education (see, for example, MCEETYA 2008), the policy technologies of compliance pull against the very notion of democratic education. Indeed, we conceive of democratic education itself as an act of resistance, providing schools and teachers with a framework for action and practice that might be employed to 'push back' against the narrow and impoverished view of education encapsulated in the compliance agenda.

The implications for school and classroom practice, however, are considerable, as are those for teacher education, both initial and ongoing. In Parts II and III we consider some of these implications through an exploration of methods for listening to and engaging student voice, with a particular emphasis in Chap. 11 on professional and research ethics in the context of this work. First, however, we turn to the topic of 'empowerment', seeking to problematise this concept that tends to lie at the heart of much discussion of student voice.

Chapter 4
Approaches to Student Voice: 'Empowerment', 'Evidence-based Practice' and Participation

> *Student voice, as it has been conceptualised in work which claims to empower students, is an oppressive construct—one that I argue prepetuates relations of domination in the name of liberation. (Orner 1992, p. 75)*

Having established a context of current efforts toward student voice, in terms of both theoretical perspectives and contemporary education policy, in this chapter we move to explore the rationale for democratic student agency. In the first section, we problematise the dual and widely adopted notions of 'student empowerment' and 'evidence-based practice' as framing devices for student voice initiatives, and consider as a cautious alternative Michael Fielding's 'patterns of partnership' model (Fielding 2011) as introduced in Chap. 1, which, we posit, provides a possible means of navigating the difficulties we see in the earlier two conceptualisations. We then consider what this approach might mean for the involvement of children and young people in research and inquiry and point to some implications of young people's active engagement in dialogue and decision making about their education for classroom practice and pedagogy, a theme to which we shall return in Chap. 9.

Problematising/Problematic Discourses
Surrounding Student Voice

Thomson and Gunter (2006), in their discussion of the discursive framing of student voice, highlighted two dominant 'frames' for student voice work, namely that of standards and school improvement, and that of rights. Reflecting on the education policy context in the United Kingdom in the mid—2000s, they suggest a privileging of the first of these frames over the second: "there is a marked tendency for senior policy makers to bring 'pupil voice' into the policy conversation as a means of achieving school improvement and higher standards of attainment, rather than

© Springer International Publishing Switzerland 2015
N. Mockler, S. Groundwater-Smith, *Engaging with Student Voice in Research, Education and Community*, DOI 10.1007/978-3-319-01985-7_4

as a matter of the UN convention, citizenship and rights" (p. 840), arguing elsewhere that "'pupil voice' has been harnessed firmly to the yoke of school improvement, rather than existing as a public good in and of itself". While the discussion in Chap. 3 underlines our agreement with this assessment, we wish here to expand on this discussion to consider the shaping of these two frames themselves.

The first, that of school improvement and standards, is largely underpinned by narrow conceptualisations of 'evidence-based practice', which initially emerged from medical and allied health fields in the late 1980s and have subsequently become embedded in discourses surrounding education policy and practice. While it might be claimed that contemporary iterations of evidence-based practice in education hit their most influential peak in the late 1990s/early 2000s, recent posturing by key politicians involved in leading education policy both in England and Australia in particular suggest that we may yet be up for a reprise. The second, the 'rights discourse', the origins of which were discussed at length in Chap. 1, is often framed by the notion of 'empowerment' (Orner 1992), wherein students are seen to require 'empowering' by teachers in order to find and express their voice.

In this chapter, we seek to problematise these two key conceptualisations and contextualisations of student voice. As an alternative way of understanding the enactment of student voice in schools, we then explore Fielding's 'patterns of partnership' model, suggesting, somewhat cautiously, its usefulness for conceptualising young people's engagement in school-based research and education and schooling more broadly.

Student Voice and 'Empowerment'

The discourse of student empowerment is embedded not only in work related to students as agents in research but also in a great breadth of the literature, both research-based and professional-development focused, on progressive and democratic approaches to education. In addressing the notion of empowerment here we do not wish to take aim at the spirit of this work, which in general, makes a compelling case for, on both a local and a structural level, enhancing opportunities for students to be agents of and for their own education. We are mindful at this point of Michael Apple's recent quip regarding progressives often lining up in a 'circular firing squad' (Apple 2012, p. 11) despite their shared aims, and wish to make it clear that our intention is to critique the concept of empowerment, arguing for a more complex and holistic understanding of power and the way it operates in contemporary schooling, rather than to mount a critique of work that makes use of the concept, per se.

Emerging predominantly from critical social movements of the 1960s and 1970s, such as those related to civil rights and feminism, the notion of empowerment implies a bringing to consciousness and 'power' of a social group previously lacking in power. In development studies over the past two decades, the concept of empowerment, particularly as linked to the capability approaches enunciated by Amartya

Sen (1999) and Martha Nussbaum (2000) has become central. Embraced by both the United Nations and the World Bank in this time as pathways to the eradication of poverty and achievement of the Millennium Development Goals, the concept of empowerment is understood in the following way in these contexts:

> Empowerment is the process of enhancing the capacity of individuals or groups to make choices and to transform those choices into desired actions and outcomes. Central to this process are actions which both build individual and collective assets, and improve the efficiency and fairness of the organizational and institutional context which govern the use of these assets. (World Bank 2011)

Sidestepping the neoliberal undertones of this definition, complete with its emphasis on choice and efficiency, it shares significant dimensions with notions of empowerment in education, particularly the emphasis on capacity for choice and engagement.

Troubling 'Empowerment'

Our issue with the use of the concept of empowerment as a rationale for the enlistment of student voice is threefold. Harking back to the quotation from the work of Mimi Orner with which this chapter began, we are concerned with the capacity for student voice, through 'empowerment', to operate as an oppressive construct, perpetuating domination rather than functioning as a tool of transformation or liberation for students. Gore (1992) suggests that 'empowerment' presupposes (1) an agent of empowerment; (2) a notion of power as property; and (3) some kind of vision or desirable end state, and each of these presuppositions relates loosely to our concerns.

Our first concern relates to the overly paternalistic nature of the notion of 'empowerment', where implicit in the process itself is the assumption that one group (in this case, teachers) holds the capacity to 'hand' power to another. Within this paternalistic conception, student empowerment occurs as a generous gesture on the part of teachers, bounded by teachers' own desires and control, while the power students already possess is minimised and disregarded in an act of 'othering'. Consistent with Freire's (1972) notion of the 'banking model' of education, where power, via knowledge, is transmitted from teacher to student, such a conceptualisation of student voice fails to take into account the complex nature of both power and knowledge as enacted within the school and classroom. Robinson and Taylor (2007) in quoting Freire, propose that

> He complicates the notion of 'empowerment' by arguing against the paternalistic view' that empowerment flows from the educator to the educand. Thus more flexible notion of power, not as the possession of one (the teacher) which is 'given' to the other (the student) is built instead on the 'moment of communiucation' between teacher/student and it is from this that the possibility of 'building a new culture' flows. (p. 13)

This notion of 'building a new culture' is a significant one for our discussion of student voice and democratic education. Retaining the hope that school or classroom cultures can be tinkered with, through notions of 'empowerment' of students, to become environments where students experience real agency, is fraught. Only when new cultures, new logics of practice and new identities are forged for both students and teachers will transformation, liberation or democracy emerge.

Our second, related, concern with the concept of empowerment regards the implicit assumption that power is a 'giftable' commodity rather than discursively constructed, and consequently, ever-changing and evolving. Rather than seeking to 'give power' to students, we might seek to *understand* power as it manifests in our schools and classrooms, recognising that the discursive production of power is highly context dependent. As Orner argues, these contexts hold significant implications for our understanding of the enablers and inhibitors of student voice:

> How power relations in the classroom manifest is crucial. How do the subject positions inhabited by one student connect with the subject positions of everyone else in the room? How do these multiple identities and positions inform who speaks and who listens? Who is comfortable in the room and who is not? Who was insulted and who did the insulting in the hall just before class? It seems impossibly naive to think that there can be anything like a genuine sharing of voices in the classroom. What does seem possible, on the other hand, is an attempt to recognise the power differentials present and to understand how they impinge upon what is sayable and doable in that specific context. (1992, p. 81)

Furthermore, understanding power as discursive and "circulating" rather than as a conferrable commodity opens the door to an understanding and consideration of Foucault's notion of 'disciplinary power', where external systems of surveillance become internalised with the effect of individuals becoming their own overseers. Such an understanding of power gives rise to questions about how far the structures of the school and the classroom play a role in the positioning of students as those with less power and what might be done about it in the context of transformative or liberatory educational practices, such as those related to the privileging of student voice.

Finally, our third concern, linked closely to each of the prior two, relates to the capacity of the concept of 'empowerment' itself to undermine the very aims of 'student voice' with regard to educational transformation. First, the premise that one group can and indeed should 'empower' another, imbued with connotations of colonialism and 'Othering' as discussed above, mitigates against the very idea of democratic schooling, which relies on a more reflexive and nuanced understanding of power as held in different forms by different individuals and groups. The notion of cultural capital is useful here—democratic education seeks to value and affirm a variety of forms of cultural capital rather than privileging one form (held by the 'empowerer') over another (held by the 'empoweree'). Such a bipolar dichotomy is unhelpful in seeking to understand schools and classrooms as complex and multi-faceted fields, and fails to support the 'empowerees' to question their own role and the ways they may be implicated in the system they seek to correct (Gore 1992, p. 61).

Furthermore, the 'flat' conceptualisation of power as a commodity implicitly denies the highly contextual nature of schooling and, in doing so, plays directly into the discourse of 'what works', as touched on in Chap. 3 and discussed more expansively below. For 'empowerment' to be conceptualised as a process whereby students, homogenously regarded, find and express their 'voice', thus reflecting such homogeneity, suggests a transferrable, transplantable process that might be 'rolled out' regardless of context. Such an approach is unlikely to be helpful, and indeed, stands in contrast to an understanding of democratic education as about communicative, dialogic space.

Student Voice and 'Evidence-Based Practice'

Despite its origin in democratic and progressive visions of education (Rudduck and Fielding 2006), 'student voice' has found a comfortable home within contemporary, instrumentalist education policy agendas, where it has been put to work as a tool for school improvement (Thomson and Gunter 2006), personalisation (Fielding 2008), and evidence-based practice (Taber 2013). As arguably "the 'buzz word' of the twenty-first century" (Cheminais 2013, p. 1), student voice has emerged as a significant force within the 'what works' policy environment, the key driver of which is the very notion of 'evidence-based practice', albeit a version utilising a very narrow view of what counts as 'evidence'.

As noted in Chap. 1, the recent history of evidence-based practice in education can be traced to 1996, when David Hargreaves, in his Teacher Training Agency lecture (subsequently published as Hargreaves 2007) lamented the lack of 'value for money' in publicly funded educational research. He called for teachers to engage in applied educational research and to concentrate their research efforts on 'what works' in the classroom, so as to systematically begin the codification of teachers' technical knowledge and skill for the purpose of cataloguing and subsequently dispersing 'best practice' amongst the entire profession. Furthermore, he conducted a lengthy comparison between the professions of education and medicine, finding education seriously wanting in its use of evidence for professional decision making:

> Today teachers still have to discover or adopt most of their own professional practices by personal preference, guided by neither the accumulated wisdom of seniors nor by practitioner-relevant research. They see no need to keep abreast of research developments and rightly regard research journals as being directed to fellow academics, not to them. Teachers rely heavily on what they learn from their own experience, private trial and error. For a teacher to cite research in a staffroom conversation about a pupil would almost certainly indicate that he or she was studying for a part-time higher degree in education or rehearsing for an OFSTED visit—and would be regarded by most colleagues as showing off. (Hargreaves 2007, p. 7)

Leaving aside Hargreaves' simplistic portrayal of the medical profession as a homogenous group of practitioner-researchers contributing to and simultaneously drawing on academic journals in their enactment of evidence-based practice, the key problem with his argument is the singular lack of clarity around what exactly counts as appropriate evidence in education, and how indeed this might be different to the kind of evidence that medical practitioners regularly draw on in their work. Embedded in Hargreaves' call for teaching to become an 'evidence-based' profession such as medicine, is a positivistic understanding of 'evidence' as leading to scientific certainty and a command of best practice in the form of 'what works'.

In subsequent works, Hargreaves further elaborated this position, naming New Labour's "pragmatic approach to 'what works' and to the rapid dissemination of 'good practice' throughout the education service" as cause for optimism (Hargreaves 1999, p. 245), bringing to mind Thomson and Gunter's assessment of Third Way policy as a "*melange* of apparently incompatible elements" (Thomson and Gunter 2006, p. 842).

The discourse of 'what works' has been roundly critiqued by many advocating a more nuanced approach, criticised in turn by Hargreaves as "postmodern hermits" (Hargreaves 1999, p. 242). Scholars such as John Elliott (2001) Martyn Hammersley (1997), Tony Edwards (1996) and Harvey Goldstein (1996) argued against the narrow definition of 'evidence' upon which Hargreaves' comparisons between education and medicine were based. Elizabeth Atkinson argued passionately 'in defence of ideas', maintaining that "a narrow focus on 'what works' will close the door that leads to new possibilities, new strategies, new ways of reframing and reconceiving the educational enterprise" (2000, p. 328). Jill Blackmore (2002a, 2002b), working from an Australian perspective,, argued that evidence-based practice, particularly the its medical iteration, fails to understand the complexity of the field of education, especially in respect to the theory-practice dynamic and the complex relationships within the field between education policy, research and practice. Blackmore argues in favour of teacher professional judgement in the enactment of evidence-based practice, that which is usually omitted in such discussions due to its 'subjective' nature. She writes:

> Research based practice works through the theory practice dynamic critically, and it is that criticality that is crucial for a knowledge based democracy which takes into account the social and cultural as well as the scientific and technological. It requires researchers to problem set and not just problem solve, to be strategic as well as relevant. It requires from teachers as practitioner researchers another level of professional judgement that derives from the theoretical underpinnings of their disciplinary field of practice. (Blackmore 2002a, p. 17)

While initially this iteration of focus on evidence-based practice emerged from the United Kingdom, since the re-authorisation of the Elementary and Secondary Education Act in 2001 (known as 'No Child Left Behind'), growing attention to what Patti Lather has termed "the politics of the science of the US accountability movement in public education" (2004, pp. 759–760) has seen an increased focus on evidence-based practice in the United States of America also (Slavin 2002). There, a focus on 'scientifically-based educational research' (Eisenhart and Towne 2003), with a particular privileging of randomised controlled trials as the 'gold standard' (Biesta 2007, 2014) of educational research, preferred and/or prescribed increasingly to the exclusion of other approaches to research, and increasingly shaping the landscape of educational research in the US (Lather 2010).

In Australia, the continuing focus on evidence-based practice has seen the notion embedded in national policy documents such as the Early Years Learning

Framework (Busch and Theobald 2013; Commonwealth of Australia 2009) and the Australian Teacher Performance and Development Framework (Australian Institute for Teaching and School Leadership 2012b). Additionally, it maintains an implicit yet strong underpinning of processes such as teacher registration and certification, where teachers are required "to evidence" (Australian Institute for Teaching and School Leadership 2012a) their practice in ways that are annotatable, demonstrable responses to the Australian Professional Standards for teachers.

Since the 2010 election in the United Kingdom and the ascendancy of Michael Gove to the position of Secretary of State for Education, evidence-based practice has undergone something of a renaissance in the UK. In June 2012, the Behavioural Insights Team, located within the Cabinet Office, produced a paper entitled *Test, Learn, Adapt: Developing Public Policy with Randomised Controlled Trials* (Haynes et al. 2012). Co-authored by two members of the Behavioural Insights Team with experience in randomised controlled trials (Haynes and Service) and two consultant academics with specific expertise in clinical and randomised controlled trials (Goldacre and Torgerson), the paper argued for the adoption of randomised controlled trials across a broad range of public policy areas, and posed a simple nine-step process for remedying the current situation in which "we don't necessarily know 'what works'" (Haynes et al. 2012, p. 15). In March 2013, Gove commissioned Goldacre, a medical doctor, epidemiologist and academic who authored the trade non-fiction book *Bad Science* in 2008 (Goldacre 2008) and has since developed a profile as a media commentator through his badscience.net website, to conduct an external review for the Department for Education "on improving the creation and use of evidence in the teaching sector" (Goldacre 2013a).

The publicly available component of the external review, a paper entitled *Building Evidence into Education* (Goldacre 2013b), argues for the adoption of randomised controlled trials by teachers (and presumably, other educational researchers), while using the concept of 'evidence-based practice' interchangeably with that of randomised controlled trials. Clearly for Goldacre, the only evidence that 'counts' is that which is generated through randomised controlled trials, and, like Hargreaves before him, the question of what actually constitutes good evidence in educational contexts remains unaddressed. Furthermore, in a similar vein to the *Test, Learn Adapt* report, the differences between scientific and social contexts for research and 'evidence' and the implications of these differences also remain unaddressed. The jump in logic from an argument that holds at its centre that we need to get better at systematically generating and using evidence in education, engaging in what Lawrence Stenhouse termed "systematic inquiry made public" (Stenhouse 1981) (an argument which goes back to the work of John Dewey in the late 1800s, incidentally, and with which we are in agreement) to the positing of randomised controlled trials as the best way to get there is essentially nonsensical. Furthermore, the suggestion that 'what works', arrived at through this narrow interpretation and use of evidence, will provide a catalyst for the teaching profession to become more enlightened and evolved betrays a deep misunderstanding of the current scope and shape of teachers' work, the role of professional judgement and joint enterprise in that work, and the context within which teachers' work is enacted.

Troubling 'Evidence-based Practice' in the Light of Student Voice

While this critique of 'evidence-based practice' in education has been broad-based, there are a number of specific issues that relate to the links between evidence-based practice and student voice, and with the framing of student voice in the context of evidence-based practice, as we see predominantly in the employment of student voice for the purposes of school improvement, for example. Three separate but inter-related concerns emerge for us.

First, the narrow interpretation of 'evidence' employed by advocates of evidence-based practice, as explored above, presents particular problems for the integration of authentic student voice. When evidence that can be counted, replicated and packaged as 'what works' or 'best practice' is privileged over that which might be richer yet more unwieldy, the risk emerges that lines will be drawn around student voice that confine it to the kind of evidence that clearly elucidates the 'what' at the expense of the 'how' and 'why'. Tightly controlled surveys that allow students' experiences to be compared across school contexts, for example, limit the ways in which students might be inclined or able to speak and the things that they might be requested to speak about.

Second, and related to the first concern is the decontextualisation of educational practice that is assumed in an evidence-based practice framing of student voice, that assumes that 'what works' can be neatly transplanted from one school community to the next. While the development of much related to medical practice relies on scientific principles and the findings of scientific studies, the field of educational practice is highly context-specific. To be authentic, student voice initiatives need to speak to the local context and to be embedded in the history and culture of school communities. Not only are national and cultural categories such as class, race, gender and ethnicity germane here, but the specific histories and cultural nuances of the community and its members, within which the best approach to engaging student voice might be negotiated. One size fits all approaches to involving students in this kind of work are likely to be superficial in nature and consequently short lived.

Finally, and of great consequence for the philosophy of student voice enactment that underpins this book, the positioning of students as 'data source' by evidence-based practice is highly problematic for us. Within this frame, gathering evidence from students and young people is construed as the province of teachers and other adults, including, in the UK, OFSTED inspectors as well as others who would wish to 'consult young people' for the purpose of improving services for them such as those working in various cultural institutions and discussed in Chap. 6., Thus the role of students in the equation is to answer the questions conceived and posed by these 'wiser others' through the mechanism of 'consultation'. Such an understanding of student voice is highly impoverished, and far from the democratic and radical aims of the student voice project, runs the risk of reinforcing rather than overturning the status quo.

Clearly a different approach is required, and it is to our suggestions regarding the desired framing that we now turn.

Framing Student Voice Differently

Neither the empowerment/rights nor the evidence-based practice/school improvement framing of student voice is adequate. Embedded as each of them are in traditional (and in the case of evidence-based practice) neoliberal conceptualisations of schooling, our desire here is to offer a framing of student voice that reflects a more generative vision of twenty-first century schooling, one that suggests a need to shape schooling differently in a more democratic mode. Our aim here is not to develop a new model for framing student voice work, but rather to examine three models which have preceded our own work in this area, explore their similarities and differences and suggest a number of implications for school communities of embracing such approaches, implications which will be taken up in more detail in subsequent chapters of this book.

Three Critical Approaches to Understanding Student Voice and Participation

Roger Hart's 'Ladder of Participation' (Hart 1992) has been used for two decades in the shaping of work related to the participation and 'voice' of young people. Developed in the context of Hart's work in the 'minority world' (Hart 2008), the ladder has been used in a wide variety of contexts, including in work in the majority or developing world. Most notably, while the model itself was developed in the early 1980s, it was through its publication in 1992 in an essay sponsored by UNICEF that it garnered a significant following, contextualised at that time within the United Nations Convention on the Rights of the Child, which came into effect in 1990.

The essay 'Children's Participation: From Tokenism to Citizenship', in which the ladder of participation was first published, contextualises children's participation within the discourse of empowerment, but also strongly within the discourse of democracy and citizenship. It opens with the following paragraph:

> A nation is democratic to the extent that its citizens are involved, particularly at the community level. The confidence and competence to be involved must be gradually acquired through practice. It is for this reason that there should be gradually increasing opportunities for children to participate in any aspiring democracy, and particularly in those nations already convinced that they are democratic. With the growth of children's rights we are beginning to see an increasing recognition of children's abilities to speak for themselves. Regrettably, while children's and youths' participation does occur in different degrees around the world, it is often exploitative or frivolous. This Essay is designed to stimulate a dialogue on this important topic. (Hart 1992, p. 4)

The 'ladder' itself comprises eight 'rungs' the bottom three of which Hart categorises as 'non-participation', while the top three he categorises as 'degrees of participation'. Table 4.1 below summarises the eight rungs and their descriptions.

In latter years, Hart has clarified his original thinking on the ladder, reflecting that his chosen metaphor has in some ways hamstrung the model, either encouraging a

Table 4.1 Hart's 'ladder of participation' (Hart 1992)

	Rung	Examples/features (from Hart 1992)
Degrees of participation	Child-initiated shared decisions	Projects initiated out of children's interests and actively engaged in by adults, genuinely sharing decision-making
	Child initiated and directed	Children working co-operatively together without the intercession of adults
	Adult-initiated shared decisions	Project initiated by adults, but decision-making shared with young people
	Consulted and Informed	Children as consultants
		Feedback provided to participants
	Assigned but Informed	Genuine informed consent
		Children have a meaningful role to play
		Children as genuine volunteers
Non-participation	Tokenism	Children asked to lend their voice but without choice regarding the subject or means of communication, and often without a chance to formulate their own opinions
	Decoration	Children used to bolster a cause of adults' choosing
	Manipulation	Coercion of students to participate
		Consultation without feedback to children

'lockstep' interpretation or else suggesting that the highest 'rung' is that which is to be aspired to at all times within communities. On this he has written:

> The ladder should be thought of as some kind of scale of competence not performance: children should feel that they have the competence and confidence to engage with others in the way outlined on any of the rungs of the ladder, but they should certainly not feel that they should always be trying to perform in such ways. (Hart 2008, p. 24)

The ladder, then is a heuristic for thinking about the possibilities of the kinds of project work that might be undertaken with children, the central idea being that an environment should be developed wherein young people and adults hold the capacity to work together in any of the ways suggested by the 'degrees of participation' rungs. We would agree with Hart, however, that the hierarchical nature of the ladder metaphor undermines the notion that different approaches to participation by young people (and indeed adults) are not inherently preferable to others. True participation can occur in a variety of configurations, so long as the capacity exists for ideas and initiations to emerge from both young people and adults within the community.

Finally, it is interesting to note that in his 2008 reflection on the use of the ladder for understanding, Hart noted that "even some schoolteachers" had used the ladder of participation to rethink their work with students (Hart 2008, pp. 22–23). Even some schoolteachers! Given that of all his nominated 'professional' groups and institutions included youth workers, television and radio directors, scout leader, play workers, street workers and health professionals, all of whom spend arguably far less time with young people in an ongoing way, and also who presumably would have far less opportunity to create the kinds of stable communities of young people and adults wherein participation might flourish, this is particularly telling. The

Table 4.2 Shier's 'pathways to participation' (Shier 2001)

Level of Participation	Openings	Opportunities	Obligations
5. *Children share power and responsibility for decision-making*	Are you ready to share some of your adult power with children?	Is there a procedure that enables children and adults to share power and responsibility for decisions?	Is it a policy requirement that children and adults share power and responsibility for decisions?
4. *Children are involved in decision-making processes*	Are you ready to let children join in your decision-making processes?	Is there a procedure that enables children to join in decision-making processes?	Is it a policy requirement that children must be involved in decision-making processes?
3. *Children's views are taken into account*	Are you ready to take children's views into account?	Does your decision-making process in enable you to take children's views into account?	Is it a policy requirement that children's views must be given due weight in decision-making?
2. *Children are supported in expressing their views*	Are you ready to support children in expressing their views?	Do you have a range of ideas and activities to help children express their views?	Is it a policy requirement that children must be supported in expressing their views?
1. *Children are listened to*	Are you ready to listen to children?	Do you work in a way that enables you to listen to children?	Is it a policy requirement that children must be listened to?

structures, norms and logics of practice of schooling work in many ways to mitigate against the establishment of such communities, and it is the implications of privileging student voice work for these that we will focus on in the next and final section of this chapter.

Harry Shier (2001) subsequently developed an alternate model for enhancing young people's participation in decision making, in his 'Pathways to Participation' approach, referencing both the imprimatur of the UN Convention on the Rights of the Child and Hart's ladder of participation. Shier is quick to suggest that his model might sit alongside the ladder as an "additional tool for practitioners, helping them to explore different aspects of the participation process" (Shier 2001, p. 109). Shier's model differs from Harts in that it begins with degrees of participation, while recognising that some of the most important work done by the ladder of participation may have been the drawing of practitioners' attention to the way in which they have in the past limited students' opportunities for participation to these non-participative categories. In addition to the five levels, which correspond loosely but not entirely with Hart's 'rungs', Shier poses 15 questions, grouped for each level into 'openings', 'opportunities' and 'obligations'. Shier's model is summarised in Table 4.2 below.

Shier conceptualises the pathway to participation as a process whereby practitioners might begin in the bottom left hand corner, working their way sequentially through the questions to determine their own, and their institution's level of readiness for student participation. He notes that level four, where children are involved in decision-making processes is the minimum level for compliance with the UN Convention on the rights of a child,

While Shier's model does indeed add a further dimension to the ladder of participation in the proffering of questions regarding processes and policies to support young people's participation, he offers little in terms of the ways in which practitioners and institutions might go about shaping adequate answers to these provocations and the ways in which tensions might be navigated. The strongly hierarchical nature of the levels and the aspirational positioning of level five makes this a less complex and nuanced conceptualisation than that of Hart (particularly considering Hart's later clarification, discussed above), and the framing of participation in the relatively narrow terms of procedures and obligations, directed at the adult members of the community, also limits the model.

Finally, Michael Fielding's typology, *Patterns of partnership: How adults listen to and learn with students in schools* (2011), proposes six approaches to interactions between adults and students within schools, in response to the call from one of us to 'interrupt' the conditions of interaction between adults and young people in schools to build a more participative and generative model (Groundwater-Smith 2009). Like Hart, Fielding's model is rooted in a desire to foster authentic, intergenerational democracy, but, perhaps symptomatic of time of writing, for Fielding this project comes with a level of greater urgency. He sees neoliberal approaches to education and social policy as deeply undermining of democratic values and processes, and suggests that genuine partnership as a bold act of resistance for teachers and students:

> Whilst the hegemony of neo-liberalism is pervasive and even totalising its ambitions, it remains vulnerable not only to the power of dispositions and values energised by motives other than those typical of a market model of human flourishing, but also to the alternatives that history offers, to the plurality of histories it so strenuously denies. (Fielding 2011, p. 62)

Furthermore, Fielding argues, in the framing of his typology, that partnership between adults and young people in schools might be regarded as a kind of "radical collegiality" (p. 66), a reciprocal learning where schools become exemplars of democracy and participation. Important within Fielding's model (summarised in Table 4.3 below) is the 'Fellowship Dimension', embracing a "relational anthropology of care" which argues for "education as the practice of humanity, of human becoming" (p. 68).

Like Shier's model, the 'top' level (level six) of Fielding's model is aspirational, but unlike Shier, Fielding's vision of that aspiration is one that moves well beyond young people having power shared with them to the development of a shared responsibility for the common good, the enactment of which might see different members of the community operating on all (participative) rungs of the ladder of participation at different times. Furthermore, this aspiration comes with a desire to, through such engagement, envision a different society. Fielding draws here on John Berger's notion of 'an otherwise':

> The culture in which we live is perhaps the most claustrophobic that has ever existed; in the culture of globalisation ... there is no glimpse of an *elsewhere*, of an *otherwise*. ... The first step towards building an alternative world has to be a refusal of the world picture implanted in our minds ... Another space is vitally necessary (Berger 2002, p. 214).

Table 4.3 Fielding's 'patterns of partnership' model (Fielding 2011, p. 67)

Instrumental Dimension	Patterns of Partnership	Fellowship Dimension
High performance schooling through market accountability	*6. Intergenerational learning as lived democracy* shared commitment to/responsibility for the common good	*Person centred education for democratic fellowship*
	5. Students as joint authors students and staff decide a joint course of action together	
	4. Students as knowledge creators students take lead roles with active staff support	
	3. Students as co-enquirers staff take a lead role with high-profile, active student support	
	2. Students as active respondents staff invite student dialogue and discussion to deepen learning/professional decisions	
	1. Students as data source staff utilise information about student progress and well-being	

We find this notion of partnerships between adults and young people, particularly teachers and students, as potentially opening up 'another space' to be highly compelling. The question that remains for us, however, is around the implications of such a vision for contemporary schools and the ways in which it might be brought about, and it is to this question that we turn for the final section of this chapter.

Generative Partnerships Between Adults and Young People: Implications for School Communities

At the outset, we wish to emphasise that we do not purport to hold the key to achieving such generative partnerships, and neither do we intend to provide a ready-made solution (or answer to the 'what works' question) that might be implemented. Furthermore, there is no process, nine-step or otherwise, that might be followed to achieve the goal. As observed earlier in this chapter, schools are complex and messy places, and the nuances of context are critical in shaping school-level strategies. There are, however, three key areas that we believe school communities might interrogate in order to critique current practices and further embrace student voice and partnership.

First, reflecting upon and developing a shared understanding of how children and young people are conceptualised within the school community is important. In some schools a de facto 'us and them' relationship exists between staff and students, while in others teachers express a fear of surveillance at the hands of students and, through them, parents. Uncovering and exploring the assumptions, expectations and outlooks that teachers hold with regard to students and building a collaborative commitment to positioning students in a different way, if necessary, might go some way toward opening the door to generative partnerships.

Second, casting the spotlight on the role of teachers within the community and the kinds of professional identities, habitus or subjectivities that might best support generative partnerships is critical. In some ways, these kinds of partnerships require teachers to make themselves vulnerable to students, to learn reciprocally and to engage in joint enterprise and negotiations. Such approaches require robust understandings of their own professional 'space' and identity on the part of teachers, a clear articulation of their role within the teaching and learning environment (for while learning may happen reciprocally, teachers and students inhabit different spaces within that environment), and strong collegial support for working in this way.

Finally, as explored at length in Chap. 3, the environment of contemporary schooling is in part shaped and impinged upon by neoliberal policy agendas which sit uncomfortably alongside the aim of building democratic school communities. Strong leadership, not only on the part of Principals and those in formal executive leadership roles, but on the part of all teachers, alongside the student body, may go some way toward speaking back, if only at the local level, to these counter-productive agendas. The more that communication strategies are clear and transparent and decision making essentially devolved and shared, the stronger generative partnerships will potentially become and the more scope for the opening up of alternative spaces, the 'elsewhere' of which Berger and Fielding speak.

We understand that these things are far more easily said (or written!) than done, and in some of the chapters that follow, we draw out these implications either in more extended discussion or through the presentation of cases drawn from our own experiences in schools and other educational settings.

Part II
Listening to Student Voice

Having mapped the theoretical, social and educational contexts of student voice work in Part I, in this second section we build on the issues and challenges raised by detailing specific, contextualised examples of institutions listening to the voice of children and young people across different educational and other settings. We draw on these narratives of practice further in Part III as we consider principles of ethical practice for researching with young people.

The four contexts from which our examples are drawn are school, learning contexts for children outside school such as museums and other cultural institutions, contexts beyond educational institutions where young people engage with in their communities, and finally, higher education institutions. We have chosen these four contexts because they represent distinctly different but important settings that young people move within and between. Furthermore, our contention, laid out in the introductory chapter, is that these four settings each offer opportunities, taken up to greater or lesser extents, for student engagement and agency in decision making. While the examples offered are drawn from the Australian context, we believe that in these times of globalised education policy and practice, they offer insights and observations that resonate in other, different, national contexts.

We are at pains to emphasise that we do not offer these examples as examples of 'what works', beacons of excellence that humanity might be well served to 'scale up' and implement across different institutional contexts. Indeed, as discussed in Chaps. 1 and 4, we remain very wary of principles of 'best practice' embedded in the 'what works' agenda. All educational practice is, for us, context dependent. Rather, we offer these examples as site specific snapshots of practice from which some principles might be drawn and adapted for use in different educational and other contexts. Furthermore, the examples provided in different chapters are of quite different orders. In the chapters on student voice at school and student voice beyond school in cultural institutions we have drawn on work conducted by one of us working as academic partner to members of the *Coalition of Knowledge Building Schools*. In the chapter on the voices of young people in the community, a range of examples is provided drawn from a breadth of literature around research with young people in the majority world, research with young people with experience of the juvenile justice system, and research with young people from less advantaged communities. Finally, in the chapter on the student voice in higher education settings, we examine the framing of 'student feedback' and student voice in universities, examining not so much the generative practices of educators but rather the policy frameworks that they operate within. It is hoped that these cases might serve not only to illustrate the perspectives about which we have written in Part I of this book but also that they might serve as useful cases in graduate education contexts where students might be interrogating the use of student voice.

Chapter 5
Student Voice at School: Participative Research as Apprenticeship, School Students as Co-researchers

In this chapter and the one that follows we present several case studies. Such studies can be seen as illuminations of practice, but should not be seen as representations of 'best practice'. Rather they provide us with what Bob Stake (Stake 1995) has named as 'petite generalisations' that allow the reader to engage in personal interpretation. Such cases are empirical in that they are field oriented and may be seen as naturalistic. They are developed so that the reader may develop insight into particular features of practice.

This chapter, then, can be seen as a narrative of practice. It serves to represent a substantial case in a single setting. It is not intended to be celebratory, although there is much of merit in what has taken place, but rather to highlight both the challenges and dilemmas of working with students over a sustained period of time.

Matters of Dialogue and Agency

The 'Students as Co-researchers Project' has now completed its fourth year in a co-educational comprehensive secondary school located in metropolitan Sydney. It is a school that faces challenging circumstances for a variety of reasons including families living in poverty; a high proportion of young people for whom English is a second language; and a number of recently arrived refugees from as far afield as West Africa and Afghanistan.

In many respects it can be regarded as a residualised school; that is one where it has become the school of last resort within a policy of school choice and the educational market place. As Campbell et al. (2009) have observed Australian middle class parents are increasingly seeking to cement their privileges, social position and educational advantage by congregating in schools that cater for those families similar to themselves. In the United Kingdom these schools have been unsympathetically named 'sink schools' being so designated on the basis of their desertion by middle class families, resulting in a form of social segregation. Students attending the school of which we write are acutely aware that there are other secondary

© Springer International Publishing Switzerland 2015   53
N. Mockler, S. Groundwater-Smith, *Engaging with Student Voice in Research,*
Education and Community, DOI 10.1007/978-3-319-01985-7_5

schools nearby that enjoy a more positive reputation than their own and that they are often stigmatised as 'losers'. Nairz-Wirth, (2011, p. 41) writes

> It becomes clear that the social space, the professional playing field and the educational playing field are all battlefields on which players with limited resources (cultural, economic and social capital) or an 'unsuitable' habitus run a high risk of being stigmatised as losers.

Nonetheless, a significant number of students aspire to finish their schooling and continue on to further education, apprenticeships and the like.

In particular the school has been working to address the significant literacy and numeracy needs of its students. To assist in this work it has been supported by a program funded jointly by the federal and state governments, known as the *National Partnerships for Low Socioeconomic Schools*. The partnership program has granted significant amounts of funding to eligible schools with the monies extending over a number of years, in this case four. Among the aims of the school's enactment of the program has been the desire that the school should not only consider strategies for the academic development of its students, but also seek to 'reform' a number of its established practices, an important one being the nature of the relationships between students and their teachers and the extent to which they can be enhanced and improved. In designing the project of which we write the school was mindful that these relationships were at greatest stress during the middle years of secondary school, that is to say Year 9, when a number of students were disengaged, even antagonistic.

With a change of government this program has now ceased, leading us later in this chapter to raise questions of sustainability in the face of scarce resources.

Dialogue is seen as central to the reform that will be discussed in this chapter. Typically dialogue in the school has positioned students as learners, rather than as speakers. As we have discussed in earlier chapters, Biesta (2010) argues that we must take a new entering stance when engaging in education. He takes as his starting point that all students can *already* speak. It is a point that "positions equality at the beginning of education, not its end point" (p. 540). Such a liberatory function of dialogue has long been argued within discussions of critical social theory. Habermas (1979, p. 97) writes "Dialogue is a gentle, but obstinate, never silent, although seldom redeemed claim to reason". It requires respect, truth, open mindedness, and a willingness to listen and risk one's own preconceptions, fixed beliefs, biases and prejudices. It requires fundamental procedures that try to reduce overt and subtle forms of power. For this reason the establishment of the students as co-researchers project can be seen as a radical interruption to the normal asymmetries inherent in school relations.

This project was concerned with student agency. We argue that the project was designed to enable participants to build and voice their own views of schooling. They were to participate through their activities as members of a social group that assisted in giving meaning to their lived lives in the school. But this is no easy matter because they also have to live with and alongside their teachers who may hold very different views to their own:

> They (the teachers) are trapped in a double-bind relationship because they are asked to establish their authority and at the same time to listen to children (and young people)

while the latter is still interpreted in many spheres as proof of professional incompetence. (Stoecklin 2012, p. 9)

Thus many teachers feel conflicted, should they listen to and consult their students or not; this, in spite of Hattie's research (2008, p. 252) that argues, in relation to student achievement, "if the teacher's lens can be changed to seeing learning through the eyes of students, this would be an excellent beginning".

Thus, while the project envisaged the students as legitimate actors with their own agency it was mindful that their teachers might see that agency as a form of resistance; forms that Lanas and Corbett (2011, p. 418) characterize as dialogical encounters in school contexts. Following Woodhead (2010, p. xxii) the participation of the students was not just about teachers 'allowing' them to offer their perspectives, it also involved the young people having a place and space to challenge adult assumptions about "their competence to speak and to make decisions about issues that concern them".

While unspoken there was an agenda of interrupting the deficit discourses that are so dominant in schools of this kind; discourses about the school, schooling and the students themselves. Seemingly, there is a certain 'script' and set of 'roles' that generally operate in schools that have a high percentage of students from low socio-economic backgrounds. There are many deficit messages, low expectations and a focus on teacher control and surveillance of students that have been well documented and which require extraordinary efforts on teachers' parts to resist and transcend them (Munns et al. 2013). Haberman has critiqued the "pedagogy of poverty" and pointed out the divide between the role of teachers as "in charge and responsible" and the role of students as subjects (2010 [1991], p. 83). Even when there is a desire to relax the 'script' of the teacher-centred lesson, it is argued by many who teach in such schools that this would only be possible if only students were more compliant, and enthusiastic about their learning. There was a definite policy in developing the students as co-researchers to be inclusive of students with not only a range of abilities but also those who are seen as resistant and unorthodox. This policy was seen as a response to Stoecklin's (2012, p. 4) concern that:

> … structured channels of consultation such as youth forums or youth councils only grasp a part of what children and young people are actually able to do, and their filtering effect increases the representational problem linked to the difficulty of reaching a diversity of voices. There are powerful social and economic forces limiting children's voice, and invisible networks perpetuate a culture of non-participation where children and young people feel that decisions are always taken elsewhere and end up frustrated or cynical.

The Architecture of the Project

The project with which this chapter is concerned was first established in 2010 (Mayes and Groundwater-Smith 2010). Its intention was to build opportunities for a selection of students (approximately 20) from Year 9 (14 year olds) who would be apprenticed into becoming participant-researchers investigating an aspect of the ways in which the school went about its work over a whole school year. This group became known as "The Steering Committee"—an important metaphor for its work, since it had little executive power in the school, but could inform the steering of reform and change. The school students were to effectively become knowledge creators, contributing to the fund of professional knowledge available on the nature of teaching and learning within the school precinct.

The focus of the inquiry for 2010 was "The school I'd like", in 2011 a new cohort of students, also from Year 9 addressed "The teaching I'd like" while in 2012 attention was paid to "The learner I would like to be." 2013, the last year of the project, included students from Years 7–11 with an interest in "What I would like to learn".

In each year students engaged in a series of research workshops conducted by teaching staff and a university based partner, one of the authors of this book. These were organised to serve a dual purpose: to familiarise students with research methods, and to provide conditions where students could also express their own feelings and orientations to their schooling. Thus the workshops were structured to both develop confidence and insight (Hill 2006).

Commensurable with the research workshop objectives to enable students to voice their responses to various aspects of their schooling the focus was upon qualitative, open-ended methods. Details of such methods and their rationale are discussed extensively in Chap. 8. In each year students became competent in: conducting focus groups; developing and analysing surveys based upon focus group findings; using visual methods (e.g. photographing aspects of the school environment); constructing scenarios using projective strategies such as cartooning, puppetry; and, observing and interviewing teachers at work. Workshop sessions were designed such that students evaluated and commented upon the various methods and how they might be best employed to address the key focus for that year.

In the case of observing and interviewing teachers, this strategy was undertaken 2011–2013 (with 2010 being seen as a pilot year) and also involved visiting other schools.

We have selected from each year critical moments and their implications for the development of the project.

Critical Moments in the Development of Students as Co-Researchers

In his work with respect to teachers and action inquiry Tripp (1993, pp. 24–25, 27) has pointed to the ways in which educators may identify what he considers to be the merit of rendering moments in practice as critical, thus enabling extended reflection.

> The vast majority of critical incidents […] are not at all dramatic or obvious: they are mostly straightforward accounts of very commonplace events that occur in routine professional practice which are critical in the rather different sense that they are indicative of underlying trends, motives and structures. These incidents appear to be 'typical' rather than 'critical' at first sight, but are rendered critical through analysis. […] To be critical, it had

to be shown to have a more general meaning and to indicate something else of importance in a wider context. Thus one can see that critical incidents are not simply observed, they are literally created.

In our account of students as co-researchers we have identified a selection of moments among many. They are not only illustrative and illuminative, they also provide us with a touchstone to discuss aspects of the project as it progressed and to raise questions regarding the 'normal' operation of the school. Following Butterfield et al. (2005, p. 483) we see that by focusing on these events as narratives we can imagine how they have promoted or detracted from the desires of the project.

2010

In 2010 two moments have been identified; the first of these is reported in greater detail.

PBIS and KERF: A Teacher's Response

During the first year of the project students explored the kind of school that they would like to attend. At the same time the school was developing its Positive Behaviour Intervention and Support (PBIS) strategy. There was a concern that the work of the Steering Committee would be directed, as a key reference group, to following the procedures required to develop that strategy, and that there would be little encouragement for the students to evolve their own agenda. However, by the end of the year the students had their own acronym: KERF: Know students, Encourage them, Respect them and have Fun. At a staff meeting they presented to the staff their findings in relation to each of these. A small sample is reproduced here:

Knowing students

A good teacher thinks that you're capable.

First day of the term—[a good teacher] asks the class what the students like- they get to know you—know what you like, what you don't like and how you want to learn.

If you've got your head on the desk, you want them to ask you if you're ok, not get angry.

If a student does something wrong, it doesn't mean that they're going to be wrong for the rest of the term. The teacher shouldn't treat that student differently. Next day is a new day. The next day have a little talk: 'yesterday was a bad day. Now is a new day.'

Teachers don't always notice when you're working hard—they're too busy with the bad students. Other students miss out.

Use the smarter kids more. Get the smarter kids to teach the people that don't know stuff. The people who know are able to explain it to others—use our kind of language. Sometimes teachers don't understand the way we understand.

Encouraging students

Saying, 'well done,' 'good work,' 'excellent'—makes you feel proud of yourself and you like the classroom better, try harder.

In maths, my teacher saw my book and said, 'I'm going to change your report because I can see it's good.' I was encouraged to keep doing homework because he noticed.

Last year when we were learning about poetry, my teacher kept encouraging me to write more and more—I could bring my writing to her—I used to be more self-conscious. She would mark and explain to me what she liked and didn't like—the feedback and direction encouraged me to do more. I felt I could write another one better than I could have before. If she had been negative, it would have discouraged me and sent me in a different direction. There is room for critical feedback—you need that with the positive feedback so you can use both. As long as you get positive feedback, you can cope with the negative."
"The criticism and the praise work together to help you work better."

Respecting students

Talk to you nice—treat you as their own. Reward you. Don't shout at you.
Don't talk down to you—makes you feel inferior—makes you want to act out/retaliate.
Ask questions and take our opinions—don't call you ignorant—listen to my opinions and explain if they think I'm wrong. Don't cut me down and say I'm wrong.
Know what to say and how to say it—don't speak to students in an offensive way. A teacher should greet the students and not just start screaming.
If a teacher moves you and you weren't doing the wrong thing, you feel that you are being disrespected. If they explain why, it's okay to move you.
If they treat us with respect, we'll treat them with respect—goes both ways.

Having fun:

Teachers should start the lesson with something fun like games.
Teachers should treat students with respect—don't expect silence and respect if you are barking at your students. Teachers make learning easier by explaining and having fun, not screaming.
To make you interested and have more fun—relate it to normal life, connect it to what's important to you (they need to ask and find out from you what's important to you). Teacher needs to think of why the knowledge is important in the real world.
Let a student teach for a bit—teach the same things, but with your own words, with your own understanding—teacher as a back up.

Some teachers found the student presentation quite confronting. Soon after the meeting, one teacher encountered a challenging student in class and publicly asked a steering committee member, "so, you know all about respect, what do you do now?" In this instance the steering committee member felt that the presentation had fallen on deaf ears. We argue that this is a critical moment because it interrupts the relationship between teachers and students. Evidently, the teacher was frustrated by the students' claims that they deserved to be respected, while dealing with what was seen as a moment of disrespect. However, rather than solve the problem, and use the moment to make explicit her professional values, she used it as an opportunity to undermine the work of the steering committee.

However, the whole group was much encouraged by the reception that they received from visiting scholars from the Netherlands.

Affirmation by Visiting Scholars

Towards the end of 2010 the Steering Committee was invited to present their KERF findings to two scholars from the University of Applied Sciences, Utrecht who were in Australia to present at the Australian Association for Research in Education Annual Conference (Smit et al. 2010). The students were greatly encouraged by the close attention that was given to their work and excited by the notion that young people in other countries were also being enabled to become co-researchers. They saw that they were part of something larger and were heartened by the ways in which the visiting scholars evidently valued their work.

2011

In 2011 two matters stood out as critical moments: one, students being enabled to watch teachers at their work and the other to present findings to the whole staff in ways that teachers found more acceptable.

Observing Teachers at Work

With the focus for the 2011 on "The teaching I would like" students were afforded opportunities to observe volunteer teachers, having first solicited their 'informed consent'. Together they designed a letter:

> We would like your permission to come to your class and collect data by watching one of your classes learning, taking notes and photographs. We would come to ONE lesson. We would also like to ask the students some questions about how you teach and how the students learn. Could we also make a time to interview you about teaching and learning after the lesson? It can be any time that suits you. When we have finished the project we will be presenting our information to (School Principal) and the Staff. We hope you will help us with our project.
> Please let us know what classes you would be happy for us to observe and a time that would be convenient for us to observe you this term.

They conducted focus group interviews with selected students from the class asking them the following questions:

> What did you learn in this lesson? How did you learn it? What did you like in this lesson and why? What was your favourite part and why? Do you like coming every day to school and learning? How do you learn best? What do you enjoy most about coming to school? Do you understand what you are learning in class? How do you know? What would make school even better for you?

The steering committee students then de-briefed with the teachers regarding the ways in which the lesson was taught and how it fitted into the teachers' normal repertoire of practice. They discussed such matters as: teachers connecting to their learners by building strong relationships and caring about them as individuals; teachers 'knowing their stuff'; teachers helping students to find more than one way to solve a problem; and teachers trusting their students.

This work could be represented as "risky business". Many teachers find themselves uncomfortable when being observed by their peers, let alone by students.

In most secondary school contexts, teaching is a private affair (Hargreaves 2010). However, both teachers and students found the conversations helpful and revealing with students believing that they developed greater empathy with their teachers when they had a sense of what it was like to "be on the other side of the desk". Normally their acquaintance with teaching only comes from being on the students' side of the desk (Lortie 1975) with many students believing in a generic comment that "they (the teachers) are only in it for the pay".

Presentation to Staff

While 2011 was undertaken with a new Steering Committee it was clear that the teachers who were managing the project had learned much from the previous year. Rather than leave students vulnerable they enabled them to pose a series of questions to the whole staff when they made their presentation at the end of the year. They asked:

- *What do you **agree with** from the Steering Committee's presentation today?*
- *What do you **disagree with** from the Steering Committee's presentation today?*
- *What did you find **interesting** from the Steering Committee presentation today?*
- *What did you find **challenging** from the Steering Committee presentation?*
- *How does what the Steering Committee said fit in with **what you know already** about effective teaching?*
- *Is there **anything you want to say** to the Steering Committee?*

In groups of three the students then met with small groups of staff to discuss their responses. By agreement these were not recorded, but students felt that staff were receptive and interested in their presentation. As Tripp (1993) has noted critical moments are not isolated. The staff presentation and subsequent discussion was developed, not only from the findings for the year, but also from the somewhat hostile reception from the previous year.

2012

Visiting Other Schools

To facilitate continuity and development, previous Steering Committee members were invited for the first four weeks of the year to mentor incoming members. This enabled them to explain what they had been responsible for and how they had proceeded. The new committee was particularly interested in the notion of interviewing staff members and since their focus for the year was upon "the learner I would like to be" they looked forward to being provided with an opportunity to visit another school and identify how young people saw themselves as learners in a different environment. Subsequently, they made two visits, one to a co-educational secondary school whose students were identified as being in comfortable circumstances, but somewhat disengaged with their schooling and the other to a primary school in an affluent 'leafy suburb'. In the first case they recorded a number of observations that they made of student responses to three specific lessons. A sample is reproduced below:

Lesson 1
Some students did not concentrate.
Students make jokes about other people's art works
Stupid comments lead to others
Students are restless
Teacher makes jokes with students to regain attention
Teacher allows each student to cooperate in class
Students talk back to each other
Students do not feel interested in class anymore.
Teacher waits for a while to gain attention
Most students do not have any equipment for art.
Student does not have his work out and he is tapping on the table
Some people talk without putting their hands up
Half of the class has not taken out their stuff
A student is talking about a different subject

Lesson 2
The whole class enjoys the activity
A student is being silly, a student is chewing gum
A student is playing with a paper
A student is making unnecessary noise
A student is playing with scissors
A student is throwing paper
Not listening to the teacher
Some students easily distracted
Students laughing
Students on warnings
Student not listening to teacher: result; teacher gives warning
Most students not ready for school (no equipment)
The whole class laughs because of a silly comment made by a student
The teacher talks to them in a kind manner
The students are all into the subject
A student comes in from the deputy and distracts the class
The same student continues to disrupt the class throughout the lesson
A student takes out an orange and scissor but no work
The class is noisy throughout the whole lesson
A student takes out paper and starts making something that has nothing to do with the lesson.

Lesson 3
The majority of girls are separated from the boys
The class was very different from our own in the fact they were following all the rules
The students are friends towards the teacher and they make jokes together
The majority of boys were seated in the middle
Most of them asked questions from the teacher at some point
The girls were less interactive then the boys

They did not go off subject
They whisper between one another when they need some help from their peers and the teacher helped. Generally, the teacher had a great way of teaching.
They were always on task
They followed all the rules
They were taught effectively by the teacher
They asked questions on the subject
The students sometimes discussed something before asking the teacher
They gave us no attention
More boys than girls
They began to go off task after the teachers were not completely supervising the whole class.
Students paid attention to the teacher while she was speaking and no-one interrupted her.
Students focused well on the task
The students listen to the teachers carefully

In their discussions the students imagined which of these teachers would most facilitate their learning and how they acted in comparison to teachers in their own school. They also wondered about the impact upon student learning.

While there were no notes from the primary school visit, there was an animated discussion regarding the notion that the young people that they encountered were universally enthusiastic about school. They were reported to have said how much they enjoyed their learning and the student researchers wondered why it was that such a positive orientation might be drained away as they progressed into secondary school. They also observed the socio-economic circumstances of the school. While also a government school it still had resources, such as an excellent library and attractive grounds well in excess of their own. They also observed that the students, although still in primary school, expressed expectations, their own and that of their parents, that they would be going on to tertiary education.

These moments were critical to the project in that students came to an appreciation that young people of their own age are not so very different, in spite of differences of opportunity and affluence; however, they were surprised at the seeming "passion for learning" among younger children and their sense of entitlement that they would receive 'a good education'.

2013

In this, the last year of the project two 'critical incidents' have been extracted; the first of these is the selection of students; the second the actual focus for the year upon curriculum. The choice of critical moments was difficult in that much of the year was taken up with students interviewing teachers from specific key learning areas regarding their curriculum decision making not only in their own school, but also in a high status independent girls school. However, we have already discussed something of student experiences in interviewing and observing teachers and having opportunities to visit other schools.

Selection of Members of the Steering Committee

To support student voice becoming a whole school initiative, it was decided by those managing the overall National Partnership Project that students from across all school years would be able to elect to participate in the Steering Committee in 2013 however, the majority of members would still come from year 9. This decision was taken to support the rationale used in the past, that it is in middle school that students tend to become disengaged and this can be detrimental for senior studies. Thus the composition of the Steering Committee would be: four students each from Years 7 and 8; ten students from Year 9; and, four students each from Year 10 and two from 11.

As in previous years written expressions of interest were sought. Initially, in 2010 and 2011 students had needed to be actively encouraged to apply, especially those who saw themselves as marginalized within the school community. However, by 2013, following a school assembly where former members of the various Steering Committees explained their work with the assistance of a video that captured the work of earlier years, the expressions of interest were many and varied.

It was decided that former members would assist in a short-listing exercise where they would interview all aspirants of whom there were over 100. They did this in teams of three having first read the relevant expressions of interest. Finally twenty-six students were selected with an additional student in both years 7 and 8.

On the one hand the selection by former members of the Steering Committee was a demonstration of the maturity of the project. The interviewers were confident and able to justify their choices, based upon their own experience of working on the committee and understanding its challenges and demands. They had also been briefed regarding the focus for 2013 and believed that it would require participants who were both able and active. On the other hand their selection meant that they tended not to choose challenging or difficult students whom the teachers might have believed should be given a voice.

The Focus for the Year

In its submission to the school's executive regarding the final year of the project it was argued:

> The Steering Committee's aim for the past 3 years has been to support the development of student outcomes through encouraging students to have an active role and voice in the operation and issues of the school. Additionally, through facilitating more active communication between teachers and students it has been hoped that these relationships would strengthen.
> The implementation of the National Curriculum affects all students in every school across the nation. Conventionally, staff are the only stakeholders to read, deconstruct, workshop, discuss and then make decisions upon the implementation of the document in the classrooms. Once again, students are the consequential stakeholders in this process bearing the consequences of decisions made on their behalf.

It must be acknowledged that it would be highly ineffective to place the responsibility of decision making regarding what will be taught and how it will be taught on the student however, through structured preparation and exposure to the behind the scenes work of what it takes to implement a change in curriculum within a school, it is hoped that students will be able to make a meaningful contribution to the process.

The subject to be selected for student inquiry into curriculum decision-making was the history component of the Human Society and its Environment key learning area. Access to "behind the scenes" decision making was to be not only to be via interviewing the Head of Department and the teachers but also by observing a departmental staff meetings where decisions were to be made and by perusing the documents from which teachers were working.

A thread that was to run through the student deliberations was the operation of the "hidden curriculum". This is a difficult concept to grasp at the best of times, As the academic partner wrote in her notes:

As it is understood in the education literature the hidden curriculum is that which is taught implicitly through practices, procedures, rules, relationships and structures that are to be found within the school and its expectations.

It is regarded as an insidious form of socialization because it is opaque and for some social groups results in a dry, thin and meager kind of education that controls rather than liberates the students. It relates to concepts of cultural capital in that students in less privileged circumstances may have funds of knowledge that are not legitimate currency in a form of school education that demands conformity to the norms established by those who are strong and powerful.

For students to identify and discuss the hidden curriculum is a daring and exciting venture.

Indeed, the young people approached it with some considerable zest. As an introductory procedure they viewed, among other resources, the music video of Pink Floyd's *Another Brick in the Wall.* Students were well able to identify the hidden curriculum as that which is not taught "on purpose", but is "the way things are taught". They saw that they were constantly in receipt of messages regarding how to speak, how to behave, what is acknowledged and rewarded, what is sanctioned. After viewing *Another Brick in the Wall* they could surmise that much of what is required is the need to conform and "not to speak back"; that for some students schooling can result in "self doubt".

When it came to presenting their groups' musings on the film clips generally students were responsive and articulate and could make judgments about the juxtaposition of that which was obvious and that which was hidden. They could see that it was "not just what the teacher teaches, but *how* the teacher teaches it". "It is the things between the lines". "It is what is obvious and noticeable as well as what we should be learning". Students saw that both the explicit and implicit curriculum were important.

They saw that both teachers and students should have a say in what is to be learnt and how; "students have a say about what they want and teachers need to know what students can do." One surmised, "the whole school community should have a say".

Parr (2010:31) quotes from David Hamilton (2005) in describing research as a "fumbling act of discovery" (p. 289). This could well characterize the progress of the students as they uncovered the ways in which curriculum decisions are made, not only within their school, but also at the behest of politicians whose views are based upon political theories and ideologies.

Questions of Sustainability

By any measure this project is a significant one, spanning four years and supported by funding that has provided teacher release and the assistance of an academic partner. As well, one teacher has progressed to become a doctoral candidate and is working with challenging theoretical tools to explore deeply and intensely the meaning of student voice and school reform (e.g. Mayes 2013a, b).

Nonetheless, with the cessation of the National Partnerships resources there are serious matters regarding sustainability that will need to be considered. The school has made clear that it cannot afford the teacher release time that a continuation of the project would require, nor the assistance of an academic partner.

Scaling up or even continuing innovative programs over time is a major challenge for schools in the absence of funding, especially in schools whose budgets are already stretched to the limit. Clearly, through its challenging nature, there are practical, professional, physical, structural and cultural barriers.

In an email to those most directly involved in the project the academic partner wrote:

> We had a very fruitful meeting considering the question of "where to from here?" in relation to the future of the Steering Committee. We asked ourselves a series of questions:
> What happens to the program?
> What are the conditions for student participative research that have been fostered and how can they be nurtured?
> How can these conditions be spread and enabled?
> What are the roadblocks?
> How can the effectiveness by evaluated?
> Who are going to be the champions?
> We believed that the conditions that had most enabled the project were based upon the productive and trusting relationship that had been built between the students and teachers most directly involved; but also the developing relationships with others across the school who may have participated by being involved in interviews, focus groups, observations and the like.
> We saw that the key to the project were the concepts associated with inquiry based learning that is currently being understood as essential to Learning in the twenty-first Century as espoused in the New South Wales Department of Education and Communities discussion paper Great Teaching Inspired Learning.
> We also understood the power of communicating the various processes and outcomes through regular presentations at the Coalition of Knowledge Building Schools and a range of local and international conference presentations—these have led us to perceive that the project has significant currency in the professional community.
> From these discussions we concluded that the most significant route for the project, as a means of embedding it in the school would be to offer it as an elective, possibly within the ambit of HSIE. The work could well be seen as an important pre-cursor to the development

of skills for students undertaking later accredited High School Certificate courses, for example in Society and Culture.

The orientation to inquiry would be very helpful in terms of overall teacher professional learning in the school—again, this is consistent with the DEC blueprint for action in relation to Great Teaching Inspired Learning that gives greater recognition to professional learning undertaken in schools.

We believe that further development of student participative research within the elective framework, ultimately spanning Years 9 and 10, would assist in making learning more visible across the school using the ideas that have evolved through the various manifestations of project based learning. We see that students could be enabled to participate in designing the course and assessing its outcomes, with research, reflections, and videos being built into it. If the proposal were acceptable, this year's steering committee could assist in the design and naming of the elective. Thus the students themselves could be the champions for the project.

We believe that the roadblocks should not be formidable, but acknowledge that the proposal would need to stand beside other electives that are competing for students.

For my own part I would have to say that this has been one of the most satisfying and engaging encounters with students and gifted teachers that I have had over a long career of educational research and professional learning/development within an action research framework. I must thank everyone for being so inclusive and open.

Thus a proposal was put forward to the school to develop an elective strand within the school, extracts from which appear below:

What Happens to the Students as Researchers Project in 2014 and Beyond?

A Year 9–10 Elective

- An elective about research inquiry with students designing their own research.
- Year 9—research inquiry could be more whole class oriented facilitated more explicitly by the teacher
- Year 10—students writing their own inquiry question, designing and carrying out their own research (potentially in groups)
- Research could be within the school, but could also be in wider community
- This elective could be a model for other schools
- Elective would be teaching students critical research tools
- 1st year (2014)—one teacher teaches a Year 9 class and develops a 'structure' for the course, could be seen as a pilot
- 2nd year (2015)—two teachers (to spread the expertise/ increase sustainability)—one teacher teaching Year 10, and another teacher teaching Year 9
- Elective to be within the HSIE faculty as it aligns with the Higher School Certificate Subject, Society and Culture, but teachers could come from other faculties to teach this elective

How Could Student Learning in this Elective be Assessed?

- Teachers could negotiate with the students how their work will be assessed. This may include:
  - Self/peer/teacher mark combined
  - Artefacts—things they've made
- Learning might also be assessed:
  - By the numbers of students who choose to do the elective/ retain enrolment in the elective
  - In reading the qualitative reflections about learning throughout the year/ self evaluation of the effectiveness of the process of inquiry

What are the Roadblocks?

- Funding, the elective may still involve some time from other classes, for example, if students had a research inquiry that involved visiting the local primary school for a morning to conduct focus groups etc.
- Staff engagement in the idea of student/ teacher inquiry
- Staff expectations—among some, there exist expectations around students experiencing an overnight 'turnaround' in engagement, and 'giving up' when inquiry based learning does not work the first time. Time and repeat experiences are needed for teachers and students to get used to a different way of working, 'giving it a go'
- Continuing induction of newer teachers and students leading to a refreshment of ideas and processes.

A roadblock that had not been anticipated was the resistance to developing an elective strand in a context, where it was argued, it takes at least a year to have one approved and the impetus by then could well have dissipated. It may be that the sustainability of Students as Researchers will be manifest in the ways that other schools in other jurisdictions, who have heard about the work, will decide that it is a viable project for them.

Sustainability in innovation is no easy matter. Is the innovation seen as an opportunity for growth and development, or a threat to the existing school ethos and the ways in which members of the school staff construct their professional identities? Clearly this project was variously received being both applauded and rejected. In many ways it takes us back to the very purposes of schooling with which we are concerned, such as: the kind of society that we want; how schools can contribute positively; what are the consequences of disparities of power and how are teachers and their students to live together. Gunter (2009, p. 101) argues:

> We can begin by stopping the demonizing of children. Giving them space to live and makes mistakes and learn from adults that they are a worthwhile new generation.

What can we Learn?

We argued, at the beginning of this chapter that it is important that readers connect it to their own experiences; that they undertake to personally reflect on its content in relation to what they already know and understand about the ways in which schools go about their business. For this reason we have chosen not to emphasise the salient matters that the chapter might be said to illuminate, but ask instead that the readers examine the multiplicity of issues that the study surfaces in student/teacher relationships and ask themselves why undertaking a project of this kind can cause practitioners to face some uncomfortable truths.

In our next chapter we shall see the ways in which children and young people can make a positive contribution to the work of cultural institutions. But even here, we are not entirely sanguine and seek to draw a line between consultation and appropriation. In the last chapter of this book we hope to draw from these many cases and arguments just how we can best work with children and young people in ways that are both sustainable and liberatory.

Chapter 6
Student Voice Beyond School

Introduction

As noted in the introduction to the previous chapter, case studies have a particular appeal in enabling the reader to develop insight into certain features of complex social practices. Stake (2005) sees that readers can learn vicariously from their encounters with a given case. It is also important to place a given case in the context of the discourses that may have a particular currency regarding the phenomenon being examined.

In the preceding chapter we looked at the specific case of students acting as researchers within one school. We used the case as a touchstone to raise some of the many issues and dilemmas that surface when, over successive years, young people are given an opportunity to examine key questions regarding the kind of schooling, teaching, learning and curriculum that they would like. In this chapter we turn first to issues in relation to learning beyond the school and then pay attention to another extended case study that is embedded in the discussion regarding the kind of pedagogy that is evolving beyond the boundaries of the school in a range of cultural institutions that offer educational experiences.

The Role of Cultural Institutions Beyond the School and Why the Voices of Children and Young People Matter

In this book we have highlighted the Convention on the Rights of the Child in terms of children and young people being listened to, but the Convention has another aspect that deserves attention in terms of the work of various cultural institutions. Article 31 states the child's right to 'participate freely in cultural life and the arts' and emphasizes, furthermore, governments' role in promoting and encouraging those rights. In other words, the rights of the child become the obligations of the

© Springer International Publishing Switzerland 2015
N. Mockler, S. Groundwater-Smith, *Engaging with Student Voice in Research, Education and Community,* DOI 10.1007/978-3-319-01985-7_6

institutions charged with meeting them. This can be realized by cultural institutions[1] consulting young people and inviting them to participate in both designing and evaluating educational functions including exhibitions and the like.

Hooper-Greenhill (2004, p. 11) argues that audience research has been 'museum-centred' taking insufficient account of the needs, likes and dislikes of those who may visit them. Thus much of the research has been to meet the concerns of those who work in cultural institutions, taking little account of the reasons why the wider community might even avoid them. As for gaining the insights and perspectives of children and young people there remains a paucity of research that has addressed their needs, likes and predispositions; that is, what they might want to know, be interested in and how they might be enabled to better understand particular events and phenomena. Even so, taking account of the insights of young visitors is not unproblematic. Later in this chapter we shall also argue that there may be a fine line between consultation and advocacy; is it possible that the voices of young people can be appropriated to become essentially a marketing tool?

Even so, there can be little question that cultural institutions are unique places for learning outside the classroom (Foreman-Peck and Travers 2013, p. 37):

> Museums offer more than an enrichment to the curriculum; museums are environments of possibility, of insight into the development and formation of ideas and the wonder of human ingenuity. The learning offered is more than a series of activities responding to a collection of objects; it could be described as an engagement with a 'collection of thoughts'.

But they are also complex environments that are required to satisfy a much wider range of audience needs than do schools. Audience engagement is vital if they are to be seen as successful, unlike schools, attendance is voluntary, and other than when visiting as part of a schooling schedule, people may leave if and when they wish. Also, it may be the case that many cultural institutions are seen rather as a kind of tourist attraction than an authentic place of learning, because as Worts (2011, p. 221) has noted "existing audiences of museums often associate museum visits with entertainment." In today's world of economic rationalism the effectiveness of such places may be determined more by the turnstile figures than as sites that deliver robust and effective learning opportunities. It is for this reason that hearing about their learning from children and young people is so critical.

Furthermore, by engaging with children and young people from a variety of different cultural backgrounds, as portrayed by Kelly and Fitzgerald (2011) who reported upon work with Pacific Island students from the *Coalition of Knowledge Building Schools* (Mockler and Groundwater-Smith 2011), it is possible to broaden and enrich the museum learning experience. Stein et al. (2008, p. 181) ask the question "How might visitor studies and audience—or community based research support museums in becoming more valuable, relevant and accessible to immigrant

---

[1] 'Cultural Institutions' is a portmanteau term that is inclusive of a wide range of facilities ranging from natural science museums, art museums, maritime museums, social history museums, libraries and the like. Hooper-Greenhill 2004, p. 3) refers to the notion of museums as a 'capacious concept' immensely varied and fluid in their design and purpose. What holds them together is their capacity to provide access to a wide range of cultural practices, both those that may be familiar to their audiences and those that are different, provocative, even exotic.

communities?" indicating that immigrants can straddle two worlds, bi-cultural and bi-lingual. In the case reported by Kelly and Fitzgerald, Pacific Island students, who had been invited to go 'behind the scenes' to see and experience the richness of the Pacifica collection, were anxious to protect their heritage and make it more widely known in their communities thus furthering and consolidating their sense of identity. As two participants put it in their concluding comments:

> Museum, thank you for being concerned about Islanders and what we have to share, including our history and how we came to be.
> Thanks for coming to our school and wanting our opinion and ideas! Yay! (p. 85)

Miller (2009) would have lauded these comments in her portrayal of museums as 'borderlands' where young people, who may be otherwise marginalized at best and treated with contempt and disdain at worst, can make an active and considered contribution.

In their discussion of the features of the responsive museum Lang et al. (2006, p. 227–228) nominated the following desiderata, among others, that are necessary for a museum to develop an authentic relationship with its community: to be audience centred; to be in dialogue with its audiences and potential audiences; to be accessible; to be learning focused; to be innovative and to creatively use information and communication technologies. These features resonate to those proposed by Worts (2011) in relation to museums re-assessing the extent to which their work addresses a range of cultural issues and realities that are relevant in today's world—a world, that is in the grip of an unprecedented information revolution.

Furthermore, it is essential that museums consider carefully both the explicit and implicit messages that are embedded in the manner in which they capture information in ways that are compelling and engaging. Anderson (2009) writes of "the listening museum" where various cultural institutions should develop more effective ways of addressing, listening and including young people. He maintained that:

> Visitors have great stories to tell. Yet in museums, as in society, it is so often analysis rather than the story that is valued. …Professionals can have a disguised contempt for narratives, as if they are for simpler minds, whereas analysis—so often the knowledge privileged by experts—is given status. Yet, genuine storytelling evokes judgmental responses, is ethically provocative, is inherently anti-authoritarian, leaves space for multiple responses and interpretations, preserves ideas, beliefs and connections, and is a counter to the accelerating rationalisation and technologisation. Storytelling is more easily remembered, and more likely to influence people's lives… Effective storytelling demands as much from the listener as it does from the teller—to imagine, to empathise, to understand, to interpret and to retell. For the most part our profession has not valued these skills highly in ourselves or our audiences, yet they are the ones we most need. (p. 40)

He goes on the question whether even this provision is enough. He asks that children and young people should be seen as partners making a contribution to what it is that museums have to offer and cites the youth forums of the British National Portrait Gallery and that of Museums Sheffield.

The Youth Forum of the National Portrait Gallery meets once a month on Thursday evenings. Participants come from various parts of London and may or may not have an arts background. The activities allow them to both engage with the works and to create their own responses as demonstrated by this blog entry:

Youth Forum at National Portrait Gallery discusses my portrait
The last time I visited the National Portrait Gallery I wondered why there were a group of teenagers gathered around my portrait of the "Golfing Sisters" staring earnestly and obviously in deep discussion. My curiosity got the better of me and I approached one of them and asked her for their feedback. She explained that they were part of the Youth Forum, a partnership with the NPG's Photographer's Gallery Forum.
They felt that the portrait represented a close and informal relationship with the photographer and that came through in the way the sisters responded to the camera and photographer, relaxed and intrigued. Overall the teenagers felt it was a very positive image that was uplifting and iconic in its Britishness! They had also been looking in to my history and finding out about First Women. It was great to hear them say that the project was an inspiration to them as young women. (Anita Cobin, 20th January, 2011)

Over the past few years, the Sheffield Museum's Youth Forum has produced a diverse range of creative responses to various works in its permanent collection and major touring exhibitions from partners, including Tate and the National Portrait Gallery. Working with professional artists, the group has produced engaging, imaginative explorations of various exhibitions in conjunction with staff and community partners. For example, the Youth Forum has explored the themes and ideas in the Museum's World Cultures collection. They selected objects and worked with designers and curatorial staff to completely redevelop the gallery. The project has enabled participants to gain a considerable knowledge of museums' practice and developed a wide range of new skills. The Youth Forum meets on Monday evenings and is completely free. In addition to the weekly sessions, the group is also involved in a number of visits to other museums and galleries, as well as a host of behind the scenes opportunities.

Arrangements such as these have certainly given voice to young people in new and creative ways, providing curators and designers with fresh insights into the management of collection development and of exhibitions.

Thus far, we have explored the rationale for consulting with children and young people and provided some examples; we are also mindful of the fact that 'visiting' may no longer be a matter of physically going to specific cultural institutions. It is now the case that many have developed access through their extensive digital resources. Tonta (2008) reminds us that museums are not longer just physical spaces but are, in effect, virtual destinations. It is increasingly of interest to know what use children and young people may make of these resources as well as the ways that they may interact with site visits and traveling exhibitions with their opportunities for object handling and specialist talks.

Working With Cultural Institutions: An Extended Case Study

The Coalition of Knowledge Building Schools (Mockler and Groundwater-Smith 2011) has contributed to audience research conducted in a number of Sydney cultural institutions including The Australian Museum, The State Library of NSW, Taronga Zoo Education and most recently Sydney Living Museums. All of these sites increasingly understand that children and young people today have been born into a digital world that they can navigate and understand. As Valenti (2002) has noted, what is required is a consultative model that is sufficiently flexible and is based upon the convergences, new knowledges and pedagogies that are interactive and responsive.

The *Coalition* is a hybrid collection of schools (Government and non-Government, single sex and co-educational) spanning Kindergarten to Year 12. It includes students from some of Sydney's most privileged families to those who are in difficult circumstances, including Indigenous and Pacific Island children, refugees and those from language backgrounds other than English. Its membership also includes the cultural institutions cited above as well as interested parties from organisations such as the NSW Commission for Children and Young People. The diversity of its membership make it appealing as a consultative group to the various cultural institutions when they wish to explore their various social and educational practices. In recent years this has been particularly so in relation to The State Library of NSW.

The State Library of NSW began in the early years of the Colony as *The Australian Subscription Library* (1826) and became the *Sydney Free Public Library* (1869). It was renamed the *Public Library of NSW* (1895) and finally took on the name of the *State Library of NSW* (1975). It houses a vast collection of over five million items including the David Scott Michell's collection of Australiana. The physical building is an assembly of wings that have been added over the years. The newest building houses an exciting and innovative contemporary learning space known as *The Glasshouse*.

When opening this space the Arts Minister of the day, paid particular attention to its commitment to "delivering inspiring and curriculum focused programs to K-12 students and teachers in real and web-based settings" (State Library of NSW 2011). It was indicated that students and their teachers would have access to a variety of electronic media including iPads, laptops, interactive whiteboards and the like; and would encourage a range and variety of partnership arrangements with those providing education services.

These aspirations accord with the key words and phrases that the State Library employs to describe its services, these being: Innovation and Engagement; Valuing People; Honour and Integrity; Energy and Teamwork.

Learning engagement in the context of such a cultural institution can be variously categorised as:

- Knowledge and understanding;
- Skills;
- Attitudes and values;
- Enjoyment, inspiration, creativity; and
- Activity, behaviour and cooperation (Hooper Greenhill 2007, p. 52)

The concept of consulting young people regarding exhibition design and the ways in which exhibitions can contribute to both actual and on-line learning has been employed as a central principle of the State Library's education officers. Thus, as a growing and changing institution the State Library of New South Wales has identified participating schools in *The Coalition* as those who not only can, but are willing and able to make a contribution to its various programs.

In this case study we shall draw upon two consultations regarding a short term exhibition featuring the history of shopping in Sydney and one in relation to a permanent exhibition.

On Sale! Shops and Shopping

The State Library of New South Wales is located in Sydney's central business district that is a flourishing shopping precinct. In spite of the growth and development of suburban centres and shopping malls the shops in the CBD still attract a large clientele. Many of them have a long history and have been functioning since the late nineteenth Century. Over the years the library has accumulated an archive of artefacts from these large stores, as well as historical records of early shopping opportunities that developed in the Colonial days.

A half day program was devised to include the perspective of young people into the *On Sale! Shops and Shopping* exhibition. This was intended to provide the State Library with valuable information about what students are interested in seeing in the exhibition itself and also allow the library's learning services to provide a rich on-line learning activity for students and teachers unable to visit the exhibition on-site. Thus the consultation would have both an evaluative and design function.

Fifteen young people took part in the consultation: Three Year 6 students from an inner west metropolitan public school; four Year 6 students from a North Shore public school; four Year 8 boys from a comprehensive boys high school; and four Year 8 girls from an independent girls school. They were supported by two State Library education officers, a teacher from each of the schools and one of the *Coalition's* academic partners.

The *On Sale! Shops and Shopping* curator oriented students to the exhibition by explaining the function of her role as one who develops and nurtures a concept and an understanding that the State Library is far more than a collection of books but a repository of a huge range of artefacts. The exhibition was six months in preparation and required her to scavenge through the library's collection to locate relevant material. She pointed out that her desire was to develop an exhibition that would touch everybody's interest from shopping for food, for clothes, for appliances and the like to the fact that shopping has been around for a long time. In thinking about shopping in Sydney she drew first of all upon the requisites brought by the first fleet, comprising mainly as convicts, to arrive as colonists in Australia and explained that generally the convicts had been accustomed to shops in their towns, villages and cities and were nonplussed to fail to find any in their new environment.

It was explained that early shipments to the colony were quite erratic and goods arrived irregularly. In 1806, for example, because of a shortage of newsprint *The Sydney Gazette* was printed on wrapping paper. Early markets were established to satisfy people's need to shop with one such being conducted in 1810 where the Queen Victoria Building (a well known local site) now stands.

Currency was a continuing story. The shortage of money in the colony led to the holey dollar where the centre was stamped out to create a separate coin. Pounds, shillings and pence prevailed until 1960 when decimal currency was launched. Credit cards grew from store charge plates with the Bank Card being introduced in 1974 and EFTPOS in the 1990s. Gift cards, vouchers, loyalty cards and trading stamps were also a part of the way in which transactions were and continue to be conducted. Originally receipts were in the form of hand-written invoices with the printed docket arriving much later. It was not until 1860 that the first cash register came into being. All this seemed quite a revelation to the young people whose imagination until this point had been limited by their own recent experience.

The curator pointed out that we take for granted shops as part of the landscape but much has changed over time. The art of window display alone required the introduction of the plate glass window. The introduction of gas light in the 1840s and electricity in the late nineteenth century also played into the ways in which goods could be displayed, sometimes at great cost, as for example when a gas explosion blew out a large glass window.

Internal arrangements also changed the ways in which people shopped; wealthy people arriving in carriages were waited upon by assistants who brought the goods to them. The introduction of ready-made clothes also affected the ways in which garments were purchased. Elevators and escalators altered the ways in which people could move around inside the buildings.

Shopping was increasingly being seen as a social activity. The development of arcades and street blocks encouraged people to take a leisurely stroll. Sales techniques began to take account of advertising campaigns with the example of National Washing Machine Month as a precursor to Mothers' Day being used as an illustration.

Finally the presentation traced the development of the weekly shop, the introduction of the shopping centre and the mall taking hold and most recently the evolution of on-line shopping.

As an icebreaking activity all participants were asked to examine a series of images responding to "When you think about shopping in the city how does it feel to you?" This strategy has been described by Colucci (2007) who recognized it as a signature practice used for focus group discussion in *Coalition* investigations.

Four responses referred to the first image, that of a dancer stretching out to hold aloft a large pearl:

- Shopping in the city feels glamorous, it's a link to the real world outside school walls. You want to show off your shopping and wear it proudly.
- It shows the stretch of the city. How people stretch everyday to find the item the want to buy. The need to find the item.
- Because it is exhilarating, freeing, fun, exciting. The city streets, the store windows, fashion, buildings. The image displays this sense of freedom and the ability to be blown anywhere.

- It feels like a heavy burden, hard work, not always easy to find what to buy and hard earned money disappears quickly.

One responded to the second image, that of a tethered goat:

- I am rather extravagant and love shopping so it is a good thing if I am tethered like the goat so that I don't overspend.

Six selected the fourth image shadows of camels crossing the desert with the words "giddy up"

- Because it is a new place where you can look around and explore. You will never know the way off by heart, there will always be a new adventure ahead of us.
- Because when I shop in the city I feel free and the city is so much bigger than other shopping centres. It is very fun and exciting.
- Because when I go shopping in the city I feel free and I am having fun. Also there is lots of space and it isn't crowded.
- Shopping is an exciting adventure like exploring the desert on camel back. You don't know what you'll find, but if you look hard enough you'll come across an oasis with bargains and sparkling things.
- I have to choose this because the city is all hustle and bustle.
- Because I don't enjoy shopping and I am always in a great rush to get it done as quickly as possible and get out of there!

Four chose the fifth image "open your eyes":

- Being aware, staying focused, scrutinising.
- Shopping in the city can be relaxing and intense. The picture shows us that when shopping in the city you should keep your eyes clear at all times because the currency in Sydney is high and being a wise consumer while shopping you could save yourself a lot of money—so open your eyes.
- Because you can't see everything so the caption at the bottom is telling you that you need to 'open your eyes' to everything around you and not stay on one thing.
- Because when I shop in the city I look with my eyes. I scan every item in my view to see whether I want it or whether it would suit me and what I would wear with it. Also I am always focused on city life observing everything.

Students were issued with individual iPads and asked to photograph themselves and initially document what excited them about the prospect of their involvement in the project and what surprised and interested them in relation to the curator's presentation. A small sample of responses are reported below:

- I feel excited about today because I am very interested in shopping and how it has evolved over time.
- What I found interesting about the presentation is that shops actually changed over time with their different layout on the interior of the shop and then there were the invention of lifts so there was then multistorey shops and the supermarket was invented so you did not have to go to the grocer you could actually look around and even be seduced by different products.

- What I find interesting so far is the history of shopping. I did not realize how much change there has been from telling a shop keeper what you wanted to browsing around a shopping centre. Shopping has changed from packing as well. They were originally in brown paper bags and are now in there own colorful packings that we can choose from.
- I feel excited because last time I came to the library it was really fun and I know coming here I will learn something of great value.
- Today I feel really excited and overjoyed that I was chosen for this excursion. I think that we are going to be very busy today and I can't wait.
- I found it interesting that in the olden days they didn't have packaged things in the grocers shop.

Students were then able to browse through the exhibition and identify their favourite item and why they had selected it. Students were then given an opportunity to further research the information attached to the item: When and where is it from? Why was it created? What does the item tell you about Australia and shopping? What would you like to know more about this item?

As an illustration of the ways in which students pursued this challenge two students were closely observed. One, a primary school boy, had chosen an early twentieth century invoice from a major department store His original reason was that he had enjoyed watching early episodes of "Are you being served?" and wanted to know more about the store. He returned to the item and examined it carefully. He was able to identify that it was written in 1910 for a Mr Johnson who appeared to be furnishing his entire house in one fell swoop. It was created so that customers could have a record of what had been purchased and the cost. He was fascinated with the way in which each page of the extensive invoice was sub-totalled and the procedures for managing pounds, shillings and pence. He identified that the most expensive item was the bedroom suite at a cost of one hundred and twenty four pounds, and although not recorded he wondered why there was no item for bed linen. He was interested in using the currency converter to see what the total spent would be in today's currency, over 100 years later. He was interested in whether other similar files existed.

A Year 8 girl selected a Department Store poster. Her favourite item in the exhibition was a poster with the poodle because it was "very eye-catching and the colours that were used were bright." It was created on the 1st September 1949. It was created to advertise the store as an elegant store and encourage customers to purchase items from it. "It tells us that everyone in Australia wanted to be posh and upperclass so they can look like they are rich. The store is advertising for upperclass customers to look fashionable, classy and rich. I would like to know why it chose the rich people mostly to go to their store instead of the lower class and the middle class people".

These examples illustrate how assiduously the students researched their items and justified their selections.

Following filming activities students, teachers and museum staff returned to the Glasshouse and recorded the ways in which their views might have changed following their exposure to the exhibition:

- I now feel that shopping in the city isn't as new and glamorous as I had first thought. The fact is that shopping is a very old activity.
- Visiting the city can be really troublesome if you don't open your eyes anything can happen. You will miss the icons, the beautiful sculptures and shopping centres if you go around with your eyes closed.
- The exhibition has provided me with an awareness one needs to have about the sellers' aim to make me buy. I need to buy what I need rather than be told what I should buy.

The young people were able to either give a message to the State Library on their ipads and suggest improvement and/or write a slogan for the Library. They suggested the ways that the library could make the exhibition even better would be by having some more interactive sections. "Kids are always attracted to things that move and that you can touch." They saw that the exhibition could be improved by adding information about why we shop in the first place. "What is it that makes us want to shop? Does the stereotype of women shopping still fit the reality of our world today? What is it that makes us want something? What is it that makes us absolutely hate something? How do retailers make us want something?"

A number of improvements could come about by using improved technology that is interactive "so children can have more fun while they are exploring the history. eg. an iPad stuck on the wall and there is someone telling a story about the item". These students were acutely aware of the affordances of a range of technologies that would enhance the exhibition for their age group.

Finally, the students constructed slogans for the State Library's shopping exhibition:

- Shopping isn't about buying something new, it's about continuing something old
- A great library with many different historical items. You must visit if you want to unlock the mystery.
- I know about libraries, they are about books. Oh no you don't—go the On Sale and see something completely different.
- Are you tired of going to the shops, then come and see the shopping exhibition at the State Library.
- Everything old is new again. So come and see On Sale! at the State Library showcasing shopping over time, seeing when things were fashionable for the first time.
- Come in and experience some extraordinary library fun.
- If you like shopping come and enjoy the history of shopping.
- The wonders of the world can't be seen better than in its centre, The State Library.
- Did you know you can shop at the State Library? See how they used to do it.
- Travel around the globe? Is it too boring why don't you visit the State Library in the morning.

- Come and look at nineteenth Century shopping—a place for a laugh and history at the State Library.
- The State Library is as good as shopping!

Through this project, young people were provided with opportunities to develop their knowledge and understanding specifically in relation to the evolution of shopping behaviours from both the merchants' and consumers' perspectives. Their responses and insights clearly demonstrate that they travelled well beyond their early concepts and beliefs. They developed skills and competence in using sophisticated equipment and employing visual communication. They were able to bring into play their attitudes and values regarding shopping well beyond a transient form of consumerism. At the same time they were appreciative of the effort and energy that had gone into planning their program for them. There was clear evidence of their enjoyment and the ways in which they willingly engaged in a range of activities and in working cooperatively to achieve the objectives for the day. This was robust and effective learning as well as sound advice to the Library.

As we noted earlier in this chapter, too often 'service delivery' in institutions created for public use is measured by monitoring the numbers who may visit with little known or understood about the engagement of participants. By consulting young people the State Library has commenced a path where the development of practices will be directly related to the ways in which they are experienced.

The 'Amaze' Exhibition and the 'Pocket App'

The most recent demonstration of the ways in which students from the *Coalition* have been able to contribute to the development of exhibitions and accompanying digital resources has been in relation to the State Library of New South Wales where they assisted in the design of a 'pocket app' that would enable visitors to the Mitchell Library and the upcoming AMAZE exhibition to decide upon which features they wished to focus and what the appropriate information level might be.

In designing an app it was believed that it must be functional and useful, it must be easy to use and hold meaning for the user. This, then, was the challenge that was set for the young people taking part in the consultation; the task being to inform, in part, the design and content of an app that could be used to access relevant information about the Mitchell Library its layout and history and the AMAZE exhibition designed to give access to some of the unusual and curious ephemera that the library had collected for over a century. The development of a mobile app was seen as part of this process for it was seen that "what connects us are our stories, every object has a story". In some ways the app would give access to these stories. But it would also be a form of technology with which young people have a familiarity through their use of tablets and mobile phones. It was to be a mobile device that could identify the whereabouts of the user and provide icons of the objects around them that could then be investigated. Users would be able to inform the Library of their likes and dislikes and would be encouraged to share information. They would be able to save their tour and find out more about specific exhibits that may have intrigued them.

As young people their input was regarded as valuable in that they would have a variety of views regarding what might be of interest and the level and kind of language that would appeal to their peers. The selection of the participating schools was carefully considered. Beside two independent girls' schools there were two Government boys' schools and one coeducational Government high school as well as one comprehensive primary school, all from Metropolitan Sydney. Finally, students from a Catholic secondary school located on the Central Coast of NSW travelled down for the day.

Sites such as the State Library of NSW are exceptional places of interest for nurturing curiosity and inspiring learners to develop understandings of the world of which they are a part. These cultural institutions are complex environments that serve a number of purposes, however a primary one among them must be to provide effective learning opportunities for young people. Over a number of publications it has been argued (for example Weill 2002; Hooper-Greenhill 2007) that the two vital questions to be addressed are how are objects and collections used by cultural institutions to construct knowledge, and how can the relationships of audiences to this knowledge be understood?

Furthermore, it has been increasingly understood in the relevant literature that educators in sites of learning other than schools, need to notice what it is that learners do and the language that they and these institutions employ in order to collectively negotiate ways ahead (Ash et al. 2012). What is desired is that a common ground is found that will engage all of the stakeholders. The educator is no longer functioning in a didactic way, but acts to enable the learning of the student, learning that may be mediated by any number of digital forms such as an app.

Students were issued with iPads that would be the main tool that they would utilise throughout the day using an 'app' that enables users to combine visual media and text, in relation to thoughts and questions arising from exposure to the objects and architecture of the Library. As a means of practising their skills the students were given free reign of the library while curators set up four actual artefacts in the learning space that would provide students with rare close-to-the-object experience.

Students were able to photograph the items with their iPads and ask the curators further questions. It was explained that these four items would be among the 60 that would go into the exhibition space. The exposure to the items was then extended through a series of photographs of the other pieces that would form the exhibition. They were asked to identify and summarise the nature of a particular item, what they had liked (or disliked) about the item, what kinds of broader opinions might be of interest, what was a 'quirky fact', what ancillary media would help (e.g. audio) and additionally did they have any provocations that they could ask—i.e. questions to which there are no ready answers but require speculation. They were reminded that the exhibition and the building itself will be caption free, so the user of the app would need to have some scaffolds by which they can examine the objects.

After a lunch break students were able to roam the building, but this time with a purpose in mind—to collect no more than ten photographs that might give access to the question "what sort of story does the building tell us?". These too were to be entered into Keynote.

On their return students began to collate their images and text. They were fascinated by a large range of points of interest from the insertions of blue glass into the leaded glass windows depicting the Seven Ages of Man in the Shakespeare room through to the card catalogue on the library floor. Indeed, the interest in the card catalogue intrigued Library staff who had not realized that these young people had been accustomed to digital catalogues and found the beautifully crafted wooden cases housing thousands of cards as an interesting relic from the past.

It was clear from the extent of student engagement across a whole day that they not only enjoyed the experience including the use of digital tools, but also that they were making a sound contribution to the Library. It has long been understood in countries such as the UK where Ofsted (Ofsted 2008) has explored the nature and impact of learning outside the classroom that visits to various institutions are at their best when they are purposeful and interactive. This consultation was all of those things and would enhance the development of the app as intended.

An unexpected outcome was that the students then decided that they too could develop an app in relation to their own schools that could be used to familiarize visitors with features of the schools' histories, architecture and design. Some months later they were invited to re-visit the Library and see the extent of the development of the pocket app and the ways in which their contributions had been incorporated.

Student Voice or Student Exploitation?

At a recent research training workshop conducted by the Australian Association for Research in Education one of the authors of this book outlined these consultations and others with which the *Coalition* had been engaged. She was asked whether this work with cultural institutions was, in fact, a cheap form of market research and did she consider that the students were being exploited. Together, we vehemently deny this charge, arguing that such a view is instrumentalist and fails to recognize the potential to interrupt the power relations that are so strongly embedded in the ways in which decisions are normally made. We strongly asserted in the introduction to this book that we would eschew the notions of 'empowerment' and suggest here that the dynamic is a very different one; what is proposed is a relationship in that the engagement of children and young people in assisting to shape the practices of our cultural institutions is more akin to the development of what Fielding (2008, p. 63) has nominated at 'person centred communities'; a matter to which we referred in our opening chapter.

Tzibazi (2013, p. 157) looks to the mores and practices of participative action research (PAR) in the context of the development of Museum policies to justify consultation and dialogue as authentic and as an interruption to regimes of power,

"The PAR approach views control of knowledge by those who are the experts as a means for reproducing unequal power relations." She argues, as we have through this book, for an inclusive and democratic ethos that can be informed by consulting young people who are able to reclaim a space that in the past denied them full participation and concludes: "If institutional transformation remains to be pursued, we risk involving young people in projects that only act as vehicles for self-development" (p. 167).

We see this as a powerful argument against the notion of consultation as exploitation. Certainly the cultural institutions themselves may benefit from the advice of children and young people, but this will be to the benefit of the wider community. As Young (2002) has noted major decisions regarding the practices of cultural institutions are taken by "experts" away from the public gaze with consultation only taking place once the plans have been completed and solidified as practice.

Kelly and Bartlett (2009) in their summation of the practice of consultation with young people, as undertaken by the Australian Museum, a member of the *Coalition,* have identified a number of key factors that enliven exhibitions and programs that are designed to attract this sector of the community. They see that young people:

Need opportunities to explore widening world and reflect on new experiences:

- so they begin to consider themselves as participants in society, not just observers
- involve them in the museum rather than anticipate passive consumers
- moving them from child museum experiences to adult ones are interested in exhibitions that include personal stories, national history, indigenous and environmental issues that are interactive, changing and aesthetically attractive

Clearly, what is being promulgated in this work is a case for collaboration rather than exploitation. Any assessment of sustained consultation with children and young people needs to take account of the attention that is paid to their ideas and the extent that they are given opportunities to voice fresh perspectives and that, where feasible, these are acted upon.

For those whose work is mainly in relation to school education this study raises interesting questions with respect to considering students as 'audiences' who deserve to be consulted regarding the arrangements that are made for them. Clearly the work goes well beyond a notion of market research and we would certainly eschew the notion of students as clients rather than as learners; but there remains a suggestion that if we are to 'sell school' to young people who may be quite reluctant learners, we need to take their views and experiences into account.

Having taken this step out of schools and classrooms in our next chapter we turn to community engagement with children and young people being involved in decisions in the streets and the parks in which they live. We also broaden the discussion by examining unfamiliar contexts ranging from Ethiopia to the Indian subcontinent.

Chapter 7
The Voices of Young People in the Community

This chapter will explore the development of sustainable and collaborative partnerships for example, those with health, social justice, recreation and environmental agencies. By moving beyond school and university education to consider the ways in which the voices of children and young people can make a meaningful contribution to services designed for them in such varied contexts as juvenile justice and town planning we believe that new models of participation can be built.

Furthermore we see that by travelling into less familiar territory beyond the majority world, consulting with younger members of the community in a range of settings can teach us much. With this in mind we have turned to a number of studies that consider forms of participative action research (PAR) in contexts as far afield as Latin America, sub-Saharan Africa and the Indian sub-continent. While these studies may seem remote from our immediate concerns we argue that they embody practices and principles that can be applied in education contexts.

Participative Action Research with Children and Young People in Different Worlds

In their voluminous and informative toolkit aimed at researchers working with children and young people with regard to their experiences of the physical and emotional punishment and discipline in South East Asia and the Pacific et al. (2004) focus upon the participation of children as the key stakeholders. They provide the reader with a range of strategies and varying references. For instance, they cited the work of Hecht (1998) who explored with street children in Brazil the ways in which they understood their experience. His two key questions were: How do these children interpret their street predicament and which ideas of childhood are revealed in their sense of self and in the social apparatus aimed at saving them? His inquiry was undertaken via what he called 'radio workshops' whereby he handed these young people, mainly boys, a tape recorder and microphone and asked them to interview each other using their own questions. He found that:

© Springer International Publishing Switzerland 2015
N. Mockler, S. Groundwater-Smith, *Engaging with Student Voice in Research, Education and Community,* DOI 10.1007/978-3-319-01985-7_7

- The children tended to view the tape recorder not with suspicion but rather as a means of getting their opinions listened to;
- They often used role play, pretending to be on the radio, as the basis of their interview technique;
- Street-children interviewers were not afraid to challenge a participant if they thought he was telling lies;
- They asked questions adult interviewers would not have thought of;
- They asked questions in words and ways that other boys understood;
- The questions they asked each other were often as interesting for the research as the answers they gave (Ennew and Plateau 2004, p. 237–238)

Thus, a simple strategy yielded interesting and valuable results that could inform those who have relied, in the past, on researcher observations and statistical data, rather than first hand accounts from those experiencing the hard life of living on the streets.

Ennew and Plateau have provided something of a blueprint for the conduct of inquiries that support the agency of children and young people and do so in the context of the rights of the child that has been paramount in our discussions throughout this book. They provide five levels containing twelve steps that will assist those wishing to develop a plan of research that addresses encounters with young people, these being:

Preparation

1. identifiying stakeholders and the research team;
2. defining the research aims and main research questions;
3. collecting, reviewing and analyzing secondary data;

Protocol Design

4. developing detailed research questions;
5. identifying research tools;
6. evolving a research plan

Data Collection

7. Undertaking 1st cycle data collection
8. Undertaking 1st analysis
9. Undertaking 2nd cycle data collection

Analysis and Report Writing

10. Analysing
11. Writing

Implementation

12. Use information

They recommend that the young people who are to be involved should be incorporated into the process as early as possible. In other words the young people themselves become instrumental in identifying who the other stakeholders might be and considering how the research questions can be structured, and are then active throughout all the steps. This is a strategy that we have strongly advocated throughout this book.

These processes have certainly been recognized by Lolichen et al. (2006) who investigated with children in India the difficulties that they encountered with transport, mobility and access within a large program "Concerned for Working with Children". The sites selected for study were underdeveloped villages, poor and lacking in transport and mobility facilities. The study was designed to enable the child participants to design and develop the methodology and tools to conduct the research. The study had the following principal objectives:

- To enable children to access, obtain, and manage information appropriately, in order to 'empower' them to become their own protagonists.
- To enable children to identify and recognise problems, access and analyse data, and use the resulting information to take control of the issues they face and, further, to develop solutions to overcome them.
- To demonstrate that children are capable of effectively participating in all democratic processes, provided that they are equipped with appropriate information and skills and that their participation in such processes can bring about structural changes in the community. (Lolichen et al. 2006: 348)

While we have been somewhat skeptical about the notion of 'empowerment' the evidence from the study suggests that indeed the 300 boys and girls aged 9–18 had gathered a body of information that could not be easily dismissed and would influence and bring about change and future decision making. Lolichen argues that information is power, especially in communities where the power has been hitherto invested in bureaucratic processes. The program was conducted through a series of workshops including: 'walkathons', mapping, interviewing and using flashcards. Each workshop was documented through field notes collected by facilitators. For example:

> Manjula, a 13-year-old working child from Nayakwadi, is able to walk to the shop, as it is close by. However, in order to get to the market or the ration store, she needs to take the bus. It is a problem for her to go to these places because it takes long time and she has a lot of work to do at home. It is also a problem for her to carry heavy loads, since there are many ups and downs, and small stones along the route that she frequents. There are forests on either side of the route that Manjula takes to get to the hospital, temple, and to fetch water. She also has to pass a cemetery, which frightens her. There is a water facility close to her house, but it does not supply water regularly. (Interview with Manjula, Gujjadi Panchayat, February 6, 2005)

Many such interviews yielded information that could not have otherwise been collected. We should understand that this work went beyond positioning young people as data sources in that they were able to act as agents for change. Seeing the world through Manjula's eyes allowed those who are responsible for designing rural transport to understand that it is not only the task to be undertaken, but the ways in which it interconnects with other issues in Manjula's hard and demanding life such as being responsible for the collection of water and goods for the family and dealing with her own fears and anxieties.

In the study of the nature of children's work in rural and often remote Indonesian communities Hastadewi (2009) also emphasizes the need for information collection that involves the young people themselves. There is a scarcity of valid information on child labour, even some dissembling, when informants believe that their disclosures might harm a profitable enterprise.

Hastadewi's research gathered 1315 pieces of data from 256 participants (165 working children, 70 non-working children, and 21 adults).

Seventeen different data-collection methods were used including: focus group discussions, story telling, body map drawings, circle diagrams of how earning are spent, 24-hour clocks of daily activities, cause–effect diagrams, Venn diagrams to explore the social elements encouraging children to work, drawings, photo essays, seasonal calendars, daily activities' calendars, neighbourhood maps, structured observations, recall sheets of how earnings were spent, role play, visual stimuli and neighbourhood walks (Hastadawi 2009, p. 481) These methods were selected as ones that the children would find engaging as well as encouraging them to be open and transparent. Because they were so diverse in their nature they enabled cross checking and triangulation to take place.

Many results confirmed what had already been suspected about the extent and diversity of child labour, however, one unexpected surprise was the extent to which children faced physical risk in their workplaces. Injuries were disclosed through the development of body maps where they were indicated upon the body, but explained through further notes and discussion. "Some injuries to hands, knees and feet were caused by sharp tools. In the garment sector, conditions such as dehydration, suffocation and headaches were caused by heat and dust. Girls cleaning jellyfish in the fishing sector sometimes suffered poisoning or blisters from using chemicals such as chlorine. High-risk work on fishing platforms at sea and in a stone quarry, had resulted in bone fractures and even fatalities" (p. 483).

For children and young people in many parts of the world less privileged than those living in what might be called over-developed communities the impacts of environmental degradation and climate change have meant that their young lives are even more difficult and stressful than hitherto. Few places can claim to be more problematic in this respect than Ethiopia, one of the world's poorest countries. Failed seasons, unpredictable rains, sometimes a complete failure of seasonal rains, requires an extraordinary resilience on the part of people facing food insecurity. It is in this context that Campbell et al. (2013) sought to investigate with young people their perspectives on the nature of their environment, both built and natural in a context where activism by those most affected is singularly absent from the debates and discussions. Using Social Representations Theory (SRT) (p. 437) as a framework for revealing shared systems of social knowledge and associated practices, the researchers worked with five students from each of six urban schools, twenty-nine students in all aged 12–16.

In order to elicit and explore students' perspectives on the environment and the meanings that they attributed to its change and degradation they used such participatory methods as photo-voice and draw-and-write techniques that would enable those young people with limited literacy skills to reflect on their inner and social worlds. Campbell et al. believed that by examining the systems of values, ideas and practices that orient young people to their physical and social worlds and engage with them in dialogue regarding how they might make sense of that world, it would be possible to construct new meanings and action plans.

The guiding questions were: What are the strengths of your environment? What are the challenges facing your environment? How do you engage and interact with the environment? In some ways in response to the first question the students idealized their environment, arising no doubt from their urban experiences; however in addressing the second, they also understood the nature of the degradation of the environment and its impact, particularly on health. Drawings included in the study were graphic illustrations of practices that would certainly endanger the health of the community, such as a number that were of people defecating and urinating into rivers and on public streets. Their emphasis was upon pollution created by people living in over-crowded and impoverished circumstances with little or no reference to the larger issue of climate change (a matter in which the researchers had an interest) possibly because they saw that there was little that they could do to address that larger concern.

As Campbell et al. (2013, p. 456) reported:

> Despite their awareness of environmental misuse and weaknesses, students largely see the damage as reversible and feel they have some role to play in tackling the issue. This belief in reversibility helps to inform students' sense of agency. Students believe they have something positive to contribute to environmental preservation and improvement. Moreover, this sense of ownership and responsibility in regards to addressing environmental degradation and misuse goes hand in hand with students' belief that they themselves have a role to play in tackling local environmental challenges.

It was argued that while the young people's sense of their place in the world was mediated by conditions of poverty, poor infrastructure and unregulated economic development they had a positive sense of hope and confidence that they could contribute to tackling environmental degradation. Such resilience cannot be easily put aside by powerful adults who will need to capitalize on the sense of hope and resilience that such studies can bring to policy and practice. But these cases are more than a process for drawing the attention of authorities to the conditions of children and young people's lives, as well as enabling active participation, for as Lolichen et al. (2006, p. 356–357) point out "They are leading the way to making the governments accountable. Children have started a revolution for change and the adult world is yet to catch up with them and respond adequately".

Being at the Margins

However, we do not have to look far from home to find that young people are leading difficult and challenging lives. One place that the adult world has difficulty in understanding and collaboratively researching with young people is that where juveniles come into contact with the law. Certainly there has been a plethora of research that has examined the experience of these young people in terms of crime statistics, family studies, institutional reviews and the like, however, few studies have actively engaged with them in exploring their lives and the consequences of involvement in illicit activities ranging from lower order crimes such as graffitiing and vandalism, to those causing concern such as drug taking and dealing, stealing, and violent assault. Other groups are marginalized by virtue of poverty, ethnicity and race. They are often difficult to reach and work with in ways that honour and respect them.

Recent years have brought to light matters of the abuse and neglect of young people in care. An Australian Royal Commission into Institutional Child Sexual Abuse, established in 2013, has heard many tales of children and young people where they were not only not listened to, but were not believed when they did manage to give accounts of their travails. This accords with the research undertaken by Tucker (2013) who engaged in the challenging task of involving young people as co-enquirers into abuse and neglect in England. Working with young people who had been subjects of many forms of abuse the research investigated how they regarded themselves and others. The sensitive nature of the study and the distribution of its participants across the country made face-to-face contact difficult; the outcome was to adopt conversation by telephone (individual and conference calls) and email exchanges. Participants became familiar with each other's perspectives by both listening and examining the transcripts of each other's revelations over several years.

> Gary: We're digging deep here and trying to get to grips with something hard. I'm starting to see this as a battle to make yourself heard when nobody wants to or can't hear you. B said something earlier about rights and that makes sense but my big question is where do the rights go to? Like they evaporate?
>
> Brendan: They go because of what you are, how they see your family. Mrs so and so's kids. Crap on someone's shoe, Lowest of the low and disrespected. Nothing going for you and the family _ shit education, shit estate, shit leave you to put your bits in there… point for me is nobody cares (p. 278)

The outcome of their enquiry was that, as a group, they evolved a 'typology of disbelief' (p. 279) being the key reasons why they were not believed; among them: background and baggage; family background; reluctance and refusal; and personal relationships. The study required participants to relive intense personal pain and it was a mark of their commitment to others in similar circumstances to persist with the study in the hope that professionals in the field would be more able and inclined to listen.

Other groups are also difficult to reach and understand often because of reticence on the part of members of the group themselves, uncertain and fearful of what will be made of any information. For example, an Australian study (White 2007) exploring the nature, patterns and causes of youth gang violence examined, in great detail, gang related behaviours, gang membership and the occurrence of violent and anti-social behaviour. The study acknowledged the diversity of gang formation and characteristics. Membership was seen to vary in terms of commitment and association and even the rites by which individuals may be initiated into the gang's activities. The review cites a range of studies that have examined procedures such as these, as well as the attitudes of young people in the community vis-à-vis gang behaviours and their own aspirations to belonging to such a group. But this research has directed itself generally to interviews and questionnaires developed, conducted and analysed by adult researchers and failed to seize an opportunity to work more deeply and systematically with the gangs themselves to ameliorate their conditions.

In his conclusion to an otherwise well informed paper the author recommended that a number of aspects of youth group participation might be explored, such as: ethnicity; patterns of activity; similarities and differences between school and street gangs; cultural and economic factors; the use of weapons; and, relationships to adult criminal gangs. Missing from the recommendations was any reference to working with young people themselves.

In contrast to this study the work promoted by Cammarota and Fine (2008:11) establishes as praxis, i.e. morally informed action, a particular form of participatory action research, namely youth participatory action research (YPAR). This they argue provides young people with opportunities to solve those social problems that impact on their lives and design actions to rectify them.

> What perhaps distinguishes young people engaged in YPAR from the standard representations in critical youth studies is that their research is designed to contest and transform systems and institutions to produce greater justice—distributive justice, procedural justice, and what Iris Marion Young calls a justice of recognition, or respect. In short, YPAR is a formal resistance that leads to transformation—systematic and institutional change to promote social justice.

Each chapter in the book edited by Cammarota and Fine (2008) takes a particular case, many co-written with participants, and places it in context along with a subsequent commentary. For example, Chapter 5 (Cahill et al. 2008) describes the ways in which a community of young researchers was formed through a process of "doing it" (p. 109) by developing a response research project that would "speak back to stereotypes that over-simplify, reduce and limit" (p. 113). The study sought to identify what is possible for young people living in cityscapes that are being increasingly gentrified and that, for them, are alienating and marginalizing. In some senses the study was a series of creative workshops. Calling themselves 'The Fed-up Honeys" young adolescent women investigated their lives in Lower East Side New York City by opening their eyes to what it was that made them mad about the ways in which they were regarded and often vilified and how that impacted upon the ways in which they saw themselves.

The participants were engaged in place-based research, seeking for an understanding of the nature of their physical and historical environment that labeled them variously as a burden to society and teen mums. The participants began by researching their own everyday lives using mental maps, behaviour mapping, taking field notes, photographing, conducting their own focus groups and brainstorming sessions that enabled data to be gathered that could be analysed and make collective sense of what members of the group shared and what was different. They discussed the lack of support and places for young people, as one put it "I am an interesting young woman who bores herself to delirium. Because there's nothing to do. I'm bored... It's like that 'I'm interesting' is going to waste because I have nothing to do with it." (p. 119). They examined the consequences of gentrification that was pushing the original community more and more to the margins. Even the term 'gentrification' was a new one to the group who discerned the power of naming what was taking place in their neighbourhood.

During the course of their investigations the Fed Up Honeys became incensed at the ways that charitable organisations stereotyped them and the ways in which these stereotypes informed the policies that were said to assist them. As a means of 'speaking back' their form of action developed. Participants sought to feed back into the community 'youth friendly' resources (p. 127) that made explicit community development strategies that would enhance education, health and housing. They did this by writing and distributing reports, by establishing a website and by saturating the community with action stickers, all of which have penetrated far beyond the specific location within which they worked. They perceived that they had established a 'pedagogy of citizenship' that demonstrated the positive outcomes when young people invest themselves in their communities.

These are not easy and comfortable studies to engage with. Academic researchers need to learn to take a back seat. Often the YPAR studies both showed the way in terms of authentic participative research with young people, but equally demonstrated that notions of power and control are interrupted and need to be renegotiated on more equal terms, an aspiration that this book clearly subscribes to.

Less contentious, but also a realm where there is much to learn about enquiring *with* children and young people is the nature of their and our natural and built environment and ways that aspects of it might be improved.

Taking Account of the Perspectives of Children and Young People Regarding the Environment

It is often the case that when children and young people are consulted regarding environmental questions it is in the context of the school. Such was the case in regard to the UK Research Council's project (L2 C) that was located in schools in socially and economically deprived urban areas in the England and that focused on how ten to twelve year olds experienced their local communities and made sense of their lives in that community and the school curriculum. An aspiration of the project was to evolve methods that would allow for collaborative and participatory research and would develop the students' capacities as researchers and their understanding of the value of sustained, inclusive enquiry (Barrett-Hacking and Barrett 2009, p. 372).

The L2 C project aimed to explore:

1. 10–12 year old children's experience in the local environment and community.
2. How the curriculum can become more relevant to children, their families and the local community, and ways of involving children in both curriculum development and action in the local community.

3. How local environmental and educational policy can change to take account of children's perspectives.

A pilot project conducted in Staffordshire found that there was a dissonance between the children's local experience and the school curriculum that had taken little account of their views. Even so, it was the case that to develop a dialogue between the young people and their teachers and the researchers much of the process continued to be out of their control and it was realized that some training was required. Thus, in early meeting the children explored what they understood by the term 'local environment and community'; they planned to enquire into how a range of children behaved in the local environment; and they sought to consider how they might research children's likes, dislikes and feelings about the community in which they lived.

An important departure in this research was to teach the participating students how to deal with data: how to read and look at maps, how to interpret audio and video materials; how to re-examine data in the light of emergent theories; how to identify key themes and share these across the group. Bragg (2010) suggested that when young co-researchers become involved in data analysis their involvement is greatly enhanced. In the case of the L2 C project it was conceded that while, within the project, the children were respected and viewed as competent, as a reform it had little impact across the school.

> Within the project children are viewed differently, however, outside of the project there's status quo. The project has come so far but there's still much to do to make it a proper reform to transfer across the school. (teacher-researcher end of project interview) Barratt Hacking and Barrat 2009: 380).

So how do we understand the matter of impact in terms of children and young people making an authentic contribution to decision making about the environments in which they live? It is important to understand that there are both differences and similarities in the ways that young people and adults view the world around them. Midbjer and Day (2007, p. 3) have noted that "adult experiences centre on how we use places, we need to know what they are *for*. For children it's more what the places 'say' how they meet and *experience* them". Thus the impact on decision making when children and young people are consulted has to be mediated through the lens of the ways in which they view both the built and natural environment. All too often young people are required to function in environments that suit adult needs and that may be quite alien to their wants and desires.

All the same, the notion of Child Friendly Cities, has been taken up by communities who have taken seriously, to the point of implementation, the ideas that were contributed by children and young people. Wilks (2010) has reported on a number of such projects undertaken in Italy and the UK. For example, schools in Cremona, Italy developed what were known as "Piccolo Guides" whereby the students collected historical information about the town and developed a tourist guide. They used these to escort their parents around the town and opened their eyes afresh to what the town had to offer. "The Piccolo Guides are now very popular because children are very creative at making games and seeing things in a city that adults do not normally notice" (Wilks 2010, p. 32).

Having worked on a number of such projects related to children and young people's participation in planning and development, particularly in terms of the urban environment, Malone (2011) undertook a project in the small New South Wales town of Dapto, a town not renowned for its responsiveness to the needs of its young people. Malone consulted with children from the first year of school to Year 5 in a local school from the very outset of a planning initiative. Using a range of both qualitative and quantitative tools including visual, verbal and textual methods she ensured the participation of the age and ability range of the students being consulted. Their task was to document the nature of available places and spaces that appealed to them in their local community. A core group of students then formed a reference group whose task was to analyse the data, make recommendations for a "dreaming play space" and design a walkable adventure pathway that would link old and newer neighbourhoods.

Through the participation in projects such as these it is possible to find children and young people developing confidence and skills in advising the power brokers in the community, the developers, the bureaucrats, local government how they might better create environments that will be used and enjoyed by all citizens, young and old.

This chapter and the ones preceding it provide us with examples and evidence of participative inquiry in a number of different settings from an individual school, through engagement with cultural institutions to broader and varied community settings. We believe that each has provided us with a range of models of practice in the ways and extent of participation in line with Hart's ladder of participation. In the chapter that follows we are more cautious about what has been and can be achieved when it comes to hearing the voices of students in tertiary settings.

Chapter 8
Student Voice in Higher Education Settings

This final and fourth chapter in part two of the book addresses the matter of listening to student voice in tertiary settings. One might imagine that it is something of a paradox to advocate for authentic procedures for consulting university and other higher education students regarding their experiences and perceptions when of all the groups that have been discussed they would seem to be both relatively powerful and articulate. However, we shall argue that while the previous cases covering: children and young people in schools; their education in cultural institutions; and more widely in the community, particularly those who are marginalized and lacking power have been promulgated as means for improving services, seemingly in higher education, the rationale has circulated around the matter of markets and meeting student needs as clients as opposed to being learners.

The systematic collection of student voice in universities and other higher education settings has become embedded as a standard procedure over the past two decades in most western countries (Newton 2010). In this chapter, we explore the landscape of 'student voice', often constituted as 'student feedback' in higher education, and generally located within the realm of 'quality assurance' of teaching and learning or the 'student experience'. We argue that while the integration of student voice in the shaping of tertiary education has become standard in the repertoire of universities and academics, that current directions in student voice in higher education are more closely linked to discourses around the marketisation and commodification of education than to anything we might recognise as genuine attempts to create and embed democratic processes such as those we have worked with in this book. Indeed, as we shall attempt to show, many of the processes and procedures used to obtain students' perspectives amount to little more than what Hart (1992, 2008) might regard as 'non-participation' and Fielding (2011) as 'students as data source'. Furthermore, and perhaps more concerning, such approaches seem to be linked more to universities seizing and maintaining a competitive edge than about furthering the public good, an idea embedded in the work of Simon Marginson and Mark Considine over a decade ago now (Marginson and Considine 2000). We argue that while they are to a great extent counter-cultural, opportunities do exist for tertiary educators to engage students in authentic dialogue beyond market research, and for the necessity of carving out the space to do so in the contemporary university.

© Springer International Publishing Switzerland 2015   93
N. Mockler, S. Groundwater-Smith, *Engaging with Student Voice in Research,
Education and Community,* DOI 10.1007/978-3-319-01985-7_8

The chapter is presented in three parts. In the first, a brief introduction is provided to the policy context of student voice work in higher education. In the second part, we explore more specifically the conceptualisation of student voice at work in the tertiary sector, using data collected in the form of publicly available policy documents from ten Australian universities. We use Fielding's work on contrasting approaches to student voice (2010) to interrogate the policies on student evaluation of teaching and learning in particular, looking for evidence of partnership beyond students as data source.

The Context of Student Voice in Higher Education

The policy context of student voice work in higher education is one informed by new public management and associated neoliberal education discourses. In providing a potted history of this context, Marginson (2013) points to the expansion of the neo-liberal market model in higher education over the past two decades, and indeed to the failure of the model to create viable markets in higher education, despite the ongoing and continuing attempts on the part of governments toward this goal. Newton (2010) has cast this as a 'quality revolution', arguing that the notions of efficiency and customer satisfaction imported to education from business in the 1980s and 1990s lost favour in some quarters in the 2000s but have recently made a return. He writes:

> Often these definitions and systems were imported from industry and business and, in the end, told us very little about quality enhancement or how we might actually improve the student experience, as opposed to improving quality bureaucracy. After all, students, we were told, were to be viewed as 'customers'. (And as an aside, in the UK we seem now to be coming full circle on this as the conference circuit again seems to be showing all the signs of a customer focus, masquerading as a concern for the student voice.) (Newton 2010, p. 52)

Elements of neoliberalism which we see as particularly creating a backdrop to the enactment of student voice work in universities include the ongoing positioning of students as consumers of an educational product, a phenomenon linked, of course, to the high cost of tertiary education, particularly in jurisdictions such as Australia where until relatively recently tertiary education was free. Second, discourses of 'effectiveness' and 'continuous improvement' have pervaded higher education to a large extent, and metrics relating to teaching and learning quality hold particular consequences for teaching staff and their academic units. As Richard Hil points out, somewhat ascerbically, in his book *Whackademia*,

> Student evaluations and surveys are among the most important elements in any university's system of teaching and learning review. That's why almost every institution goes to extraordinary lengths to ensure that the process is raked over for internal consistency and 'reliability'. Both staff and students are given copious quantities of information and advice on how to approach and reflect upon the educational process. For instance the University of Tasmania's 'Student Evaluation of Teaching and Learning' web page contains a truckload of information about teaching evaluation for both staff and students. The staff site includes

all manner of information relating to how academics might go about evaluating the reception of their teaching by students. This student site on the other hand contains a mass of
information on dealing with 'feedback from staff on changes made to unit assessment,
content and delivery as a direct result of previous evaluations'. the invitation seems to be
that if you don't like of course complain about the invitation seems to be that if you don't
like of course complain about it and the university will fix it. The customer is always right,
after all. (Hil 2012, pp. 211–212)

Our contention, therefore, is that 'student voice' initiatives implemented on an
institutional level within higher education institutions, are more closely linked to
discourses of improvement and effectiveness than those of transformation, which
seek to generatively form and re-form the community in democratic ways, or of
'translation' (Cook-Sather 2007, 2009), which seeks to create new understandings
of educational spaces through a process of "duplication, revision, and recreation,
with meaning lost, preserved and created anew" (Cook-Sather 2006, p. 28). We turn
now to explore this contention in relation to data collected from a range of Australian universities.

'Student Voice': Market Research in the Neoliberal University?

Michael Fielding (2010) whose insights have been widely cited in this book has
identified three contrasting approaches to student voice at work in educational institutions, largely dependent on the acknowledged purpose of engaging with student
voice in the first place along with the broader institutional goals. Table 8.1 below
highlights the contrasts between these three approaches in terms of philosophy,
aims, relational context and arrangements for listening that most often take form.

Fielding's thesis is that student voice is enacted in different ways according to
the 'type' or organisation, with a growing emphasis on shared commitment and
responsibility for dialogue on the right hand side of the table. He posits a series of
evaluative questions over the domains of speaking, listening, skills, attitudes and
dispositions, systems, organisational culture, spaces and the making of meaning,
action and the future, through which, he argues, the conditions for student voice
might be assessed. Table 8.2 below sets out these evaluative questions organised via
these nine domains.

Using Fielding's evaluative domains and questions, policy and/or procedure
documents related to student evaluation of teaching and learning in 10 of Australia's
39 universities were analysed. Universities were sampled not randomly, but pur-
posively, taking into account location—at least one university from each state and
territory was sought[1], and a balance of urban and regional universities. Additionally,
a proportional representation of 'Group of 8' universities, predominantly Australia's

---

[1] Although the one university located in the Northern Territory was unable to be included as the
related policy document/s are not publicly available.

Table 8.1 Contrasting approaches to student voice (as represented by Fielding 2010, p. 8)

High Performance Learning Organisation	Person Centred Learning Community	Democratic Fellowship
The personal is for the sake of the functional	*The functional is for the sake of the personal*	*The political is for the sake of the personal*
Student Voice—How and Why	*Student Voice—How and Why*	*Student Voice—How and Why*
Wide ranging formal + informal consultation making current arrangements more effective	Wide ranging formal + informal mutual engagement in order to develop wise persons	Shared responsibility for + commitment to the common good
Relationships	*Relationships*	*Relationships*
Instrumental use of trust and relationships	Mutual trust, care and respect	Shared commitment to deepen democratic living and learning together
Arrangements for Listening	*Arrangements for Listening*	*Arrangements for Listening*
Multiple managed opportunities for staff and students to listen to young people's views of what staff are interested in	Reciprocal listening resulting in emergent foci and wide-ranging agendas	Importance of community Meeting + range of smaller spaces that foster diverse identities

oldest and wealthiest tertiary institutions was sought. Table 8.3 below summarises the universities included in the sample.

Australian universities where chosen to be included in this analysis because of the readily and publicly available policy documents that guide the implementation of student evaluation procedures at the highest level. Each of the policy documents was analysed using Fielding's framework as a guide.

Speaking

The policy documents analysed ranged in scope from those positioned to oversee course management and quality assurance generally, such as Curtin University's *Course Approval and Quality Manual: Consolidated Policies and Procedures* (Curtin University 2013) and the University of Sydney's *The Management and Evaluation of Coursework Teaching* (University of Sydney 2001) to those more specifically related to student evaluation of courses and/or teaching (see, for example, Federation University Australia 2012; Griffith University 2012; University of the Sunshine Coast 2012). In some universities, student evaluation of courses or units of study is regarded separately to student evaluation of teaching or teachers (University of Wollongong 2007b, 2008), while in others the two sets of 'evaluations' are seen as linked parts of the one process (Flinders University 2012; University of Tasmania 2010; Victoria University 2007). In most cases there exists a separation of some kind between student feedback on the delivery of courses themselves and on the provision of teaching by academics, and different parameters exist as to what participants are permitted to speak about in each case.

Table 8.2 Evaluating the Conditions for Student Voice. (Fielding 2001, p. 134, also in Fielding 2010, p. 11)

Speaking	*Who* is allowed to speak?
	To whom are they allowed to speak?
	What are they allowed to speak about?
	What *language* is encouraged/ allowed?
Listening	*Who* is listening?
	Why are they listening?
	How are they listening?
Skills	Are the skills of dialogue *encouraged and supported* through training or other appropriate means?
	Are those skills understood, developed and practised within the *context of democratic values and dispositions*?
	Are those skills *transformed* by those values and dispositions?
Attitudes and Dispositions	How do those involved *regard each other*?
	To what degree are the *principle of equal value and the dispositions of care* felt reciprocally and demonstrated through the reality of daily encounter?
Systems	*How often* does dialogue and encounter in which student voice is centrally important occur?
	Who *decides*?
	How do the systems enshrining the value and necessity of student voice mesh with or *relate to other organisational arrangements* (particularly those involving adults)?
Organisational Culture	Do the *cultural norms and values* of the school proclaim the centrality of student voice within the context of education as a shared responsibility and shared achievement?
	Do the *practices, traditions and routine daily encounters* demonstrate values supportive of student voice?
Spaces and the Making of Meaning	*Where* are the public spaces (physical and metaphorical) in which these encounters might take place?
	Who *controls* them?
	What *values* shape their being and their use?
Action	What *action* is taken?
	Who feels *responsible*?
	What happens if aspirations and good intentions are not realised?
The Future	Do we need *new structures*?
	Do we need *new ways of relating to each other*?

While some universities noted in their policies that the formal process of gathering student feedback on courses and/or teaching was merely one way of conducting evaluation, which may be supplemented with other means of gathering student voice such as informal or formative feedback, focus groups etc (see, for example, Australian National University 2013; Curtin University 2013), clearly and consistently articulated in these policies was a conceptualisation of these formal feedback mechanisms as the most important (and thus mandated) means of utilising student voice within the institution.

Table 8.3 Universities included in the sample

University	State/Territory	Characteristics
Australian National University	ACT	Go8, Capital city
Curtin University	WA	Capital city
Federation University	Vic	Regional centres
Flinders University	SA	Capital city
Griffith University	Qld	Capital city
University of Wollongong	NSW	Regional centre
University of the Sunshine Coast	Qld	Regional centre
University of Sydney	NSW	Go8, Capital city
University of Tasmania	Tas	Capital city
Victoria University	Vic	Capital city

Interestingly, while these policies are all about the provision of opportunities for students' voices to be contributed and listened to, in a number of these policies, students are positioned as having a responsibility to participate in feedback activities, as illustrated in the following example from the Griffith University policy:

Under the Griffith University Student Charter students are expected to provide constructive feedback on teaching, learning and other academic activities through participation in quality improvement activities such as providing feedback through [Student Evaluation of Courses] and [Student Evaluation of Teaching] surveys and other surveys. Students are expected to respond to open-ended questions in a constructive manner, focusing on learning and teaching issues, and avoiding content of a personal or inappropriate nature. (Griffith University 2012, p. 4)

Similarly, the Australian National University, in laying out responsibilities of the university, students and teaching staff in relation to student surveys and evaluations, suggests that students hold the following responsibilities:

a. Contribute constructive, honest and thoughtful feedback
b. Provide feedback which is not derogatory or vindictive
c. Recognise their important role in contributing to improvements in teaching, learning and the broader student experience (Australian National University 2013, p. 1)

This positioning of students as holding a moral responsibility to participate in the process of consultation—for, as we shall argue later, on the whole these student voice processes amount to little more than student consultation rather than to anything we would point to as furthering the cause of democratic education—is a tactic that while perhaps attempting to connect with notions of participatory democracy and the moral responsibility of citizens to actively participate, for us represents more a demand on the part of the institution for students to participate in what is essentially a non-participatory research endeavor, where they are expected to respond on the institution's terms to questions determined by the institution. Student consent is taken as given when they complete a survey. In some ways it could be argued that it is a coercive strategy by which students are led to believe that they will contribute to course development and improvement in spite of which, they are rarely provided with any consistent and authentic feedback regarding the results.

Listening

Issues of who is listening, why they are listening and how they are listening are reasonably consistent across the ten universities. In the vast majority of cases (the single exception being the University of Wollongong teacher evaluation procedure, which will be discussed below), the dual audiences for student feedback are on the one hand, university administration (including those responsible for co-ordinating and administering courses, School and Faculty leaders and University administrators) and on the other hand, teaching staff who are responsible for making 'improvements' to their practice as a consequence of student feedback.

The University of Sydney's *Management and Evaluation of Coursework Teaching Policy* is clear about the ways in which this 'listening' informs action at an institutional level:

> Results will be aggregated to faculty- and University-level and provided to all members of the University. Results inform the distribution of performance-based funds through the University's teaching performance indicators and the assessment of the quality of teaching at faculty and university level. They identify areas where further review and intervention is indicated to make quality improvements, and measure progress towards targets specified in Faculty and University Teaching and Learning Plans. An annual report by the Deputy Vice-Chancellor (Education) will summarize the results and highlight progress and areas for improvement. (University of Sydney 2001, p. 13)

At Curtin University, the dual audience of teaching staff and university administration is made clear in the following extract:

Learning and teaching evaluation data will be used to:

a. Improve learning and teaching experiences for students and teachers;
b. Assist staff to engage in a scholarly review of their teaching by reflecting on unit design, delivery, student engagement, and assessment;
c. Provide data to benchmark learning and teaching quality within and beyond the University;
d. Provide evidence for teaching staff to use as indicators of teaching performance when discussing work plans with line managers; and
e. Provide evidence for academic staff promotion, performance management processes, and teaching portfolios (Curtin University 2013, p. 68).

In all ten universities, formal student feedback processes stand outside university human research ethics committee frameworks, but all policy documents make explicit statements about anonymity of student participants and confidentiality of results. The Flinders University policy, for example, indicates that responsibility for ethical action regarding student feedback resides with the staff members responsible for accessing the results of feedback exercises:

Due care will be taken by Deans of School and topic coordinators (or other University staff with authorised administrative access to the SET instrument) to ensure that information derived from evaluations of learning and teaching is used in an appropriate manner, and that actions are taken, as appropriate, to protect the anonymity of individual staff members or students who have participated in the evaluation process. (Flinders University 2012, p. 4)

Results of student evaluation of courses/units are generally made available at Department/School/Faculty/University level, and in most cases results of student evaluation of teaching are made available to supervisor/line manager of the academic undergoing evaluation, in some cases with results being made available to Pro Vice Chancellors, Deputy Vice Chancellors and Vice Chancellors under certain circumstances.

At the University of Wollongong, results of teacher evaluations are available only to the staff member requesting the evaluation:

Results of UOW Teacher Evaluations are confidential to the UOW Academic who has requested them and are only provided to the Academic Probation and Academic Promotion Committees at the written request of the UOW Academic. (University of Wollongong 2007b, p. 2)

Unlike most other universities, agency for evaluation of teaching rests entirely with staff members at the University of Wollongong, with the process existing purely for the purpose of academic development rather than to feed into the machinery of 'quality assurance' or 'continuous improvement'. In this single case, the 'who is listening' is the academic whose teaching students are being asked to evaluate and only this individual, and furthermore in this case there is no requirement for evaluation of teaching to be undertaken in a particular timeframe, nor a sense of students' responsibility to contribute.

Skills

Contrasting with Fielding's notion that student voice initiatives should seek to build skills and capacities, particularly related to dialogue and the development of democratic values and dispositions within the community, no evidence was identified in any of the policy documents to indicate that student feedback initiatives seek to build these kinds of skills and capacities. Rather, students are positioned as contributors to 'evaluations' conducted at an institutional level whereby their perceptions and perspectives will be used by teachers and administrators to improve teaching and learning offerings for subsequent cohorts.

Attitudes and Dispositions

Fielding's critical questions in the domain of attitudes and dispositions relate to how those involved regard each other and the degree to which the principle of equal value and the dispositions of care are felt reciprocally and demonstrated through the reality of daily encounter. In the context of these policy documents, the 'regard' with which the institutions hold their students is primarily indicated by the way in which they are positioned as participants in the evaluation process. As noted above, a number of universities position student participation as a responsibility to which students should submit, both in terms of the quantity and quality of responses provided. Some universities note the problem for students of being 'over surveyed', while the University of Wollongong alone conveys a sense in their policy on student evaluation of teaching (University of Wollongong 2007b) that evaluation of teaching is a process best used sparingly as a tool for authentic and robust academic development, in the best interests of both students and teachers.

None of the policy documents examined suggest that the principle of equal value and dispositions of care are felt reciprocally or enacted through the reality of daily encounter: in all cases, despite the suggestion that informal and other means of feedback and perhaps dialogue might be pursued on an individual course or teacher basis, the 'formal' process was privileged as a true indicator of quality and set deliberately outside the boundaries of daily encounter.

Organisational Culture

While each of the policy documents examined locates the importance of integrating student voice into evaluation processes as an integral part of organisational culture, predominantly through practices of 'quality assurance' and 'continuous improvement', and thus the centrality of student voice is proclaimed within the organization, there is little evidence in these documents that this takes place within an understanding of education as a shared responsibility and shared achievement. Student participation is generally limited to lending their voice to the regular consultations undertaken, and there is no evidence of values at play within these institutions that are aligned with the kind of generative and authentic student voice efforts for which Fielding is arguing.

Spaces and Meaning Making

The spaces, both physical and metaphorical, within which this student voice work is conducted are generally controlled by the institution administering the evaluation instruments. Increasingly these spaces are metaphorical, with students invited to contribute to online surveys, and while in some cases, such as at the University of Wollongong, where academics undertaking evaluation of teaching are required to have a colleague or student administer the survey and not be present when the evaluation instrument is completed, still in these (fairly limited) instances, the spatial parameters of the student voice work are controlled by the staff or institution itself.

Action

Beyond claims that student feedback will be used to inform improvements to the quality of teaching and learning, along with feeding into performance management and professional development/promotion applications for academics, which are consistent across most of the ten universities whose policies were examined, is the requirement that the 'feedback loop' to students be closed. Most universities have made this explicit reporting of 'action' to students mandatory. In some cases, the conditions under which this should occur are left open, such as at Curtin University and Flinders University:

> Students will be informed how student feedback has been used to maintain or improve the quality of learning experiences. (Curtin University 2013, p. 68)
> Staff are encouraged to make known to students any improvements that are to be implemented in the teaching and learning environment in response to feedback derived from student evaluations. (Flinders University 2012, p. 4)
> A critical component of this Policy shall be the provision of feedback to students about the results of student evaluation processes. Faculties/ VU College will be responsible for developing appropriate systems for ensuring that feedback is provided to students on how previous surveying has been used to improve the quality of unit offerings. (Victoria University 2007, p. 4)

In other institutional contexts, the means by which the 'feedback loop' should be closed is explicitly nominated in the policy document:

> Co-ordinators, Heads and Deans must provide a summary of the results of the most recent student evaluation of units on a unit of study website or in handouts. This summary will refer to actions taken in response to student comments. (University of Sydney 2001, p. 14)
> Selected data at the discretion of the Course Convenor is used within the Previous Student Feedback section of the Course Profile to demonstrate use of student feedback for course improvement and to foster student-teacher partnerships. (Griffith University 2012, p. 5)
> Teachers and Course Coordinators must provide a summary to students on outcomes arising from their review of the reports of both Course and Teaching SETAC surveys they have conducted, in accordance with the associated procedures. (University of the Sunshine Coast 2012, p. 2)

At the University of Wollongong, the process of communicating to students the actions taken on the basis of previous students' feedback is illustrated with examples of how this feedback might be provided in the subject outline document that forms the basis for the subject or course:

> Efforts will also be made to communicate to students some of the actions which have been taken to improve individual subjects as a result of feedback provided through the Subject evaluation. Academic staff will be required to assist and contribute to this communication process through the Subject Outline as stated in the Code of Practice—Teaching and Assessment. Suggested examples of feedback include:
>
> a. Recent improvements to the subject include requiring students to write a reflective journal as part of the assessment. Reflective journals are often used in professional learning settings including the health and teaching professions to encourage self- awareness and conscious skill development.

    b. The tutorial activities have also changed to introduce a number of practical, but not directly assessed, tutorial activities in the first half of the subject. These activities will build on and reinforce the lecture material in a practical way, and give students confidence as communicators before formal assessment begins.

    c. In 2009 this subject will be using two different textbooks to those used in recent years. In particular students provided feedback indicating that they would like to use a bioethics text that was written in a language they found more accessible and that more overtly acknowledged the ethical challenges faced by registered nurses engaged in clinical practice (University of Wollongong 2008, pp. 5–6).

Beyond this transactional 'closing the loop' dimension of action, and general claims about the use to which the information provided by students will be put on both an individual academic and broader institutional level, no commitment to action is made within these policy documents. In terms of Fielding's question of who feels responsible for action out of student feedback, we would argue that as long as such initiatives are fashioned, implemented and driven at an organisational level, toward quality assurance and continuous improvement goals, a disconnect may exist between these and the responsibility felt by individual academics to respond to the feedback. In a limited number of cases, Victoria University and the University of Sydney included, individuals and organisational units are able to fashion course-specific consultation questions to be included in student surveys, as opposed to implementing a generic student survey designed for university-wide use. While this may go some way toward providing individuals and teams with feedback on critical local issues, the problem of these initiatives being largely top-down responses to questions set at an organisational level is still in play in these cases.

The Future

Student voice initiatives as articulated in these ten university policies are very much about maintaining but 'improving' current structures and organisational ways of being. In both the conceptualisation of the initiatives as 'evaluation' and 'feedback', along with the parameters for reporting actions to students discussed above, a strong sense of the preservation of current structures and processes is conveyed. Furthermore, the kind of collaborative strategic work suggested by Fielding's questions in this domain sit far outside the boundaries of this work. Embedded in all of the policy documents examined is an understanding that the University's role is to shape and implement improvement, while the role of students is to provide their perceptions on the status quo when required, and in relation to the questions established by the organisation. The following subject evaluation questionnaire questions from the University of Wollongong (chosen as the only such questionnaire with questions publicly available on the University website) serve to illustrate these observations.

Multiple Choice Questions

The scale for questions 1 to 7 is: Strongly Agree, Agree, Mildly Agree, Mildly Disagree, Disagree, Strongly Disagree, Unable to judge/Not applicable

1. In this subject the learning outcomes were made clear to me
2. The assessment criteria were clearly stated at the beginning of the subject
3. Feedback on my work was provided to me in time to prepare for other assessment tasks
4. This subject helped me gain a better understanding of an area of study
5. My learning in this subject was well supported by:

   Access to teachers
   Access to other assistance
   Learning tasks
   Learning resources
   eLearning (if used)

6. Overall I was satisfied with the quality of this subject
7. Optional question (A)
8. Choose one or more main reasons for taking this subject:

   Required part of my program
   Fitted my personal timetable
   Seemed an interesting subject to do
   Relevant to my career plans
   The reputation of the subject
   Only subject available

9. Average hours I spent on this subject each week (including class time):

   0–4, 5–8, 9–12, 13–16, 17–20, 21+

10. Choose those aspects of the UOW Graduate Qualities fostered by this subject:

    Understand a field of knowledge
    Think critically or analytically
    Find and evaluate information
    Investigate new ideas
    Acknowledge the work of others
    Develop problem-solving skills
    Communicate with others
    Value other perspectives
    Work collaboratively
    Be aware of ethical issues
    Understand international/global issues

(Please note that the survey includes the University's Graduate Quality statement)

Free Text Response Questions

1. What are the best aspects of this subject?
2. What aspects of this subject would you suggest could be improved?
3. Optional question (B)
4. Do you have any comments about this survey? (University of Wollongong 2007a)

Universities and Student Voice: Transformation or Transaction?

The above analysis suggests that while higher education institutions regard the incorporation of student voice as an important dimension of a business model that includes customer feedback and continuous improvement, there is little about such initiatives in universities that respond to the call for intergenerational democracy embedded in Fielding's work, or indeed, in our own conceptualisation of generative student voice explored in this book. Indeed, it seems that rather than strategies designed to transform learning environments or provide students and teachers with the opportunities for the agency required for the 'radical collegiality' (Fielding 2011) that should, one might argue, be more readily accessible in the post-compulsory world of higher education, the student voice strategies mandated in universities are more transactional than transformative. Conforming in most cases to quality assurance and review timelines and processes, standardised and generic survey instruments where students are positioned as 'responsible' for participation do not appear to fit within the model of radical collegiality or generative student voice. Likewise, the transactional nature of the 'closing the loop' process whereby students are encouraged to view the feedback they provide as contributing to instant change rather than making a contribution to sustained conversations about good practice necessarily limits the scope of this particular approach to student voice work which dominates in the current landscape of higher education.

This is not to say that student voice work with a transformative intent is not possible nor indeed happening within universities and other higher education institutions. Indeed, in our own university contexts and through our networks of colleagues not only in Australia but further afield in the United States, United Kingdom, New Zealand and continental Europe, we can point to examples of practice that seek to engage students as co-enquirers, knowledge creators and joint authors, and that build toward a shared responsibility for the common good in our institutions. Alison Cook-Sather, Catherine Bovill and Peter Felton's recent book (2014) provides an overview of the different ways that authentic partnerships between teachers and students in higher education might be built and enacted. Such work, however, remains largely counter-cultural in this neoliberal age, requiring a tenacity and fortitude in tertiary teachers similar to that discussed in school contexts in earlier chapters. With the increasing push toward effectiveness and efficiency in higher education globally, it is likely that transactional approaches to student voice will become further entrenched, requiring academics and other tertiary teachers with a commitment to authentically engaging with student voice to think and act increasingly critically and creatively about ways of engaging student voice within and beyond the classroom.

It is to these methods of engaging student voice that we now turn, hoping that they may provide alternatives that will lead to a greater engagement of all students in the shaping of not only their educational experiences and opportunities, but also their educational and broader communities.

Part III
Engaging Student Voice

In this final section, we explore both practical and philosophical perspectives on engaging with student voice across different educational and community contexts. From the examples and discussions drawn in Part II, we elicit some principles of practice which, we argue, might be used to guide the development of ethical and generative student voice work in these varying contexts.

While we do not aim in this book to provide a specific guide for researchers or educators wishing to take up the challenge of student voice work in their practice, we do offer some practical advice on methods for engaging student voice, drawing attention to some research methods that we and others have used to great effect with children and young people. We encourage expansive thinking about the ethics of research with young people, arguing that researchers, whether practitioner researchers or those located within university contexts have a responsibility to think beyond harm minimisation to the ways in which research ethics and the ethics of educational practice might be brought together in the practice of research. We look to the affordances and the limitations of various ethical guidelines in the United Kingdom, United States and Australia and ask what ethical practice in research with children and young people might look like 'beyond compliance', making the case that the very conduct of high quality research in this context requires the adoption of a sound and well-thought out ethical approach.

By way of arguing that listening to and taking account of student voice should not be confined to settings beyond the classroom, we examine in the final exploratory chapter the implications of student voice for classroom and pedagogical practice. We argue here that a commitment to the privileging of student voice holds particular implications for pedagogy, curriculum and assessment, and that alignment of these three message systems of schooling, as defined by Basil Bernstein, in ways consistent with the participatory and democratic aims of authentic student voice work is the particular challenge. Furthermore, we consider the shaping of these message systems by globalised education policy discourses and the ways in which student voice work might provide a means for teacher, students and community members to 'push back' on these.

In the brief concluding chapter, we offer a charter for authentic student voice work within and beyond schools, engaging the ideas and frameworks developed and discussed in this book, and suggesting a way forward for student voice work in what might be seen to be troubling educational times.

Chapter 9
Methods for Engaging Student Voice

This chapter addresses not only a range of methods that allows the emergence of student voice and the involvement of children and young people in the design and analysis of inquiries, as well as participating in subsequent actions, it also re-invigorates the arguments in relation to evidence and the ways in which that term is understood and employed. It proposes that much of the current discussion regarding evidence is embedded in the problematic area of defining 'best practice' with little attention given to the ways in which students can contribute to authentic improvement.

Evidence that Matters

'Belling the cat' is an oft-told tale, frequently attributed as one of *Aesop's Fables*. It portrays a group of mice that work together to deal with a marauding cat who threatens to decimate their number. By placing a bell around the cat's neck the mice will be warned of its approach—a fine plan, until one asks who will take on this formidable task. The story is invoked in order to illuminate the gap between having a troubling idea and executing it in a dangerous and difficult world. The sense is that good counsel may be readily called upon, but without a means to translate it into practice it is rendered of limited use and value. Such is the current discourse surrounding matters of 'best practice' and the evidence that is privileged in informing what is meant by this elusive and often misleading term, a matter that has already been raised, at some length, in Chap. 4.

In earlier chapters in this book we have discussed the difficult issue of the ways in which evidence may be assembled and used in relation to working with children and young people while in Chap. 10 we also return to matters of evidence in relation to ethical considerations when researching alongside children and young people. Later, in this chapter, we shall be outlining innovative ways in which evidence may be collected where the agency for its gathering does not rest exclusively with adults. However, the concern to which we now return is in relation to the question of 'what counts as the evidence that matters' in the context of a dominant

© Springer International Publishing Switzerland 2015
N. Mockler, S. Groundwater-Smith, *Engaging with Student Voice in Research, Education and Community,* DOI 10.1007/978-3-319-01985-7_9

discourse surrounding evidence based practice where the evidence is associated with discussions regarding 'best practice'. We have a desire to bell this particular cat in an age where too often it is argued that "there seems to be a prima-facie case for basing professional action on the best evidence available" (Biesta 2010, p. 492). Biesta is not, in fact, arguing for the adoption of an unproblematised best practice model. That is, one that seeks to reduce complexity, but instead he appeals to our understanding of the ways in which values can and should provide a stronger foundation for action. Furthermore, we would argue that the evidence arising from quasi-scientific trials and a positivist paradigm that has been posited as the most satisfactory basis for policy making in the practice of education, may not be sufficiently nuanced to be of real assistance. We shall make the case that this discussion is most salient when it comes to the matter of engaging children and young people within an inquiry context.

The belling of this specific cat that links evidence to best practice to government policy becomes quite critical when the 'what works' agenda is linked to government funding that can "define the topics to be studied and the methodologies used to study them" (Furlong 2013, p. 41). As we have maintained earlier in this book there has been an increase in activity that elicits from children and young people their perspectives on their school and tertiary environments but with insufficient attention paid to the ways in which such consultation may be achieved.

Indeed, it has been pointed out that the evidence-based and outcomes-focused paradigms for research being so strongly advocated and discussed in Chap. 4 is detached from policy and practice rather than inextricably linked with "inherently entangled" relationships between knowledge and power (Vandenbroek et al. 2012, p. 548). This in recognition that research is influenced by the the historical, social and political environment in which it takes place and that in turn the research influences this environment. So that in a 'what works' discourse the research is informed by pre-defined, measurable outcomes rather than in keeping with a process that is open and unpredictable. Efficiency then enters into the equation with the inference that once best practice goals have been established then the next step is to implement them at the least possible cost irrespective of whether what works for this one may not be the case for that one.

Furthermore, there is a certain irony when the evidence that is collected is conflicting and contradictory. Groundwater-Smith and Mockler (2009) in their chapter concerned with professional knowledge production in the context of teacher professional learning in an age of compliance, pointed to the ongoing literacy debates with appeals made on the basis of 'good research evidence' for one strategy or another for teaching reading. They examined over 170 references in their review of research literature and found that there was negligible overlap between the studies that were cited when employing different paradigms. So that while there is a superficial appeal to the phrase 'evidence-based practice' and that it would seem difficult to argue against determining action that is fully informed by carefully structured studies of, *inter alia,* procedures, resources and human capabilities, it remains critical that great care is taken regarding what will count as evidence, who will provide it and in what form it will take.

The Rationale for Re-conceptualising Evidence

In order to address the question of what kinds of evidence can be usefully gathered and employed when addressing matters of concern to children and young people we turn first to a somewhat neglected issue in relation to many traditional educational research practices that are, in the main, based upon surveys and questionnaires. Such methods are much favoured by quantitative researchers, rarely in consultation with those who are providing the responses. The issue that concerns us is that of the motivation and engagement of those who are responding to such methods of gathering information.

We address the question of motivation first and ask why children and young people should choose to put effort into responding to surveys and questionnaires. What drives them to want to provide their insights and understandings to strangers whose own motivation may not be clear to them? After all, as Mitra (2006) has noted collecting students' perspectives from afar will do little to capture their concerns in well-informed and authentic ways. Are the surveys and questionnaires of such interest that the young people will put in the energy, time and commitment that is required? Or are they persuaded by some kind of reward? While we are not specifically addressing high stakes testing it is interesting that a number of schools and jurisdictions in various countries around the world have sought to ensure students' motivation to take international standardised tests often to little avail, especially in relation to those who are low or underachievers, as Stiggins (2004, p. 24) has observed, after reviewing a number of studies:

> Now consider those students whose academic record reveals a chronic history of failure. Their reality is different. For them, the realization that the bar is going even higher—that now it will be even more difficult to succeed in school—is neither invigorating nor motivating. On the contrary, it is deflating, discouraging, and defeating. These students will regard the entire movement to embrace high standards and high-stakes testing and the intimidation-driven school improvement process as representing yet another occasion when they lose.

Clearly, motivation precedes engagement. If motivation is problematic in the high stakes testing environment then it may well be that in relation to anonymous surveys, opinionnaires and the like, where the stakes are not evident, then students may well lack motivation and hence engagement in completing them in good faith. Fredricks, Blumenfeld and Paris (2004, p. 58) recognise that engagement is multi-faceted and malleable and includes: behavioural engagement; emotional engagement and cognitive engagement. The first of these refers to participation, are the students doing the work of completing various research instruments because they are compelled to? The second relates to affiliation and valuing the task and the third to intellectual investment. Engagement can, then, vary in commitment, intensity and duration.

We argue that for children and young people to positively identify with a given project and commit themselves to it they need to see it as purposeful. Such an example is given by Taines (2012) who evolved a program in urban Mid-Western United States schools designed to facilitate urban students' activism for school reform.

The students themselves assisted in the design of the research and were agents in selecting what they believed to be the most important school problems and worked at developing solutions. Contrary to the expectations of the academic researchers, the students focused more on material facilities such as bathrooms and canteen food, than on the pedagogical practices of their teachers. Indeed, they saw that the poor provision of facilities acted as a signifier of how the school regarded, or disregarded them. Poor facilities were seen to be a distraction that led to student disengagement from school. This was not the evidence that was expected and leads us to now ask how, if we are to transcend legitimation and guardianship, two concepts that we have discussed throughout this book, we might re-conceptualise the kinds of evidence that can be collected that will give authenticity to the consideration of the voices of children and young people. Indeed, in Chap. 5 we have demonstrated that a sustained research apprenticeship undertaken by young people over four years clearly has an impact upon policy and practice in a school considered to be challenging and where students were, hitherto, disenagaged.

Evidence that Matters

Our first emphasis is that we are looking for ways in which evidence may be collected that is not *about* children and young people, but is *about how children and young people see themselves, others and the world around them.* The distinction here is that the former is the kind of inquiry that separates the young people from their world and makes them the object of someone else's study. We are more concerned with the development of strategies that enables them to have a persistent and authentic voice as free as is possible from manipulation, decoration and tokenism as understood by Hart (1992) who argues that as the ladder of participation is ascended the relationship moves through consultation and the exchange of information towards shared decision making.

These are views echoed by Fletcher (2003) when he writes:

> Students do not inherently know how to be meaningfully involved in their schools. Likewise, most educators struggle to figure out how to meaningfully involve students. Meaningful Student Involvement requires focused learning for all participants to learn the potential of their individual and collective roles. For students, developmentally appropriate learning is needed to increase their capacity for empowered participation; for teachers, administrators and school staff, learning is focused on developing the school system's ability to involve students as well as individual teachers' ability to meaningfully involve students in different kinds of learning opportunities.

In earlier chapters we have discussed cases where children and young people have acted as clients and consultants through to being pro-active inquirers, whose role it has been to not only inform, but enact a range of education policies. Here our task is to set down a number of strategies and the ways in which they can be developed and adopted as creative and engaging work undertaken by young people to good purpose. That is, they are researching not as a task to be undertaken as proxies for others, but one to which they feel a genuine commitment in recognition of their status and authority. They are all methods that rest upon the conditions of dialogue as set out in Chap. 2. Many form part of an iterative cycle of inquiry that allows further methods for collecting evidence to emerge as new and different questions are posed. To this end we shall discuss methods that engage children and young people as "strategic actors" (Greig et al. 2009, p. 207).

The literature that acknowledges and recognizes the ways in which participatory research may take place often cites what has become known as the Mosaic Approach (Clark and Moss 2001). The approach adopts a multi-method process that brings together a range of tools that include both verbal and visual procedures that will provide pieces of evidence that can ultimately be fitted together to form a full and comprehensive picture. An example of the ways in which the mosaic approach works can be found in an Australian project known as *The Nest* (Australian Research Alliance for Children and Youth 2012) designed to engage a range of stakeholders including children, adolescents and concerned adults by eliciting perspectives on the needs and preferences of each party with respect to examining the concept of wellbeing. The project sought to explore the following questions:

1. **What is important for children and young people and why?**
   What things help or contribute to a good life for children and young people, what do these look like, and why are they important?
2. **How are we, as a country, doing in relation to these?**
   How are children and young people in Australia faring in relation to the things that are important to them?
3. **Where are we heading and where do we want to be?**
   If we continue as we are, where will we be? Is this where we want to be? If not, what outcomes would we like to see for children and young people?
4. **How do we get to where we want to be?**
   What actions can be taken to get to these outcomes, based on what we know works well, including who is responsible and what is needed for this to happen?

We acknowledge that there are many creative and imaginative tools that may be used; what is critical is that they are purposeful and understandable as seen and employed by the participants. Indeed, as we have argued elsewhere, a significant step is taken when they are employed following careful and thorough support of the children and young people as the primary researchers who have a voice, not only in using the tools, but also in selecting which ones are the most appropriate to the questions to be addressed. Greig et al. (2009, pp. 229–230) provide a helpful summary of the steps and questions that might be asked and taken to ensure that participative research with children and young people is well conducted and valid, they include, *inter alia*:

> *Project planning:* deciding with all parties upon who will steer the project, determine its aims and research procedures;
> *Gathering data:* in what ways will be participants be involved—as main researchers, as partners, as peer researchers, as respondents only?
> *Analysis of data:* who will undertake the analysis, what framework (s) will they employ?

Reporting findings: what forms will the reporting take, what will be the key messages, who will be responsible?

Policy development and campaigning: how will findings be disseminated, how will key messages to communicated to different interest groups, how will participants judge the success of their endeavours?

In their planning advice the Commissioner for Children and Young People, Western Australia (2009) suggests the following:

- using creative, engaging and fun presentations and activities
- asking children and young people to help plan activities
- encouraging and training children and young people to be co-facilitators or peer researchers
- presenting information in easily understandable ways suitable for different learning styles (for example, use everyday language, pictures and diagrams).
- Ask children and young people to write, edit or review it before distribution
- selecting child and young person friendly venues and facilities—children and young people can give good advice on this
- scheduling plenty of breaks and variation in activities
- seeking feedback from children and young people about what they enjoyed, what they would like to see more of and what could be better.

If we wish to construct evidence that matters, each of these steps needs careful consideration; however, our main emphasis for the remainder of this chapter is upon a range of fresh and innovative ways that have been shown to have appeal to young people as participant researchers. They include: developing submissions; focus group discussions; co-interviewing; role playing; collages and drawings; photography and integrated digital media; concept mapping; storying, diaries and logs.

Developing Submissions and Advice

We commence with developing submissions and advice because it is often the case that children and young people are excluded from early planning. However, with an increasing trend to consult before enacting a project it is interesting to note how such business is conducted when young people are enabled to develop a submission that will inform later action. Although we must concede that at the tertiary level course designers are trammelled by many restrictive regulatory frameworks as a means of protecting institutions from 'client dissatisfaction' so that every course outline is required to be met without deviation, let alone consultation with students (Hil 2012), a matter much discussed in Chap. 8.

However, many projects may begin with questions that might arise from some kind of development plan of those who are wishing to make an organizational change and see the process of consulting young people as a form of assistance. For example the Australian Youth Forum (AYF 2012) was encouraged to make a submission to the Australian Curriculum and Reporting Authority (ACARA) on the proposed national curriculum area of Civics and Citizenship. The AYF was established as a key communication channel between the Australian Government and young people aged 15–24. An online survey was developed about shaping the curriculum area followed by the establishment of an AYF website that was designed to discuss the intended subject, what should be left out and how it should be taught. Additionally, a Facebook page was established which invited responses. In reply to one question regarding voting and young people one respondent reported:

> Because without voting the people wouldn't be able to choose a different path for Australia than the one those in power want. Also it's a lot of fun to feel part of such an important event. (AYF 2012, p. 13)

An outcome of the consultation was that young people, while being interested in teaching about Civics and Citizenship were keen that any program should be practical and not employed as an avenue to shape students' political thought. Indeed, the extract quoted above could signal that the person who responded welcomed an opportunity to express a point of view that may not have been of the kind that ACARA anticipated. We are reminded of an anecdote related by Studs Terkel (Terkel 2007) the master story teller, where he recounts the words of Mary Lou Wolff, wife of a telephone lineman and mother of eight who was fighting to save her neighbourhood from destruction during the sixties, "I realised I was saying things I never dreamt about … I began to realise that rules are made by some people and the purpose of these rules is to keep you in your place. It is at times your duty to break some of these rules. This is such a time." (pp. 251–252). Might it be that in seeking assistance in relation to Civics and Citizenship what was encountered was covert resistance or seen by respondents as an opportunity to break some rules?

In a very different context Seiler (2011) sought to reconstruct the science curriculum for a Philadelphia inner-city high school through consultation with those who were to engage with it. The study found that sound practice[1] was based upon providing conditions where students could connect science with their lives. The argument was put that while teachers and curriculum developers may have difficulty identifying topics that students see as relevant to their lives, when the topics emerged from consultation with the students more promising foci emerged, as one student reported, "I mean you can't think that just cause *you* think it's fun, *we* gonna think it's fun"[2] (p. 369). As well students were provided with opportunities to pose questions that were of interest to them, some emerging from the tough and difficult lives that they led. They were able to nominate forms of participation and scope and sequence and how they would go about their learning. Thus they contributed to both the planning and enactment of the curriculum. As Seiler observed "school curricula rarely connect to students' funds of knowledge" (p. 378) and that, furthermore they often contain an implicit deficit stereotype in relation to minority students.

Clearly, neither of these examples are essentially radical in nature, what is surprising is that providing opportunities for young people to contribute to planning

---

[1] While Seiler uses the designation 'best practice' we choose to eschew it and refer instead to 'sound practice'.

[2] Our emphasis.

in any serious and sustained way is still considered to be unusual. As Whitty and Wisby (2007) in their examination of school councils in the UK noted, more often than not they support managerialism rather than providing students with a liberatory voice.

We move on now to methods that do have the potential to be more open and negotiable.

Focus Group Discussions

As we have already observed the employment of any method is not an end in itself. Our interest is in the way that this procedure can bring to the surface perspectives and insights that can be further explored using a range of additional inquiry processes. The merit of the focus group discussion is that it creates conditions for interaction and debate. Furthermore, as we shall demonstrate, it is feasible to train young people to conduct focus groups themselves. This latter point is an important one in that in school settings teachers are accustomed to, when leading discussions, correcting and evaluating student responses. While this may be less of a problem when structuring focus group discussions with tertiary students or those in later adolescence in the community it is still valuable to consider having the conduct of the groups managed by the young people themselves who may not have the same agenda as those who are seeking the information.

There are many strategies for initiating a discussion. Colucci's paper (2007) is of particular value because she outlines a number of strategies that encourage engagement through activity and it is our belief that children and young people find activity based practices will give them scope to open up and express their ideas. She argues that it is important to create the conditions that will allow those taking part to be reflective and unhurried especially when sensitive topics are being uncovered. In her case she has been interested in the cultural meanings that are attributed to youth suicide in Italy, India and Australia. Among the strategies that are covered are:

- Free listings—where participants commence by making individual lists in response to a particular question, with the lists then being considered by the group;
- Rating scales—where a number of relevant statements are collected (either from participants or the moderator) and are given a rating that can then be compared and contrasted;
- Rankings—statements are given a ranking and the order of ranking becomes the focus of the discussion;
- Pile sorting—cards, pictures, cultural icons and the like can be sorted in terms of similarities and differences with the results then further discussed;
- Choosing among alternatives—where a range of possible solutions to a given issue are presented and the alternatives considered according to various criteria such as, most effective—to least effective;
- Labeling—participants write short statements or descriptions with respect to a given topic with labels then being sorted and categorized;

- Picture sorting—selections of pictures are provided and participants sort and select those that match a given category;
- Magic tools and fantasy—participants may step outside the present world and propose what might take place if, for example, they had a device that could make a problem solvable;
- Storytelling—an incomplete vignette or scenario can be offered to participants who then can construct alternative endings;
- Role playing—where a selection of participants act the ways in which a particular concern plays out with the role play becoming a catalyst for further discussion;
- Drawings—where participants draw a reaction to a given provocation, thereafter discussing and annotating responses; and
- Projective techniques—using metaphors and analogies as a commencement to a discussion.

In her consideration of such projective techniques Colucci cites the work of Groundwater-Smith and Mockler (2003) where they draw upon the ways in which a hybrid collection of schools have worked together to develop practices that are more enabling for children and young people to speak of their various experiences (Mockler and Groundwater-Smith 2011). Over more than a decade those members of the *Coalition of Knowledge Building Schools* have developed, in particular, projective methods that combine the concept of analogies and images. The focus group discussion commences with students recording their response to a given image and then listening to the reactions of others.

The question route that follows any one of these ice-breaking strategies can well be negotiated ahead of time with a group who have taken part in such activities before, who understand how they progress and are able to manage the discussion themselves. Students can act in teams of three, one of whom puts the questions, one observes and ensures the distribution of questions and assists the third who records responses. Teams can then meet together to identify themes, item stems and scenarios.

Below is an example of a question route that was developed by students from the school portrayed in Chap. 5 with the assistance of the school's academic partner. In this case the focus group discussion followed a survey, in other instances it can be designed to inform a survey.

1. How do you feel about school at the moment?
2. If you could change one thing about school that is changeable what would it be?
3. A lot of Year 9 students recorded that they found school 'boring'; what is it that makes it like that for them?
4. A student wrote "Teach us the way we want to learn"—what do you think that means?
5. What could the school, teachers and students do to make learning 'hard fun'?
6. If you could change one thing about yourself as a learner, what would it be?
7. If you could change one thing about your fellow students, as learners, what would it be?

Co-interviewing

In spite of the best efforts of focus group moderators it is the case that some students may be quiet or intimidated. While it may seem helpful to interview such participants separately this too raises issues about who will interview and thus who may have the power over the other. This can be solved by students interviewing one another—in effect they become involved in a structured conversation that will be governed by the normal requirements of interviewing with respect to matters of confidentiality and disclosure. This process can be constructed as a powerful response to Fielding's 2008 series of questions that form the framework for analysis of tertiary student feedback discussed in Chap. 8:

- Who is allowed to speak?
- To whom?
- What are they allowed to speak about?
- What language is encouraged or allowed?
- Who decides the answers to these questions?
- How are those decisions made?
- How, when, where, to whom and how often are these decisions communicated?

A Government secondary school for girls in Sydney's northern suburbs as a member of the *Coalition of Knowledge Building Schools,* focused for several years on student-led studies regarding bullying. By involving young people who may have experienced bullying and who had agreed to tell each other their stories it was possible to elicit a series of scenarios that, once anonymised, could be responded to not only by other students, but also by their teachers. Events that may seem trivial can be uncovered and become a part of an investigation of those aspects of school culture that are not always visible to their teachers.

> There was a time when as I went to sit down in class someone knocked my books off the desk. OK so it wasn't a big deal. Except it happened in the next class and the next. The fourth time it happened I began to cry (big mistake!). The maths teacher couldn't see what the fuss was about, but then she hadn't been there for English, or History or Italian. (Year 9 student)

Role Playing

Role playing can be conducted to serve a number of different purposes:

- Participants imagining that they have the power to design a provision for themselves and their peers;
- Participants working through what they see to be dilemmas that have arisen in their particular circumstances; and
- Participants demonstrating their concerns.

The Nest Toolkit (Australian Research Alliance for Children and Youth 2012) provides a number of strategies for ensuring that participants are carefully prepared to play out their roles, such as: developing over-arching scenarios, having character cards, imagining the time and place of the action.

A matter that requires careful consideration is related to the impact upon the audience of the role-play. It is possible that stereotypes can be developed, or that the whole exercise becomes comedic. Without careful preparation the role-play may be counter productive. In the school portrayed in Chap. 5, a significantly challenging school (Mayes and Groundwater-Smith 2013) students presented their results to the school staff at the end of each year. When presenting the results regarding the teaching they would like they had developed a video-recorded role- play of a teacher who was sympathetic to students and one of a teacher who was dismissive. The subsequent discussion indicated an antagonism by some teachers to issues centred on mutual respect. A number of teachers believed that students were disrespectful and unsympathetic to the behaviour management strategies that they were required to employ. While it may be an exaggeration to suggest lasting damage was done it raises questions regarding the ethical issues that such situations may encounter as discussed in Chap. 10. Nonetheless, in spite of these reservations it is possible to extract important evidence not only from the role play itself, but also in relation to the ways in which it is seen and understood by the audience.

Collages and Drawings

Not all children and young people are highly verbal in their capacities to express their responses to matters that concern them. A well-known study was built around "draw a scientist"(Chambers 1983) in which children drew their images of scientists at work; they were more often than not male, white coated and preparing to blow something up. Drawings can be a powerful way of eliciting stereotypes, which in turn gives insight into how they might be addressed. Although we would argue that they cannot stand alone. Drawings need to be explained and annotated. With very young children it is possible to support older students to act as their 'secretaries' who can then make the notations.

Drawings that make comparisons can be particularly revealing. Groundwater-Smith, Ewing and LeCornu (2015) provide a number of examples where children have drawn themselves learning in different contexts. For example, reading at school and reading at home demonstrate different practices. Children reading at school tend to do so as part of a group, reading at home is a more solitary activity. Frisch et al. (2012) invited young people in an affluent Parisian neighbourhood to draw their surroundings and subsequently interviewed them about the nature of their portrayals. They concluded:

> Putting the drawings of the neighbourhood in perspective with the discussions conducted with the children reveals the richness of the graphic method for analysing their relationship with their neighbourhood. Unquestionably, these drawings, which are the result of a

complex filtering process (as repeated research has shown in recent decades), are hetero-
geneous, even though they were produced by children of the same age living in the same
urban environment. Some are 'detailed', that is to say dense and meticulous, whereas others
are 'sketchy' and offer few elements which enable the relationship with the neighbourhood
to be characterised; some are plans, others are pictorial maps, and others even belong to an
intermediary category (pictorial plans). This diversity, which can initially seem disconcert-
ing, is worth being interpreted in the light of outside information. (p. 33)

The diversity of the drawings not only revealed the varying competencies among the
children but also demonstrated how differently they experienced their mileau. This
is evident in the earlier work of Whetton and McWhirter (1998) who employed a
"draw and write" approach to uncovering how children perceive and explain health
and safety related concepts. Through the wealth of material that they obtained they
were able to evolve a developmental spiral of children's changing perceptions of
"being healthy and staying healthy" (p. 277).

Helpful as drawings may be it is the case that older students may be loathe to
draw or contribute to a collage, but may feel more comfortable engaging in a pho-
tographic exercise.

Photography and Integrated Digital Media

The accessibility of cameras in phones, laptops, tablets and the like make it possible
for users to immediately see the results of their endeavours. However, earlier use of
photography as a tool for children and young people to document their experiences
has been available for many decades. Groundwater-Smith and Kelly (2003) reported on a study conducted on behalf of the Australian Museum whereby students in
small groups from a range of schools were provided with disposable cameras that
they employed in a visit to the Museum to documents those things that assisted
and impeded their learning. They then assembled their photographs into collages
that demonstrated their responses to the Museum environment. An unexpected and
widespread response was in relation to the students' emotional engagement with
a number of the exhibits. As part of its audience research the Museum had never
considered this perspective; the study led to a more sensitive policy in exhibit-
ing and explaining various displays. Thus photography allowed those working with
children and young people to re-appraise their policies.

In their study applying visual research to policy and practice across four countries
facing challenging circumstances Walker et al. (2008) asked their young participants to photograph "the opposite of violence" (p. 165). Many of the photographs
were representations of calmness in domestic settings and of places that the children
saw as "special" for them. Discussions and interviews would not have uncovered
these responses. Having a camera gave significant agency to the young people to
identify what mattered to them with little direction or steering by adults.

Indeed, reversing the normal order of things becomes possible when students can
take the initiative. Primary school students from a member school of the *Coalition*

of Knowledge Building Schools negotiated with their teachers to take a digital photograph of them every minute over a forty minute period. They then laid out the sequence and asked their teachers what they noticed about themselves and the way in which they interacted. Each had a different style, ranging from frequently getting down to the students' level to placing themselves strategically where children would come to them for assistance. This led to a later class discussion regarding the student preferences for interaction with their teachers. This anecdote is unreported in the literature because it was not a part of a research study, but was representative of a school policy that regularly honoured student voice that allowed for students themselves to propose ways of addressing issues in relation to teaching and learning.

Most recently there has been an increase in attention being paid to capitalising on the burgeoning of social networking as a means of enhancing the participation of children and young people in circumstances that matter to them. Collin et al. (2011) in publishing the benefits of social networking as a means of giving young people a voice have been supported by the *Inspire Foundation*, an international non-government organisation that brings together 63 partners in a mix of youth researchers across 13 universities, thinkers from industry and business, and mental health and youth advocates across the non-government and government sector. The research agenda has been developed with over 600 young people. It focuses on achieving change through collaboration and partnership between researchers and end-users, defined as young people, parents, professionals and members of the community. The report by Collin *et al* is seen to provide a base for youth based organisations looking to incorporate social networking into their programs. For our purposes we are particularly concerned with social networking uses in terms of civic engagement and political participation. As well as the most commonly understood adoption through the updating of profiles, commenting on photos or other posts, young people have the skill and capacity to post public messages and create information walls.

As the report observes:

> Creative content sharing practices (such as blogs, animations, videos, photos and digital collages) form an increasingly integral part of young people's communicative exchange and play a significant role in young people's developing sense of identity and community. Creative content production and sharing *empowers* individual young people through the following demonstrated benefits:

- fostering the development of literacy and technical skills;
- developing a sense of aspiration, personal achievement and self-worth, and fostering further creativity and self-expression;
- encouraging exploration and experimentation with new or different aspects of their identity; and,
- reinforcing aspects of identity, such as ethnicity or cultural background. (p. 15)

Some five years ago, Livingstone (2008) observed the 'explosion' of young people's engagement with the internet and the dearth of understanding among researchers who have failed to listen to what it is that they actually have to say. Young people do not wish to use all of the power of social media to merely reproduce what an older and more conservative generation may have to say. Harris (2008) suggests that young people "turn their backs" on the invitations that target them and instead engage in much more creative blogging, networking and the making of e-zines as a form of activism.

While it remains speculation at present we wonder whether, with their competence in managing social media, young people in countries such as the United States and the UK might question the social policy that is built on lower spending, lower debt and market led growth. In England, they can see their schools converting to academy status thus by-passing local education authorities' representations of them and their needs. Brooks (2013) in her analysis of the Conservative and Liberal Coalition's Social Policy Documents in the UK reveals that they construct young people as: "friends and students of business; active consumers; dutiful citizens; the children of authoritative parents; 'good characters-in-the-making'; and a unitary group" (p. 321). This is not necessarily a view shared by the young people themselves.

Concept Mapping

Ordinarily, concept maps are defined as a graphical tool used for organizing and representing knowledge and ideas (Kane and Trochim 2007). The concepts are arranged into circles or boxes identified by the creator with linking words and phrases demonstrating relationships. Formal concept maps created by adults also encompass a hierarchical ordering ranging from the most inclusive, general concepts at the top with more specific concepts branching out below. However, concept maps can also be employed by children, less as a planning and evaluation tool and more as a means of uncovering the ways in which they understand a phenomenon and its component parts by making them visible.

In the early days of the widespread adoption of information and communication technology (ICT) in the classroom Pearson and Somekh (2003) used concept mapping as a research tool to better understand the ways in which young children related the use of ICTs in their schools. The young people were able to 'practice' concept mapping on familiar topics such as 'holidays' or 'our school'. They were then introduced to the task of mapping computers in today's world. They were encouraged to experiment with their ideas and to make them sufficiently visual that other young people from different language groups would understand the ways in which ICTs connected up with learning.

> We want you to think about your world and all the types of computers within it.
> What would you say was the most simple computer system, and the most complex computer system you can think of? Where are computers placed at home... at school... in the outside world... or in the work place? Are they connected in any way? Think of all the people who use them. And why they use them. Take a minute of two to think before you start drawing. (p. 7)

The researchers were able to identify a range of mapping configurations: *unconnected,* without links; *linear,* with the nodes linked in a sequential fashion; *one-centred*, with one central node; *several centred*, with two or more nodes; *spaghetti,* highly distributed; and, *not a concept map*, lacking any coherence. (pp. 10–11). The adoption of concept mapping as a means of better understanding the ways in which young people understand a phenomenon was seen as providing a fluid and dynamic picture and, importantly, a medium over which they had considerable control.

While there are few studies that employ the use of concept maps exclusively, a number, particularly in the area of young people's contribution to town and community planning have incorporated concept maps and regular maps as inquiry tools. A long-time advocate for children and young people's participation in planning and development in terms of the urban built and natural environment Malone (2011) undertook an ambitious project in the small New South Wales town of Dapto where she and her team consulted with children from Kindergarten and Year 5 in a local school from the very outset of the planning. A number of both qualitative and quantitative tools were employed including visual, verbal and textual methods such as concept and regular mapping that allowed for the range of abilities and competencies of the participating students. Their brief was to document the nature of available places and spaces that appealed to them in their local community. Following broad consultation a smaller reference group of the children was formed to undertake three activities: to analyse the data in order to construct a children's report that would make design recommendations; a "dreaming play space" that would recommend key elements for a playground site; and, the design and development of a walkable adventure pathway between the old and newer neighbourhoods. In the preface to the final report one of the reference group children wrote:

> Our Dapto Dreaming report is about the things we like about our neighbourhood and the things we think could be changed to make it even better. It's about making sure adults listen and value us and include our dreams in their designs for our place. (p. 33)

Storying, Diaries and Logs

Narrative accounts of events and experiences are a natural human form of communication. Telling stories to others enables opportunities to empathise and co-create as we seek for the common ground between us. Children and young people can through narrative make sense of their own world and that of others.

Students in a *Coalition of Knowledge Building Schools* Middle School visited the National Museum in Canberra to view *Yiwarra Kuju: The Canning Stock Route* that related the narrative of the stock route's impact upon Aboriginal people and the importance of the country that surrounds it. The exhibition told the story of contact, conflict, survival and exodus as demonstrated through voices, art and new media.

Such was the impact that on their return to Sydney the students elected to tell their own stories of the journey of transition from their previous primary schools through to early secondary classrooms. This should not be taken as a form of appropriation or trivialization but rather that the students came to understand the power of narrative. Of course some routes and journeys are more difficult and painful. Sikes and Gale (2006) report on Goodson and Sikes study of the storylines of working class children who gained entry into further and higher education and the challenges and encounters that they faced that were often difficult and discouraging.

Others have turned to a melding of image and text. Lysaght et al. (2009) discussed an international research project, *Voices of Children,* where images and texts were constructed independently of one another but nonetheless related each to the other. The young people aged 6–18 years of age took photographs of their everyday lives. Written logs and diaries were kept of the contexts within which the participants lived. The process allowed a reading between the two media. Thus a playful and happy photograph of a family was accompanied by a text of a different kind as exemplified by this extract from a young girl from the U.S.A.:

> There are 4 people in my family. My mom, my dad, my sister, and me. I am the younger sister. I am 10 years old. My family can be weird sometimes, and I sometimes get mad at them. My family can embarress (sic) me and my sister. We can always wish that we were somewhere else. My sister sings non-stop. Our family does hang out some, and when we do we have so much fun together. My sister is so annoying she usually isn't my friend, but is sometimes. I have the best family in the world in my opinion. I love them a lot. (p. 5)

"Storying" as it has become known, can also provide an opportunity to document experience in ways that contribute to the learning of the story-teller and of the listener or reader. Carr and Lee (2012) have collected together a range of such learning stories in early childhood education in New Zealand. They are recorded by adults, but are representations of their engagement with young children. Below is an excerpt from a conversation as Zeb dictates a commentary for his portfolio:

> Z: That was my hammerhead shark. That was the shark day. We drew lots of pictures of sharks and I drew a volcano that just blew up and it went into the sea the killed the shark. The ash went into the sea and killed a shark.
> Z: That's me touching the shark with my Bob the Builder shirt on.
> Z: Hey, what's that one called? A bluenose and my Mum was sill 'cos she thought it was a blue cod … And I was right.
> Z: … I didn't want to pick it up because there was blood leaking from it, just want to touch the smooth parts not the drippy part.
> Z: I touched the eye and there was all black stuff coming out of the eye. I can feel the eye, it's squishy. (p. 45)

Table 9.1 below summarises these methods, when they might be employed and some of the key challenges they present.

And so we have it. An array of means of gathering a range of "evidence" that contribute to a learning democracy. That is, a condition described by Fielding and Moss (2011, p. 78) as intergenerational learning where transformation "that emphasises a joint commitment to the common good and include occasions and opportunities for an equal sharing of power and responsibility" can occur and which is further

Table 9.1 Summary of Methods

Method	When to use	Challenges
Focus group discussions	Where participant interaction and debate is essential	Moderating the range of contributions
		Staying on task
		Handling digressions, confusion and pacing
Co-interviewing	Where peer group interaction is less governed by issues of power and control than when adults are interviewing	Providing strategies for reporting back on matters of sensitivity and confidentiality
Role-playing	Where participants have a sense of agency in addressing matters of concern to them	Production of stereotypes and 'acting for acting's sake'
Collages and drawings	Where high level verbal skills are not required, and where imaginative responses can be elicited	Students' perceptions that they 'can't draw', especially older students
Photography	Where efficient capturing of multiple images can be undertaken, free of adult supervision	Selectivity may result in a distorted representation
Social media	Where civic engagement that is change-oriented is desired	Requires relatively sophisticated understanding of the medium and its impact
Concept mapping	Where relationships between elements of a phenomenon can be uncovered	Analysis can be challenging when accumulating data
Storying, diaries and logs	Where imagination can be brought into play and experience documented on an individual basis	Students' written and audio verbal skills may be relatively limited

discussed in our concluding Chap. 12. With the help of children and young people who have so much to offer us in terms of their testimony of practice we can bell the cat; we can together better understand what constitutes a good education, not 'best' education, but an education that is just and fair and fit for purpose.

At the heart of the matter, being fair and just in our dealings with each other, as adults researching alongside children and young people, our first consideration must be towards translating this aspiration through the set of ethical precepts that we discuss in the chapter that follows.

Chapter 10
Ethics in Researching with Children and Young People

In some ways, our argument in this book has been 'all about ethics', in that we believe, along with others whose work we have drawn on (see, for example, Fielding 2011b; Hart 2008; Shier 2001), that genuine engagement with the voices of young people in the ways we have been suggesting, is a deeply ethical endeavour. Our aim in this chapter is to explore some of the specific issues related to the ethics of researching with children and young people, especially in school contexts; although we do take up in Chap. 6 ethical issues around appropriation and exploitation in relation to working with cultural institutions. We do not strive here for a practical guide or description of how to navigate the ethics of conducting research with young people: there are many of these that take up the practicalities of research ethics, such as Alderson and Morrow (2011) and (Fraser 2004). Rather, in this chapter we examine the ethical implications for researching with children and young people that emerge not only from the UN Convention on the Rights of the Child but also from a number of national research ethics frameworks, in the United Kingdom, United States and Australia in particular. Second, we consider what ethical practice might look like 'beyond compliance', briefly returning to our earlier work on ethics as a framework for quality in applied research in education (Groundwater-Smith and Mockler 2007), before entering into a discussion of praxis as a framework for researching with children and young people in school contexts. We suggest here that what is required is a bringing together of "research ethics and everyday ethics" (Mockler 2013) in the context of student voice work. We argue throughout that the basic ethical axiom of 'doing no harm' is a baseline aim rather than a magnanimous goal, that enacting democratic education requires a more nuanced understanding of power relations and that the notion of 'praxis' with its strong ethical dimension, might provide a useful framework for this approach.

© Springer International Publishing Switzerland 2015
N. Mockler, S. Groundwater-Smith, *Engaging with Student Voice in Research,
Education and Community,* DOI 10.1007/978-3-319-01985-7_10

Ethics Guidelines, Statements and Frameworks: Working with Children and Young People

We began in Chap. 1 with a consideration of the United Nations Convention on the Rights of the Child (United Nations 1989) and its implications for listening to and working with the voices of children and young people in schools and other educational settings. We observed that, among others, the Convention ensures the entitlement of children to the rights:

- to express views in all decisions that affect them and the opportunity to be heard in any court or administrative proceedings;
- to freedom of expression and the right to seek, receive and impart information of all kinds;
- to have their best interests treated as a primary consideration in all actions concerning them, including decisions related to their care and protection;
- to free education available on the basis of their capacity; and
- to enjoy the highest attainable standard of health and an adequate standard of living.

Specifically relevant to the current discussion of ethics and student voice is the provision in Article 12 that:

> States Parties shall assure to the child who is capable of forming his or her own views the right to express those views freely in all matters affecting the child, the views of the child being given due weight in accordance with the age and maturity of the child.

Stemming from these provisions is, we believe, a set of moral and ethical considerations that researchers, teachers and others working in the field of student voice might do well to observe. As Harry Shier points out in his 'pathways to participation' model (Shier 2001) (discussed at length in Chap. 4), an obligation to establish policies and procedures by which children might express their views in the ordinary turn of events should exist within schools and organisations that are committed to implementing Article 12 of the convention. Furthermore, the Convention clearly positions children as active agents in the provision of information, which, coupled with the indication that children's best interests should be treated as a primary consideration in all actions concerning them, suggests that subject to informed consent, children and young people should be not only encouraged to participate in research, but that at a local level, mechanisms of informed consent and participation should be embedded in practitioner inquiry and indeed all aspects of educational practice itself.

Notwithstanding our firm belief that ethical praxis involves a commitment to what Cochran-Smith and Lytle have termed 'inquiry as stance' (2009a, b), we wish also to address here the act of engaging student voice in research that is initiated in the academy. To this end we examine three national frameworks for the conduct of social research involving humans, by way of exploring their positioning of children and young people within the research enterprise and the complementary (or otherwise) nature of their relationship with the Convention. In the United Kingdom and Australia, research conducted by university-based researchers is governed by the *ESRC Framework for Research Ethics* (Economic and Social Research Council 2012) and the *ARC/NHMRC/AVCC National Statement for Ethical Conduct in Research Involving Humans* (Australian Government 2007) respectively, while in the United States, research ethics are governed by a series of federal laws, and Part 46 of the Code of Federal Regulations on the Protection of Human Research Subjects (Office for Human Research Protections 2009). We explore each of them here in turn.

The *ESRC Framework for Research Ethics* (Economic and Social Research Council 2012) is the only of the three documents that does not include a separate section on research with children, choosing instead to integrate discussion about children's involvement in research into the general discussion of research which "involves potentially vulnerable groups" (p. 8). While the Framework makes a distinction at one point (and only one point) between children and young people, after this initial mention the umbrella term 'children' is used presumably to cover both groups. A technical definition of 'children' within the framework is not provided, and as a consequence we can assume that 'children' is used in reference to legal minors, defined as people under 18 years of age in the United Kingdom.

The most expansive discussion of research 'on children' (sic) occurs in relation to the issue of informed consent, where the Framework states that "every effort should be made to secure actively given informed consent from individual participants" (p. 30). It continues:

> In the case of research on children, one cannot expect parents alone to provide disinterested approval on their children's behalf. In such cases, every effort should be made to deal with consent through dialogue with both children and their parents (or legal equivalent). Again, there may be circumstances where seeking consent from parents could jeopardise the research (for example, in research into teenage sexuality or teenage pregnancy). In such circumstances, researchers will need to regard the potential risk to the principal participants of the research as a priority. (p. 31)

In the case of the ESRC Framework, then, children are conceptualised as vulnerable individuals for whom, other than in extraordinary circumstances, participation in research requires the consent of their parent or guardian along with, ideally, consent from individual children as well.

The US Code of Federal Regulations on the Protection of Human Research Subjects (Office for Human Research Protections 2009) contains a 'Subpart' (D) entitled "Additional Protections for Children Involved as Subjects in Research" (pp. 12–13). Within the Code, children are defined as "persons who have not attained the legal age for consent to treatments or procedures involved in the research, under the applicable law of the jurisdiction in which the research will be conducted" (p. 12).

Clearly in this, the Code is oriented toward research focused on medicine and health sciences, and given the assertion of the UN Convention that children have a right to express their views in appropriate contexts, we wonder how this applies in studies where the 'treatments or procedures' are, for example, the completion of surveys or participation in interviews[1]. The Code makes no distinction between children and young people of varying ages and in all cases, including research not involving greater than minimal risk; research involving greater than minimal risk but presenting the prospect of direct benefit to the individual subjects; research involving greater than minimal risk and no prospect of direct benefit to individual subjects, but likely to yield generalizable knowledge about the subject's disorder or condition; and research not otherwise approvable which presents an opportunity to understand, prevent, or alleviate a serious problem affecting the health or welfare of children, it requires: "adequate provisions [to be] made for soliciting the assent of children and the permission of their parents or guardians" (p. 12, 13).

The Code requires Institutional Review Boards (known in other national contexts as Human Research Ethics Committees or Research Ethics Committees) to make a judgement as to whether children are capable of providing assent to participate, taking into account the "ages, maturity, and psychological state of the children involved" (p. 13). Interestingly, the final clause in the item related to requirements for permission by parents or guardians and for assent by children is: "When the IRB determines that assent is required, it shall also determine whether and how assent must be documented" (p. 13). Thus, the requirement for children's assent could be interpreted as being the exception rather than the rule, particularly when laid alongside the edict that "even where the IRB determines that the subjects are capable of assenting, the IRB may still waive the assent requirement" (p. 13).

Similar to the UK Framework, the US Code positions children and young people as 'vulnerable' research participants. Quite differently from the UK Framework, however, the Code does not stipulate that in the normal process of events, researchers should require active consent from children for research participation, leaving the requirement for assent up to the judgement of individual IRBs and in particular circumstances.

Like the US Code, and unlike the UK Framework, which relates only to research conducted within Economic and Social Sciences, the Australian Statement (Australian Government 2007) cuts across research conducted with humans in all contexts and disciplines. Within the section on 'Ethical Consideration specific to participants' (p. 51), the Statement contains a chapter on research with children and young people. The Statement differentiates between four groups of children and young people:

a. infants, who are unable to take part in discussion about the research and its effects;
b. young children, who are able to understand some relevant information and take part in limited discussion about the research, but whose consent is not required;
c. young people of developing maturity, who are able to understand the relevant information but whose relative immaturity means that they remain vulnerable. The consent of these young people is required, but is not sufficient to authorise research; and

---

[1] We note, however, that the United States has signed but not ratified the UN Convention, and consequently has not undertaken to implement the Articles of the Convention into domestic law.

d. young people who are mature enough to understand and consent, and are not vulnerable through immaturity in ways that warrant additional consent from a parent or guardian (p. 55).

Additionally, it notes that membership of one or more of these categories is complex, and depends on both the individual characteristics of the child and the nature of the research project in which they are potential participants:

> It is not possible to attach fixed ages to each level—they vary from child to child. Moreover, a child or young person may at the one time be at different levels for different research projects, depending on the kind and complexity of the research. Being responsive to developmental levels is important not only for judging when children or young people are able to give their consent for research: even young children with very limited cognitive capacity should be engaged at their level in discussion about the research and its likely outcomes (p. 55).

In the Australian context, consent is required to be obtained from "the child or young person whenever he or she has the capacity to make this decision" (p. 56), along with consent from the child's parent/s and/or guardian. At the same time, "an ethical review body may approve research to which only the young person consents if it is satisfied that he or she is mature enough to understand and consent, and not vulnerable through immaturity in ways that would warrant additional consent from a parent or guardian" (p. 56).

The Australian Statement, then, stands alone amongst the three in its recognition of the complex differences between individual children and young people, their growing maturity and the implications of these as they relate to consent. While the Statement does not explicitly position children and young people as 'vulnerable groups', through its persistent focus on issues of consent, such a de-facto positioning results, and in this the Statement is consistent with the UK Framework and the US Code. As guidelines or 'rules' for researchers, this focus is perhaps unremarkable and to be expected, however it necessarily positions children and young people as potential victims of unethical researchers rather than more overtly as agents and active participants with a right to lend their voice to research on issues that concern and impact upon them. To explore what such an approach might look like beyond the compliance mandates of these frameworks and guidelines, we need to think in terms of the ethics of educational practice, and it is to this approach that we now turn.

Ethics Beyond Compliance in Student Voice Work

In this section we ask what it might be to look beyond these frameworks, which are essentially tools for compliance with a basic level of research ethics, in work involving children and young people. We begin with a discussion of ethics as a framework for quality in practitioner inquiry, building on earlier work to consider what this might look like in the context of inquiry-based work focused explicitly on the involvement of students and young people. We then move to consider the notion of praxis,, and what this might entail for practitioners and researchers wanting to engage in ethical approaches to student voice work.

Ethics as a Framework for Quality in Student Voice Work

Several years ago now (Groundwater-Smith and Mockler 2006, 2007), we developed a series of broad, overarching ethics guidelines for practitioner research that, we argued, take up both traditional conceptualisations of research ethics and contemporary expressions of ethical educational practice. They were:

- *That it should observe ethical protocols and processes*: Practitioner research is subject to the same ethical protocols as other social research. Informed consent should be sought from participants, whether students, teachers, parents or others, and an earnest attempt should be made to 'do no harm'.
- *That it should be transparent in its processes*: One of the broader aims of practitioner research lies in the building of community and the sharing of knowledge and ideas. To this end, practitioner research should be 'transparent' in its enactment, and practitioner researchers accountable to their community for the processes and products of their research.
- *That it should be collaborative in its nature*: Practitioner research should aim to provide opportunities for colleagues to share, discuss and debate aspects of their practice in the name of improvement and development. The responsible 'making sense' of data collected from within the field of one's own practice (through triangulation of evidence and other means) relies heavily on these opportunities.
- *That it should be transformative in its intent and action*: Practitioner researchers engage in an enterprise which is, in essence, about contributing to both transformation of practice and transformation of society. Responsible and ethical practitioner research operates in such a way as to create actionable, actioned outcomes.
- *That it should be able to justify itself to its community of practice*: Engaging in practitioner research involves an opportunity cost to the community. To do well, requires time and energy that cannot be spent in other professional ways. The benefits must be commensurable with the effort and resources expended in the course of the work which necessarily will require collaboration and communication (Groundwater-Smith and Mockler 2007, pp. 205–206).

These guidelines, however, were offered in conjunction with three focus areas for quality. The first of these was *quality of evidence*, related to the "ways in which [evidence] has been collected and the purposes to which it will be put, evidence collected under duress, evidence collected covertly, evidence that is not validated by triangulation and evidence that has not been debated, in our view is evidence that is invalid" (pp. 206–207). The second was *quality of purpose*, related to the conceptualisation of the research project: how far it originates from the concerns of practitioners themselves as opposed to being imposed in a 'top down' manner which denies teacher agency and serves the system more than the teachers involved.

The third was *quality of outcome*, related to the knowledge generated by practitioner inquiry and the use to which it is put. Here we have argued that to pass the quality test, outcomes need to move 'beyond celebration' to transform the environment in some way, however small (Mockler and Groundwater Smith, Forthcoming).

While this work was largely developed in thinking about the role of practitioner research as inquiry-based teacher professional learning, it holds particular implications for teachers and other researchers wishing to explicitly engage in student voice work. When laid alongside the frameworks discussed in Chap. 4, it suggests that at the very least, students need to be brought into the research enterprise as 'co-enquirers', but more desirably, as 'knowledge creators' and 'joint authors', to use Michael Fielding's nomenclature (Fielding 2011a). In this context, quality of evidence relates to the opportunities available for students to express their perspectives, how these opportunities are initiated and how far the young people themselves are able to engage in the robust debate that is inevitably part of the 'making sense' of the evidence. Quality of purpose in this context concerns how far students and young people are involved in the conceptualisation of the inquiry—how does the focus emerge from a joint concern held by students as well as teachers as opposed to one that is purely the province of teachers' professional concerns. At the most basic level, quality of outcome in this context is about the way that genuine feedback is provided to students, such that the 'ethical contract' between researcher and research participant is delivered upon. As Hart notes in his 'Ladder of Participation', also discussed in Chap. 4 (Hart 1992), 'consultation' without providing feedback is tantamount to manipulation of young people as research participants. At a more sophisticated level, attending to quality of outcome in student voice work might include the involvement of both young people and adults in conceptualising the use to which the research might be put within the community, such as to contribute to change and transformation.

Student Voice and Educational Praxis

In our discussion of praxis, we draw on the widely accepted definition of praxis as "morally informed action" (Carr and Kemmis 1986), and furthermore, on Carr and Kemmis' particular conceptualisation of the relationship between educational practice, praxis and phronesis:

> ...educational practice can only be made intelligible by reference to the Aristotelian concepts of *praxis*—morally informed action aimed at achieving some ethical 'good'—and *phronesis*—the mode of practical reasoning appropriate to deciding what, in any particular concrete situation, would constitute an appropriate expression of this 'good'. (Carr and Kemmis 2005, p. 352)

This articulation of the relationship between praxis and phronesis is particularly pertinent to this current discussion, for as we have argued throughout this book, the enactment of student voice work, in the context of democratic approaches to education, can never be confined to the research endeavour or the 'extra curricular' domain and must necessarily also be enacted in the domain of classroom practice.

To enact praxis, in the context of educational practice necessarily rooted in the realm of both professional and research ethics, suggests a bringing together of the research ethics we have discussed at length in this chapter and the ethics of democratic classroom practice.

Furthermore, to understand student voice work in this way as embedded in educational praxis is to understand it as part of an orientation to educational practice that values inquiry and indeed, places inquiry at its centre. Such an orientation has been described by Marilyn Cochran-Smith and Susan Lytle as 'inquiry as stance':

> Fundamental to the notion of inquiry as stance is the idea that educational practice is not simply instrumental in the sense of figuring out how to get things done, but also and more importantly, it is social and political in the sense of deliberating about what to get done, why to get it done, and whose interests are served. Working from and with an inquiry stance, then, involves a continual process of making current arrangements problematic; questioning the ways knowledge and practice are constructed, evaluated and used; and assuming that part of the work of practitioners individually and collectively is to participate in educational and social change. (Cochran-Smith and Lytle 2009a, p. 121)

Taking an inquiring stance while at the same time being committed to seeking out and listening to student voice requires bringing students in to the conversation about the problematic nature of the current arrangements and the construction of the practices at the centre of classrooms and schools.

Elsewhere, building on our joint earlier work referenced above, one of us has suggested that the enactment of praxis involves five critical ethical dimensions, reflected both in the context of practitioner inquiry and the context of classroom practice, namely:

- Informed consent;
- Striving to 'do no harm';
- Privileging student voice;
- Understanding power dynamics; and
- Exercising sound judgement (Mockler 2013, pp. 8–11).

In this particular discussion of the ethics of working with student voice, we believe these ethical dimensions to be no less important. The first two of these dimensions we have dealt with in the discussion above relating to research ethics, and also at some length in Chap. 9 on pedagogy and classroom practice. Clearly the privileging of student voice is the focus of this book, and to that end our entire argument throughout has centred on the idea that student voice can and should be privileged in schools. Each of these critical dimensions, however, holds complex implications for the 'what', 'who' and 'how' of student voice work enacted within a framework of praxis, and it is in this way that the ensuing discussion will be structured.

Ethics and the 'What?' of Student Voice

The 'what' of student voice work relates largely to the quality of evidence, purpose and outcome discussed earlier in this chapter. There, we argued that the ethical enactment of student voice work is the benchmark of quality: in short, there can be no 'quality' in practitioner research (or indeed, we would argue, any type of research, much less educational practice) without attention to ethics. Good research, like good practice, occurs within a framework of ethics.

A central ethical consideration relating to the 'what' of student voice concerns the nature of student voice itself: what we refer to as 'student voice' is in fact rarely a number of voices singing in unison, but more often a cacophony of voices, some singing in harmony while others might be regarded as discordant. Some voices are highly melodious while others are more dissonant, and some voices are very loud while others are exercised very softly, if at all. Working with student voice, authentically listening to the voices of students, whether in research endeavours or in the day-to-day of classroom life, requires that we develop an understanding of the nuance of their voices. Without privileging the harmonious over the discordant, for example (or, indeed, the discordant over the harmonious), a relational balance between the collective and the individual, similar to that suggested in Noddings' notion of an 'ethic of care' (1988, 2003, 2010), is required.

On an organisational level, attending to the ethics in terms of the 'what' of student voice requires the establishment of structures and processes that allow students to 'take up' their voice. Student Representative Councils and the like provide one avenue for this to occur but necessarily limit both the membership and the scope of decision making in ways that can generate cynicism and distrust rather than have the desired effect of opening spaces for genuine conversation (see the discussion below about the 'who' of student voice). A whole-of-school commitment to the development of student voice initiatives such as that depicted in the work of Eve Mayes (Mayes 2013; Mayes and Groundwater-Smith 2010, 2011) requires structures that are broader in scope, fearless with regard to the 'unwelcome truths' (Kemmis 2006; Mockler and Groundwater Smith, Forthcoming) that might be raised and inclusive of a diverse range of students.

Structures and processes, however, do not exist in a vacuum. They are necessary but not sufficient for ensuring the viability of the kind of student voice work we advocate. As Fielding (2011a; Fielding and Moss 2011) suggests, 'lived democracy' in schools is as much about school cultures that are open and welcoming of the voices of both young people *and* adults "not only is away of meeting individual needs and arriving at collective decisions and aspirations but also as a way of living and being in the world" (Fielding 2011a, p. 73). On this, he continues:

> Fellowship readings of lived democracy foreground the importance of rich involvement of all participants in pursuit of communal aspirations. Thus, the kinds of school meetings for which I am arguing are not those that attend with forensic energy to matters of procedure or the minutiae of form. Rather they are those which acknowledge that democratic living requires more than procedural fidelity. It transcends justice: it is more-than-political; it is a way of life within which democratic fellowship is both the raison d'etre and the means of its realisation. (Fielding 2011a, p. 73)

Attending to the ethics of the 'what' of student voice, then, within school and classroom communities, is a complex and holistic task that requires a cultural shift rather than the strategic addition of a few mechanisms and processes that allow for the voices of *some* students to be listened to *some* of the time on *some* issues regarded as appropriate by the adults within the community.

Ethics and the 'Who?' of Student Voice

Listening to the voices of students who agree with us and affirm current practice is hardly a difficult task. Likewise, listening to the voices of compliant students conditioned to participate raises few challenges for teachers and schools committed to student voice work. Indeed, it can be tempting to engage only those students who are 'willing and able', engage them in genuine and authentic ways and then be self-congratulatory about our commitment to intergenerational democracy evidenced in our student voice work. Such an approach, we would argue, is a fine place to start but a poor one to finish in.

Thompson (2010, 2011) explores the construction of 'the good student', observing that:

> Schools could be freer places for young people, but much of what in constructed as 'good' in the good student is best thought of as a set of discourses that, perversely, limit the possibilities for students to be creative and experimental of their selves. (2010, p. 413)

He identifies, through his research in three diverse secondary schools, six different rationales of constructions of 'the good student':

- *The docile and disciplined good*, disciplined by the system and consequently self-disciplined into 'good behaviour';
- *The pastoral good*, where behaviour is regulated through students' expectations of that which is right or morally correct;
- *The bureaucratic good*, exemplified by students who 'fly under the radar' by consistently complying with the requirements of learning and assessment tasks;
- *The gendered good*, where different measures of 'good' exist for male and female students;
- *The conflictual good*, where students who 'push back' on authority nevertheless win the regard of teachers for their 'liveliness' or perceived growing critical consciousness; and
- *The affiliated good*, where students who appeared as most successful were also those with high levels of public 'attachment' or affiliation with the school (2010, pp. 421–427).

Thompson's rationales remind us that the 'good student' comes in many guises, from the 'well behaved' to the 'academic achiever' to the larrikin-pushing-the-boundaries to the representative sports star. When we confine student voice efforts to engaging only these students, either via design or by happenstance, we do not attend to the ethical demands of the work, and furthermore, increase the chances that what we find will further affirm and entrench current practices rather than problematise and consequently transform them.

Students who are disengaged, disaffected and disconnected from their school experience are undoubtedly difficult to engage in student voice work. We do not suggest that the task of genuine inclusivity (i.e. where the invitation is not only offered to students, but taken up by them) is easy, nor that it can be achieved overnight, but we do suggest that attending to the ethics of the 'who' of student voice requires that a sustained effort be made in this regard.

Ethics and the 'How?' of Student Voice

The 'how' of student voice relates to those governing principles and processes that guide the work. Attending to ethics at this level relates to the overarching framework of inquiry and practice, and goes to 'macro' issues such as informed consent and the dictum of doing no harm, but also at a 'micro' level to issues such as the understanding and navigation of power relations within the classroom and the ways in which sound judgement is arrived at and executed.

In Chap. 4 we explored the notion of 'empowerment' and our own particular reticence to frame student voice work within the discourse of empowerment. Our argument there, as it is here, was that a more nuanced understanding of power relations between adults and young people in schools is required. Patti Lather suggested two decades ago a need for researchers to "learn to attend to the politics of what we do and do not do at a practical level" (Lather 1991, p. 13), and we believe that these words are particularly salient when navigating a desire to listen to student voice whether as practitioner researcher, classroom practitioner or both. In Chap. 9 we discussed some of the ways in which this might occur in the context of classroom practice, and here we reiterate that attending to the ethics of the 'how' of student voice requires us to engage deeply with the issue of power, ultimately exploring ways that power might be genuinely shared between adults and young people in schools, not because power has been 'given' to one group by another, but because the conditions for genuinely shared power have evolved.

Finally, the ways in which conclusions are reached and decisions enacted matters. Both individually and together we have written much over the years about the importance of teacher professional judgement, the responsibility and privilege that constitutes professional judgement, and teachers' right to develop and exercise their professional judgement (Groundwater-Smith 1998, pp. see, for example,; Groundwater-Smith and Mockler 2003, 2009; Mockler 2013). In one of these instances, one of us wrote:

> A commitment to the development and exercise of sound professional judgement raises questions about what evidence is used as the basis for judgement and how it is used, about how judgement might be shared and critiqued within the teaching community, and also about the countercultural nature of the very exercise of teacher professional judgement in these neo-liberal times. (Mockler 2013, p. 11)

In the context of a desire to seek out and listen to student voice, and in attending to the ethics of the 'how' of student voice work, this might be broadened to ideally include not only the teaching community but the 'community of practice' represented by both adults and young people in the school. Sharing in the 'making sense' of evidence, whether it originates from students, teachers, others or a combination of community members, developing a shared understanding and judgement of the evidence, and together discerning a course of action is a key part of honouring the ethics of the 'how' of student voice work.

Conclusion

We recognise that we have raised far more questions than we have solved in this chapter, and indeed, the intention was exactly such. The terrain of ethics is not smooth and we would do our reader a disservice to suggest that the answers to ethical questions related to student voice work were simple. Instead, we have aimed to problematise the what, who and how of seeking out and listening to student voice, to suggest some 'thoughtlines' that those embarking on (or indeed, further developing) this work might follow. We argue that the best form of ethical engagement in such work is that which occurs when we push 'beyond compliance' to consider not what the baseline of ethical engagement might be, but to explore the possible and indeed, reasonable aspirations of such work. It is our belief that robust engagement with ethical questions, particularly on the part of teachers and students jointly, is likely to yield rich conversations about students' experience of school and learning that will in turn drive forward the endeavor of listening openly and authentically to student voice and reach toward the goal of school as 'lived democracy'.

Chapter 11
Curriculum, Pedagogy, Assessment and Student Voice

So far, our discussion of seeking and listening to student voice particularly within schools has been located within the context of practitioner inquiry, and indeed this is the primary focus of the book, even admitting to other instances where children and young people deserve to be listened to and their voices acted upon. We are most interested in how teachers, working as practitioner inquirers might push beyond notions of legitimation and guardianship which so often frame 'student voice' to draw students into authentic dialogue about their experiences of schooling. We wanted also, however, to explore the implications of this kind of authentic student voice work in classroom practice, not in the sense that there is necessarily a causal relationship between practitioner researchers working with student voice and adopting classroom practices conducive to student agency (although we do believe there should be), but because there are particular approaches to curriculum, pedagogy and assessment that align more closely with the kinds of student voice practices we are advocating.

We are not alone in this concern. A number of authors (see, for example, Rudduck 2007; Serriere and Mitra 2012), have considered this very question in relation to the classroom impact of student voice work, focusing on the specific integration of student voice initiatives or 'consultation' into classroom practice through, for example, "teachers partnering with students to discuss teaching and learning, including inviting students to provide feedback on instructional styles, curriculum content, assessment opportunities and other issues in the classroom" (Serriere and Mitra 2012, p. 226). Indeed, the four year project that we portrayed in Chap. 5 had this very purpose. We see these as vital elements of practitioner inquiry when conducted at classroom and school level: teachers investigating their practice, engaging with the voices of young people to inform their practice, building mutual engagement and dialogue within their classrooms. What we wish to explore in this chapter, however, are the 'macro' level factors associated with this work, the approaches to curriculum, pedagogy and assessment that sit most comfortably alongside these practices, that might indeed be adopted by some practitioners as a consequence of their involvement in practitioner inquiry, but that also might lead others to embark on practitioner research endeavours in an attempt to become more systematic and/or

© Springer International Publishing Switzerland 2015
N. Mockler, S. Groundwater-Smith, *Engaging with Student Voice in Research, Education and Community,* DOI 10.1007/978-3-319-01985-7_11

collaborative in their inquiry. In this we are mindful of Stenhouse's definition of research as "systematic inquiry made public" (Stenhouse 1983).

Recently, one of us has begun to explore this issue in a paper entitled *'When 'research ethics' become 'everyday ethics': the intersection of inquiry and practice in practitioner research'* (Mockler 2014). In this work, she explores the 'classroom implications' of five ethical dimensions of practitioner inquiry, asking for each 'what would this look like in the realm of ordinary classroom practice?'. The five dimensions of informed consent, the maxim of 'doing no harm', the privileging of student voice, the understanding of power dynamics and the exercising of sound judgement are then examined for their logical consequences in the classroom, the argument being that 'cross-field effects' (Lingard and Rawolle 2004) take place, whereby the 'logics of practice' (Bourdieu and Wacquant 1992) of the research field impact upon the field of classroom practice as practitioner researchers' habitus is shaped and formed by the practice of teacher research. In relation to the dimension of 'privileging student voice', she argues:

> In the context of classroom practice, this might involve an emphasis on student agency in learning, through support of student decision-making in terms of the content, processes and products of learning. Furthermore, it requires teachers to foster authentic dialogue with students regarding their learning experiences and a willing-ness to adapt and tailor learning experiences according to the experience, needs and preferences of students. The notion of privileging student voice in the context of classroom practice raises questions for practitioners regarding supporting students to 'find' and express their voice in relation to their learning, not necessarily a simple task, and also developing strategies for themselves that lead to good listening, an equally complex endeavour. (Mockler 2013b, pp. 9–10)

In this chapter, we push beyond this initial suggestion of what the classroom implications of student voice work might be. Using Bernstein's (1971) notion of curriculum, pedagogy and assessment as the three message systems of schooling, we first of all draw on Bob Lingard's recent work to reflect on the shaping of these three message symbols in contemporary times through neoliberal educational discourses (Lingard 2012). We then consider each of the three message systems in the light of a desire to privilege student voice within the classroom. Of each, we ask three critical questions, namely 'What vision of this message system is promoted here?', 'How does this work within/against dominant conceptualisations of curriculum, pedagogy and assessment?' and 'What structures and processes, identities and practices does it demand of schools and teachers?'. We conclude by locating our 'picture' of the message systems of schooling shaped by a concern for student voice within broader pictures of democratic or 'radical' education.

Curriculum, Pedagogy and Assessment as 'Message Systems' of Schooling

Bernstein's seminal work on the classification and framing of educational knowledge (Bernstein 1971) identified curriculum, pedagogy and evaluation as the three 'message systems' of schooling:

> Formal educational knowledge can be considered to be realized through three message systems: curriculum, pedagogy and evaluation. Curriculum defines what counts as valid knowledge, pedagogy defines what counts as valid transmission of knowledge, and evaluation defines what counts as a valid realization of this knowledge on the part of the taught. (1971, p. 47)

Notwithstanding critiques of 'transmission' approaches to teaching and learning mounted by scholars of critical pedagogy over the past 40 years (see, for example, Christensen and Aldridge 2012; Freire 1972, 1974; Gore 1993; Hattam and Matthews 2012; Macrine 2010) and consequently the contemporary implications of the word 'transmission' in the early twenty-first century, Bernstein's conceptualisation has informed a variety of thinking about curriculum, pedagogy and assessment since the 1970s (Hayes et al. 2000; Hayes et al. 2006; Newmann et al. 1996).

Bernstein argued that the 'shape' of the teacher/student relationship was impacted upon by both the classification of the curriculum (the relationships between the various contents of the curriculum) and the 'framing' of the curriculum (the extent to which teacher and student have 'control' over what is learned). He describes the impact of these on this relationship in the following manner:

> Where classification is strong, the boundaries between the different contents are sharply drawn. If this is the case then it presupposes strong boundary maintainers. Strong classification also creates a strong sense of membership in a particular class and so a specific identity. Strong frames reduce the power of the pupil over what, when and how he receives (sic) knowledge and increases the teacher's power in the pedagogical relationship. (1971, pp. 50–51)

The three 'message systems' hold a reflexive relationship with each other, and alignment of curriculum, pedagogy and assessment, both in terms of overarching philosophy (as expressed at a broad social level in the development of state or national curriculum, pedagogical guidelines, standardised assessment, for example) and in terms of local implementation (as a consequence of decisions made at local area, school and teacher levels), is required in order for coherent and effective schooling systems to be realised.

The three message systems are, of course, open to shaping and re-shaping over time. In a recent essay, Bob Lingard (2012) has explored the re-shaping of the message systems of schooling in the UK, although his observations with regard to the schooling systems of England, Scotland, Wales and Northern Ireland are, we believe, pertinent to those in other parts of the developed world subject to the forces of the 'global educational reform movement' (Sahlberg 2011). At a meta-level, Lingard points to the increasing positioning of 'human capital' at the centre of education policy, and the removal of the policy process from teachers, who are increasingly distrusted within regimes of new managerialism and evidence-based policy and practice (2012, p. 2). Within this framework, he points to the re-shaping of curriculum and the broad aims of schooling in some parts of the world such that they are oriented more closely toward national testing and closely-related national curricula than toward the espoused aims of schooling as expressed in documents such as *The Melbourne Declaration on Educational Goals for Young Australians* (Ministerial Council on Education Employment Training and Youth Affairs 2008).

Pedagogy, he argues, has been impacted upon by the recent rise in popularity of discourses of 'teacher centrality' (Larsen 2010), characterised by a narrow focus on 'teacher quality' (Mockler 2013), which has become manifest in policy in a variety of ways. Furthermore, he suggests that high-stakes testing is currently impacting upon and re-shaping pedagogy in the UK, a claim that is borne out in recent research in Australia (Polesel et al. 2013; Thompson 2012) and elsewhere (Darling-Hammond 2010, 2011). Finally, Lingard's argument in relation to the message system of assessment is that national standardised testing and the use of international standardised tests on a national level has seen the rise of a 'comparison mode of governance' in education and ongoing struggles over what Stephen Ball, after Lyotard, has termed "the field of judgement" (Ball 2000, 2003), the field within which assessments regarding "what counts as a valid realization of … knowledge on the part of the taught (Bernstein 1971, p. 47) are made.

While we recognise that on a national and international level, the shaping of the message systems of schooling in one direction at the hands of neoliberal education policy regimes, is indeed taking place as Lingard suggests, represented in the global education reform movement, we also understand this not to be the whole story. In our own work with schools as academic partners and researchers, we see many examples of schools and teachers 'pushing back' on the GERM in the enactment of their desire to authentically engage with student voice. Furthermore, we recognise these as local acts of resistance to broader policy trajectories: schools and teachers finding 'space' within the prevailing constructions of curriculum, pedagogy and assessment, to connect local actions closely to local beliefs about the purposes and aims of schooling, on a school and/or classroom level. We understand that such actions can be regarded as highly subversive, and that there are complex factors that mitigate against schools and indeed, individual teachers engaging with them. Nevertheless, we offer here some suggestions for the shaping of the message systems of schooling at a local within contexts where the privileging of student voice and the pursuit of democratic education has become a priority. As noted above, for each of the three message systems, we pose three critical questions, namely 'What vision of this message system is promoted here?', 'How does this work within/ against dominant conceptualisations of curriculum, pedagogy and assessment?' and 'What structures and processes, identities and practices does it demand of schools and teachers?'.

Curriculum

As Apple and Beane noted in their 1995 book *Democratic Schools*, "local decision making is glorified in political rhetoric at the same time that legislation is introduced to put in place national standards, a national curriculum, and national tests" (Apple and Beane 1995). Local decision-making in relation to curriculum can be difficult to navigate, and a privileging of student voice in terms of the curriculum requires a level of negotiation and differentiation that sits uncomfortably with a standardised one size fits all approach and lists of curricular 'dot points' to be 'covered' for the purpose of testing.

Privileging student voice and putting democratic concerns regarding education at the centre of discussions of curriculum demands that particular attention be paid to the learning needs, interests, prior and background knowledge, cultural knowledge and life outside school of the students being taught. It requires students to play an active role in determining what will be learned and how it will be learned, and furthermore in order for this to occur, it requires students to have been supported to develop capacities to make wise and sensible choices about their learning, with reference to their age. Working in this way necessitates the development of strong and mutual learning relationships between teachers and students such that "teacher and student must know each other well enough for trust to develop" (Noddings 1988, p. 223).

Much mitigates against all of this in the context of contemporary schooling. First, the narrowing of the curriculum noted above by Lingard at the hands of ever-shrinking aims of schooling increasingly dictated by standardised testing which should, of course, be a means to an end rather than an end in themselves, but that in these globalised times have taken on ever more importance in the measurement of international competitiveness. Second, the common-sense of standardisation and the desire for certainty drives curriculum construction in many parts of the world. Recently announced curriculum development and review initiatives, for example, in the United Kingdom (Garner 2013) and Australia (Tovey 2014) position the school curriculum as something of shopping list of facts and figures that students are required to remember in order for the education system itself to maintain legitimacy. Such approaches ignore the role of teachers in the enactment of the curriculum, and also the reflexive nature of curriculum, assessment and pedagogy and their seamless integration in good teaching and learning. At a local level, what can also mitigate against approaches that seek to maximise student agency and voice in discussions around curriculum is a failure on the part of schools and teachers to bring parents into the conversation about curriculum choices and how they can and should be made.

Success in negotiating student agency in curriculum choices requires on the part of teachers an evolved understanding of the role of state-developed curriculum and their own role in the design and enactment of the curriculum. In schools where standardisation is privileged and divergence from the script is frowned upon, taking such a stance can be a difficult task indeed. The negotiation of curriculum and tailoring of curricular choices to local needs requires a nuanced understanding of the processes of curriculum design, a deliberate scaffolding of student decision making, a stance on pedagogy and assessment that takes into account the many pathways that students may take in terms of content to demonstrate their learning in relation to chosen outcomes, and a willingness to allow students to make poor decisions from time to time and to suffer and deal with the consequences. On the part of school leaders it requires a willingness to bring parents and other community members into the conversation about the purposes of schooling and how the curriculum fits into this picture, while at the same time engaging in parent and community education about the power of the negotiated curriculum to support student learning and deep connection between young people and school.

Over time in most western countries, school curriculum has become increasingly overcrowded with less and less space available for teachers to engage as designers, intentionally carving out space for student agency and decision making (Taubman 2009). Privileging student voice in terms of the message system that is curriculum requires us to push back on this in the way we understand and enact curriculum, flipping the central focus from teacher coverage to student understanding, such that the curriculum documents themselves become broad guides to essential knowledge rather than a total representation of the knowledge and understanding to be developed by the schooling system. It is only through pedagogy, however, that curriculum is enacted (Ladwig 2009), and it thus to the second message system of schooling, pedagogy, that we next turn.

Pedagogy

A desire to seek out and listen to student voice in schools has significant implications for pedagogy as the enactment of curriculum, particularly, drawing on Bernstein's notion of 'framing', the critical relationship between teachers and learners that shapes the teaching and learning interaction.

The past two decades have seen a proliferation of pedagogical frameworks adopted by curriculum authorities, departments of education and individual schools. The work of Fred Newmann and associates at the University of Wisconsin-Madison in the 1990s, reported in *Authentic Achievement: Restructuring Schools for Intellectual Quality* (Newmann et al. 1996) gave rise some years later to the *Productive Pedagogies* framework in Queensland, Australia (Hayes et al. 2000; Hayes et al. 2006; Lingard et al. 2003), and some years after that to the *Quality Teaching Framework* in NSW, adopted by the NSW Department of Education and Communities as the NSW model of pedagogy (Ladwig et al. 2007; NSW Department of Education and Training 2003, 2006a, b). In a very different vein, approaches such as Direct Instruction (Adams and Engelmann 1996) or multiple intelligences (Gardner 1985, 1993, 1999; Gardner and Hatch 1989) offer an in-built pedagogical framework that each suggest particular framings of the teacher-student relationship.

Our intention here is not to examine in depth a range of pedagogical frameworks and their possible alignment with student voice work, but rather argue that close alignment between the philosophies and aims of student voice work and pedagogical practice is more likely to occur via pedagogical frameworks informed by critical, student-centred pedagogy. As a case in point, we will very briefly explore the NSW Quality Teaching Framework, drawing links between its underpinning philosophy and features and the intent of student voice work in schools as discussed in previous chapters.

The Quality Teaching framework is predicated upon the understanding that student learning is best supported by pedagogy that focuses on high levels of intellectual quality and high levels of significance to students, enacted within a high quality learning environment. These three 'dimensions' of quality teaching form the basis of the model, with 18 'elements' or pedagogical strategies working as descriptors across the three dimensions. Table 11.1 below shows the elements within each of the three dimensions, with abbreviated descriptions of application to classroom practice, drawn from the 2003 discussion paper *Quality Teaching in NSW Public Schools* (NSW Department of Education and Training 2003).

Emphasis across all three dimensions is placed on student agency and the sharing of responsibility for learning between teachers (who frame and shape the learning) and students. While some elements such as Students' Self-regulation and Student Direction, overtly speak to the capacity of students to make active decisions about their learning, others, such as Explicit Quality Criteria, High Expectations and Social Support, point to strategies teachers might use to support students as agents of their own learning. Furthermore, elements such as Background Knowledge, Cultural Knowledge, Connectedness and High Expectations require teachers to develop and maintain a rich understanding of their students as people and as learners, in order to engage with them to develop appropriate teaching and learning strategies. Such a requirement presupposes a willingness on the part of teachers to engage authentically with their students, such that students' voices are sought out and heard.

We would see that the desire to seek out and incorporate student voice in the classroom sits very comfortably alongside a faithful interpretation and implementation of the Quality Teaching framework and other similar pedagogical models. While there is clearly support for such approaches in some educational jurisdictions, with either overt or de-facto endorsement of pedagogical frameworks or models, in other contexts the shape of curriculum or assessment pulls pedagogy in a different direction. The current situation in the US with the adoption of Common Core Standards, assessed via standardised testing the 'space' between curriculum and assessment increasingly filled with textbooks and other resources developed by Pearson (Ravitch 2013), for example, has the capacity to work as a kind of 'teacher proofing' of the curriculum, where pedagogy becomes highly standardised in the name of 'improvement'.

A genuine desire to engage with student voice and to do so in ways that bring classroom practice into alignment with student voice work that takes place outside the classroom requires of teachers and schools a commitment to supporting young people to take control of their learning, to make good decisions about what, how and with whom they learn, and to shape learning such that it is relevant, deeply connected to students' experiences and interests and appropriately aspirational for all students. In current times, where so much of learning is driven by less than expansive assessment practices, this can be a difficult task, and it is to assessment, the final 'message system' that we now turn.

Table 11.1 The NSW Quality Teaching Framework. (Adapted from NSW Department of Education and Training 2003, pp. 9–15)

Intellectual quality	Quality learning environment	Significance
Deep Knowledge The knowledge being addressed is focused on a small number of key concepts and ideas within topics, subjects or KLAs, and on the relationships between and among concepts	*Explicit Quality Criteria* Students are provided with explicit criteria for the quality of work they are to produce and those criteria are a regular reference point for the development and assessment of student work	*Background Knowledge* Lessons regularly and explicitly build from students' background knowledge, in terms of prior school knowledge as well as other aspects of their personal lives
Deep Understanding Students demonstrate a profound and meaningful understanding of central ideas and the relationships between and among those central ideas	*Engagement* Most students, most of the time, are seriously engaged in the lesson or assessment activity, rather than going through the motions. Students display sustained interest and attention	*Cultural Knowledge* Lessons regularly incorporate the cultural knowledge of diverse social groupings (such as economic class, gender, ethnicity, race, sexuality, disability, language and religion)
Problematic Knowledge Students are encouraged to address multiple perspectives and/or solutions and to recognise that knowledge has been constructed and therefore is open to question	*High Expectations* High expectations of all students are communicated, and conceptual risk taking is encouraged and rewarded	*Knowledge Integration* Lessons regularly demonstrate links between and within subjects and key learning areas
Higher-order Thinking Students are regularly engaged in thinking that requires them to organise, reorganise, apply, analyse, synthesise and evaluate knowledge and information	*Social Support* There is strong positive support for learning and mutual respect among teachers and students and others assisting students' learning. The classroom is free of negative personal comment or put-downs	*Inclusivity* Lessons include and publicly value the participation of all students across the social and cultural backgrounds represented in the classroom
Metalanguage Lessons explicitly name and analyse knowledge as a specialist language (metalanguage), and provide frequent commentary on language use and the various contexts of differing language uses	*Students' Self-regulation* Students demonstrate autonomy and initiative so that minimal attention to the disciplining and regulation of student behaviour is required	*Connectedness* Lesson activities rely on the application of school knowledge in real-life contexts or problems, and provide opportunities for students to share their work with audiences beyond the classroom and school
Substantive Communication Students are regularly engaged in sustained conversations about the concepts and ideas they are encountering. These conversations can be manifest in oral, written or artistic forms	*Student Direction* Students exercise some direction over the selection of activities related to their learning and the means and manner by which these activities will be done	*Narrative* Lessons employ narrative accounts as either (or both) a process or content of lessons to enrich student understanding

Assessment

The question of what kinds of assessment practices might be consistent with a desire to seek out and listen to student voice is an interesting one. While on the one hand, assessment that aligns with the approaches to curriculum and pedagogy discussed above might take into account student agency and a desire to create spaces and opportunities for students to *demonstrate* their learning against a set of outcomes and/or standards, we understand assessment to be a complex process rather than a case of one-size-fits-all.

Stobart's (2008) call to 'reclaim' assessment in the final chapter of his book *Testing Times: The Uses and Abuses of Assessment* comes with a five step 'reclamation program', comprising:

- Step 1: limit assessment ambitions, focus on achievement: "Having modest ambitions for assessment means that its principal role is to provide soundings about where somebody is in their learning" (p. 173).
- Step 2: interpret results more cautiously: "The reclamation here is in order to reduce the distorting dependence on narrow assessment measures and targets, and to avoid the simplistic interpretation of results" (pp. 176–177).
- Step 3: acknowledge the context: "Reclaiming assessment means a fuller recognition of situational factors. Whether and how students learn is largely a product of context, not of genes. part of being a self-regulated learner is to accept responsibility for learning, just as teachers must take responsibility for creating a context which helps learning" (p. 179)
- Step 4: recognise the importance of interaction: "Effective feedback is essentially about effective interaction—a difficult achievement, given that so much can get in the way…[also important is] negotiation around what is to be learned and what successful performance would look like" (p. 181).
- Step 5: create sustainable assessment: here, Stobart draws upon David Boud's notion of 'sustainable assessment' (2000), wherein "any assessment act must also contribute in some ways to learning beyond the immediate task … assessment that meets the needs of the present and prepares students to meet their own future needs" (Boud 2000, pp. 8–9, as quoted in Stobart 2008, p. 182).

Stobart argues that "reclaiming assessment therefore means obtaining a better balance between the summative assessment of present knowledge and skills and the sustainable assessment that will encourage learners to keep learning" (2008, p. 184). In this, his work is reminiscent of that of Harry Torrance and John Pryor on 'divergent' and 'convergent' assessment, where convergent assessment is constituted as *retrospective* in nature and divergent assessment as *prospective* in nature (Torrance and Pryor 2001). His work also sits well with that of Black and Wiliam (Black et al. 2004; Black and Wiliam 1998) around the powerful role that formative assessment can play in the improvement of student learning and the 'raising' of educational standards, and speaks to the not insubstantial literature on 'authentic assessment' that stretches back into the mid-1990s with its emphasis on the seamless integration of content knowledge, pedagogy and assessment in authentic tasks (see, for example, Costa and Kallick 1995; Darling-Hammond 1995; Hart 1994; Wiggins 1990, 1993).

The phenomenon by which standardised tests become 'high stakes' is well documented. Policies of deeming schools to be 'failing' are at play here, such as those adopted in the UK in the 2000s (Stoll 2002). The closure of 'low-performing' schools in the US as a consequence of the No Child Left Behind and, later, the Race to the Top policy frameworks (Lipman 2004; Taubman 2009) might be cited as another example, as can the public dissemination of schools' results via a website designed to enhance 'parent choice' and raise educational standards, as is the case in Australia (Gorur 2013; Lingard 2010). As observed above, these practices hold significant consequences for the three message systems of schooling, shaping curricular choices in particular ways that serve the purposes of the tests (Stobart 2008); shaping pedagogical decision making in directions that support the kinds of learning measured in the tests (Thompson and Cook 2012, 2014); and shaping the very practice of assessment itself such that testing becomes the privileged and practiced form of assessment outweighing other forms that might also be practiced. Stobart notes that the high/low stakes status of standardised tests impact upon the amount of time spent in test practice: "American evidence shows that, in states with high-stakes testing, more time is spent on test-practice than in low-stakes states, Teachers in high-stakes settings also begin practice earlier in the year, and are more likely to use specific types of materials that closely resemble the state tests" (2008, p. 124).

It would be naïve of us to suggest that teachers might 'just ignore' or employ a zero-tolerance approach to the impact of high stakes testing on their schools and classrooms. The machinery of neo-liberal education policy is pervasive and opting out can, for schools and teachers, be at least difficult, if not impossible. Understanding standardised testing as one data source on student learning among many, a means to an end rather than an end in themselves, is one strategy of resistance that teachers might mount. Another is to work collaboratively with colleagues (and indeed, students), to develop assessment programs that employ a wide range of strategies to assess different knowledge and skills for a variety of different purposes. Actively resisting assessment cultures that seek to cast testing as the only 'valid' form of assessment and consequently replicate the processes of standardised testing on a local level as the default mode of assessment is another. Putting teacher professional judgement to work on the task of assessing students' learning, within the context of the kinds of learning relationships discussed earlier in this chapter is a further strategy. It is important to recognise here that the vast majority of assessment undertaken is, one way or another, based on 'subjective' judgement made by one human being about another's performance. This is true of standardised testing regimes as much as of other forms of assessment, and it is critical that educators develop their professional judgement through critical and collaborative professional learning, and be prepared to defend both the judgements they make and the use of professional judgement as a valid (indeed, we would argue, the most valid) tool for assessing learning.

It seems to us that in terms of assessment, a desire to listen to and genuinely respond to student voice, might give rise to processes that draw students and teachers into dialogue about the purposes of assessment, that provide students with opportunities to make decisions about how to demonstrate their learning in different contexts, and that privilege the provision of good-quality feedback on learning contextualised within well developed and trusting student-teacher relationships. Such an approach has been adopted and refined by netowrks of schools such as those in the Coalition of Essential Schools in the US (Benitez et al. 2009) and Big Picture Education in Australia (Down and Hogan 2012).

Aligning Curriculum, Pedagogy and Assessment in Challenging Times

Increasingly, schools and teachers face attempts to constrain and 'lock down' practice related to curriculum, pedagogy and assessment. From common sense assessments of what curriculum should contain peddled by politicians to the growth of multinational corporations operating as 'edu-businesses' (Hogan 2013) to control and shape curricular and pedagogical practices (Apple 2011; Ball 2012), these attempts are many and varied.

For teachers and schools determined to work with student voice in the manner we have outlined in this book, and to develop congruence between student voice practices outside and inside the classroom, the shaping of curriculum, pedagogy and assessment in line with this desire is essentially about congruence of purpose and deed. In work built over more than a decade, Starratt (1994, 2003) developed the metaphor of 'the school as onion' as a heuristic for understanding the issue of congruence or alignment on a whole school level. His argument is that effective, healthy and ethical school communities exhibit a high degree of congruence emanating from the core of the 'onion', where the community's values reside, in Starratt's words, the "myths and meanings by which people make sense of their lives" (2003, p. 18), to the outer rings of the onion where the structures, artefacts and other observable manifestations of the learning community are visible. Figure 11.1 below our own adaptation of Starratt's model.

The key task for leaders of educational institutions and communities, then, is not merely the articulation of vision or values, but rather the embedding of these in the outer layers of the 'onion', such that congruence is achieved between values, priorities, programs, strategies, structures and artefacts. In the words of Starratt:

> The leader's work is not completed when the school community has articulated its communal vision. The vision must become embodied in the outer layers of the school organisation. The onion must be energised by its core. (Starratt 2003, p. 19)

While Starratt's heuristic relates to development of culture and identity generally, following Starratt it is possible to use the 'onion' metaphor to conceptualise the ways in which the 'values' associated with student voice work might be articulated

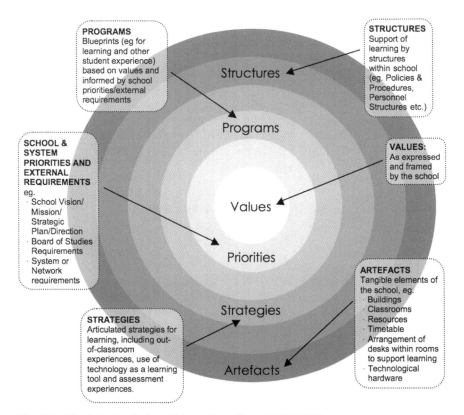

Fig. 11.1 'The School as Onion'. (Adapted from Starratt 1994, 2003)

and enacted through the priorities, programs, strategies, structures and artefacts related to curriculum, pedagogy and assessment.

In this chapter we have sketched out some of the ways that we believe these message systems of schooling might be informed by the kinds of educational philosophies that seek to privilege student voice, and the challenge here is to seek the congruence or alignment that would find classroom practice working with rather than against such initiatives, to take student voice out of the realm of practitioner inquiry and embed it in the 'everyday' of school and classroom practice. We do not suggest that this is an easy task, but it is, we believe, a necessary one if the promise of a focus on student voice is to be realised on a whole school and classroom level. We see this penultimate chapter as a 'signature' one that embodies the fundamental rationale for the book itself. In our concluding chapter we shall seek to evolve a 'charter of reform' taking us into the realm of transformational practice.

Chapter 12
A Charter for Reform

As a means of evolving a charter of reform for engaging in participative research and inquiry with children and young people in education and the community; reform based upon respect, responsibility, reciprocity and trust leading to transformation and hope, we turn first to conceptualising such a contract as a democratic enterprise.

Reclaiming the Democratic Project

At the heart of this book has been an aspiration for the democratic project. At a number of points we have evoked the work of Jurgen Habermas and later in this concluding chapter we shall align that with the writing of Michael Fielding, in particular Fielding and Moss (2011) to whom we have also consistently turned.

For a moment we shall 'borrow' some ideas from a recent piece written by Habermas (2013) in which he reflects on democracy, solidarity and the European crisis—a far cry some might say from considering student voice beyond legitimation and guardianship. However, throughout the discussion we find matters with which this book resonates. Habermas wrote of the European parliament constructing a bridge between the political conflict of opinions at the nation state level and decisions taken in Brussels, "a bridge almost devoid of traffic" (p. 1). We are concerned that the opportunities for children and young people to participate in contributing to decisions that impact upon their own experiences and futures relies on bridges being built between them and the apposite communities. We have argued that while such bridges do exist and have provided evidence of them, we are also concerned that they too are almost devoid of traffic. For most young people the chasm between those who make decisions on their behalf and themselves is deep and difficult to traverse.

Further into the article Habermas argues that the conceptions of the European Union and ideas of its future development have remained diffuse among the general population and remains the intellectual property of the political elites. This too is the case in terms of listening respectfully to children and young people and acting upon

© Springer International Publishing Switzerland 2015

N. Mockler, S. Groundwater-Smith, *Engaging with Student Voice in Research,*
Education and Community, DOI 10.1007/978-3-319-01985-7_12

their perceptions. While ideas are generated and supported by participative inquiry and research, the decisions regarding what is to be done, whether in the school, the university, or on the streets continues, in the main, to be vested in those with greater authority. Certainly there is, as Habermas suggests, an incrementalist agenda, but a comprehensive perspective is lacking. He puts the position that democratisation is presented as a promise, "like a light at the end of the tunnel", but is nonetheless endlessly postponed. "Processes are planned *for* the people, but not *by* the people" (p. 3) with asymmetries in accountabilities. This too has become a familiar cry through the book.

Habermas insists upon the viability of interpersonal linguistic communication. However, he argues that much communicative competence has been weakened by features of the *system* world that is driven by economic, legal, administrative and bureaucratic subsystems and is increasingly colonised and "uncoupled from its foundations in *life-world*, foundations that are necessary for shared sense-making, fair social relations and mutual solidarity" (Groundwater-Smith et al. 2013, p. 7). This we see in education with the increased standardisation and bureaucratisation of which we have written in preceding chapters whereby what little control children and young people have in educational institutions is more often than not ceded to the elites—politicians and bureaucrats.

In Chap. 2 we wrote of the Habermasian concept of the "ideal speech situation" (ISS) where he identified four conditions for authentic dialogue: that no one who is capable of making a relevant contribution has been excluded; that all participants have an equal voice; that they are free to speak to their opinions without deceiving others or themselves; and, that there is no coercion built into the processes or procedures of the discourse. We indicated that the most systematically distorting feature for Habermas (1984, p. 332) is the extent of the participants' desire to succeed in socially competitive situations versus the desire to reach understanding, "Such communication pathologies can be conceived of as the result of a confusion between actions oriented to reaching understanding and actions oriented to success".

In the democratic project that we wish to reclaim, we believe that the contribution that can be made by children and young people, not only as a right, but as a social, ethical norm, can and should first contribute to our understanding but may also contribute to the success of the educational enterprise as praxis—that is to say, morally informed action. This position is one taken up by Fielding and Moss (2011, 37) when they "want to see a richer, deeper public discourse about education that moves beyond the tyrannies of improvement, efficiency and standardisation". In their writing they too put democracy at the heart of authentic activism and participation.

They take democracy as their starting point because it has, inherent in its values, the opportunity to develop a kind of social intelligence that unfortunately is seen as having "low visibility in the English education system" (p. 58). Such a capacity is not to be taught, but is embodied in daily practices as a form of lived citizenship. In this book we have cited a number of instances and cases wherein students, mainly children and young people, have been enabled to partially engage in the democratic project. But we have also been wary of just how much they have been able to interrupt the deeply embedded asymmetry that exists in institutions and systems. Thus we turn now to our own charter for reform based upon respect, responsibility, reciprocity and trust leading to transformation and hope.

A Charter for Reform in Engaging in Participative Research with Children and Young People

Many chapters in this book have pointed to the challenge of contemporary times where the neo-liberal agenda is in the ascendancy. In our desire to reclaim the democratic project we have made the case to develop a more inclusive, just and sustainable research milieu that honours the capacity of children and young people to engage in inquiry as partners rather than as subjects, or even objects. We believe that matters of respect, responsibility, reciprocity and trust are the essential elements of such an enterprise.

Respect

In a speech delivered in St Louise, 1916, attacking the universal military training policies of President Wilson, Theodore Roosevelt made reference to weasel words. "When a weasel sucks an egg the meat is sucked out of the egg; and if you use one weasel word after another, there is nothing left of the other" (Roosevelt 1916, p. 2). What was being signalled is that some words can lose their potency when all the meaning is sucked from them through over-use, misapplication, or confabulation. When we turn to the use of the word 'respect' as it applies to researching and inquiring with children and young people it is in danger of becoming such a word. Young people cry out for respect, teachers and parents demand respect—but what exactly do they mean?

Todd and Safstrom (2008) argue that a cornerstone of a democratic education is respect for others who may hold a different point of view. They recommend that we take pluralism seriously and recognise the legitimacy of opponents. They ask for a generosity, a condition of hospitality, and a more active response than mere tolerance. They do not eschew conflict, but see it as the moment when new settlements might occur. This is no easy matter in the classroom where the norms of respect held by teachers may vary from those held by their students. As we saw in Chap. 5 the teacher believed a misbehaving student to be lacking in 'respect' but failed to respect the member of the students as co-researchers group. By way of contrast, in Chap. 6 we found that a large and prestigious organisation sufficiently respected the unexpected feedback that they received from students to cause it to make a costly adjustment to a display.

Respect is not to be commanded or demanded. The internet is replete with advice on ways to 'command the respect of students' ranging from professional preparedness to radiating confidence, but admonitions say little about developing mutuality or empathy. Engaging in participative research and inquiry with children and young people is tricky business, not the least because it requires the exercise of that difficult behaviour—respect.

For respect to be a building block of our Charter of Reform we require more than tolerance; we ask for all parties to show consideration for the other, to listen and seek to hear and comprehend.

But we do not wish to romanticise the notion of respect, but wish to tie it to another fundamental human practice—responsibility.

Responsibility

Taking responsibility for an action is often considered in a contractual context. The service provider is responsible for this or that; the user is responsible for functioning within the contractual arrangement. However, we are concerned to locate responsibility within an ethical framework; that is not acting in a particular way because it is required, but because it is ethically right to do so (Alderson and Morrow 2004). Following Leeson (2007) and building on Chap. 11, we see that ethics should be seen as contextual, emergent and situational, and encompass caring and solicitude.

Crebert, Patrick, Cragnolini, Smith, Worsfold and Webb (2011) in their toolkit for Griffith University graduates, working in many fields of practice, emphasise interconnectedness and an understanding that taking responsibility for one's conduct and actions can and does impact upon others. We would amplify this in relation to engaging in participative research with children and young people by pointing to the notion of duty of care, meaning not putting them at risk, not only in terms of their health and safety, but also their vulnerability. Having written that we are also mindful that responsibility is a two way street, promoters of research with children and young people can also be vulnerable; participants need to care for each other.

Responsibility requires that all who participate to accept the consequences of their behaviours and actions as best they are able and in consideration of the needs of 'the other'.

Reciprocity

More than two decades ago Patti Lather (1986, p. 263) wrote: Reciprocity implies give-and-take, a mutual recognition of meaning and power. It operates at two primary points in emancipatory empirical research: the junctures between researcher and researched, and between data and theory". Even more pertinent, when the relationship between the researcher and the researched becomes blurred as it does in participative inquiry, is the notion of giving and taking.

Furthermore it is not merely a question of research, as Fielding and Moss (2011, p. 78) remind us, intergenerational learning is at the kernel of participatory practices. While they place this matter in the context of schools we would go further in imagining its possibilities in the wider community. Generations learning from each other is not necessarily a new phenomenon, but requires each to honour the other: older/younger; younger/older. This is surely the way forward for building cultural and practical wisdom. Curiously, it is in the current digital age that such intergenerational learning has become increasingly pertinent, as young 'digital natives' explain the mysteries of social media to older citizens, not only on the basis of how they may be used, but what constitutes their power and mis-use. But beyond the technical, the young and old are equally committed to the present and the future and to building a desirable society, as illustrated by a number of examples embedded in Chap. 7. To do this they must be able to communicate in such ways that each can fully comprehend what the other has to say, how they say it and why they say it.

Reciprocity transcends cooperation; it is to do with the capacity of each party to share and explain in ways that are mutually understandable. It requires all to be willing to invest in trust and hope.

Trust

Throughout this book we have intimated that when parties work together to transform practice, whether it be in the classroom or beyond, the engagement of mutual trust is critical. For example, Chap. 3 captures what happens when there is a loss of trust in teacher professionalism and in the capacity of children and young people to be responsible learners. We quote from Onora O'Neill's Reith Lectures (2002) that argue for the building of social trust and the ability to take risks. How difficult is this in the context spelled out by Apple (2006) who points out that more and more the only agency to be trusted is the marketplace that will control and manage teachers and, for all intents and purposes, ignore the voices of children and young people.

We outlined the scepticism of some teachers in Chap. 5 when students presented them with their findings regarding the school that they would like. We would argue that such a stance arises out of a lack of trust of the young people and the authenticity of their voice.

Establishing trust is critical to any reform process. Like respect, trust has to be earned. It is not a commodity to be traded, neither is it an obligation. It is the keystone of the principles that we have outlined above.

Conclusion

Contemporary society constantly holds education, both within and beyond schools, accountable for results. But the results that are sought for lie within an economic discourse.

Groundwater-Smith and Mockler (2012) quoted from the ambitions of the Organisation for Economic and Cooperative Development (OECD), the most influential and ambitious of international agencies in this way:

"On its homepage the OECD describes its formation and function thus:

The OECD vocation has been to build strong economies in its member countries, improve efficiency, hone market systems, expand free trade and contribute to development in industrialised as well as developing countries.

After more than four decades, the OECD is moving beyond a focus on its own countries and is setting its analytical sights on those countries—today nearly the whole world—that embrace the market economy. The Organisation is, for example, putting the benefit of its accumulated experience to the service of emerging market economies, particularly in the countries that are making their transition from centrally-planned to capitalist systems. And it is engaging in increasingly detailed policy dialogue with dynamic economies in Asia and Latin America.

But its scope is changing in other ways too. The matrix is moving from consideration of each policy area within each member country to analysis of how various policy areas interact with each other, across countries and even beyond the OECD area. How social policy affects the way economies operate, for example. Or how globalisation will change the world's economies by opening new perspectives for growth, or perhaps trigger resistance manifested in protectionism.

As it opens to many new contacts around the world, the OECD will broaden its scope, looking ahead to a post-industrial age in which it aims to tightly weave OECD economies into a yet more prosperous and increasingly knowledge-based world economy.

Its mission, then, is to promote policies and practices that will contribute to a globalised world economy, including education policies, as espoused through its Directorate for Education. It is an unabashed call for the development of human capital in the most instrumental of terms.

In this book we have sought to interrupt and penetrate this discourse with an appeal to consider educational practices, including research and inquiry as liberatory and transformational. We have argued that this is only possible when all who are engaged are cognisant of what it is to be fully human rather than what it is to be an economic cog in a gigantic global wheel of production. Instead of the human capital argument embedded in much of the current neoliberal education discourse, we have argued for an approach to student voice work built on an appreciation of the rights of children and young people, and an authentic desire to share decision making and agency intergenerationally. Thus, our emphasis has taken us beyond legitimation and guardianship to an alternative vision of student voice within and beyond schools.

References

ABC Radio. (2013). Inside robbers' cave. http://www.abc.net.au/radionational/programs/hindsight/inside-robbers-cave/4515060. Accessed 6 March 2013.

Adams, G. L., & Engelmann, S. (1996). *Research on direct instruction: 25 years beyond distar*. Seattle: Educational Achievement System.

Alderson, P., & Morrow, V. (2004). *Ethics, social research and consulting with children and young people*. Barkingside: Barnardo's.

Alderson, P., & Morrow, V. (2011). *The ethics of research with children and young people: A practical handbook*. Thousand Oaks: Sage.

Alegounarias, T. (2011). *Address to the NSW teacher education council annual conference*. Macquarie University, June 2011.

Anderson, D. (2009). The listening museum. In K. Bellamy & C. Oppenheim (Eds.), *Learning to live: Museums, young people and education* (pp. 28–42). London: Institute for Public Policy Research and National Museum Directors' Conference.

Antidote News. (22 February 2010). Shaping a culture where everyone contributes to school improvement February 22, 2010. http://www.antidotenews.org.uk/?p=288. Accessed 16 March 2013.

Apple, M. W. (2001). *Educating the 'right' way: Markets, standards, god and inequality*. New York: RoutledgeFalmer.

Apple, M. W. (2006). *Educating the 'right' way: Markets, standards, god and inequality* (2nd ed.). New York: RoutledgeFalmer.

Apple, M. W. (2011). Democratic education in neoliberal and neoconservative times. *International Studies in Sociology of Education, 21*(1), 21–31.

Apple, M. W. (2012). *Can education change society?* New York: Routledge.

Apple, M. W., & Beane, J. (1995). *Democratic schools*. Alexandria: ASCD.

Arnot, M., & Reay, D. (2007). A sociology of pedagogic voice: Power, inequality and pupil consultation. *Discourse: studies in the cultural politics of education, 28*(3), 311–325.

Ash, D., Lombana, J., & Alcala, L. (2012). *Changing practices, changing identities as museum educators Understanding interactions at science centers and museums* (pp. 23–44). Dordrecht: Springer.

Atkinson, E. (2000). In defence of ideas, or why 'what works' is not enough. *British Journal of Sociology of Education, 21*(3), 307–330.

Australian education act. (2013).

Australian Government. (2007). *National statement on ethical conduct in human research*. Canberra: A Joint Statement of the National Health and Medical Research Council, Australian Research Council and the Australian Vice Chancellors' Committee.

Australian Institute for Teaching and School Leadership. (2012a). Aitsl website—Certification evidence. http://www.teacherstandards.aitsl.edu.au/certificationevidence. Accessed 30 Jan 2013.

© Springer International Publishing Switzerland 2015
N. Mockler, S. Groundwater-Smith, *Engaging with Student Voice in Research,
Education and Community,* DOI 10.1007/978-3-319-01985-7

Australian Institute for Teaching and School Leadership. (2012b). *Australian teacher performance and development framework*. Melbourne: AITSL.

Australian National University. (2013). Student surveys and evaluations policy. https://policies. anu.edu.au/ppl/document/ANUP_004601. Accessed 23 Jan 2014.

Australian Research Alliance for Children and Youth. (2012). The nest toolkit. http://www.thenest-project.org.au. Accessed 20 April 2013.

Australian Youth Forum. (2012). AYF submission on the Australian civics and citizenship curriculum. http://www.youth.gov.au/sites/Youth/ayf/weHearYou/Documents/AYF_Sub_ACA-RA_Civics.pdf. Accessed 24 April 2013.

Ball, S. (2000). Performativities and fabrications in the education economy: Towards the performative society? *The Australian Educational Researcher, 27*(2), 1–23.

Ball, S. (2003). The teacher's soul and the terrors of performativity. *Journal of education policy, 18*(2), 215–228.

Ball, S. (2012a). *Global Education Inc.: New policy networks and the neo-liberal imaginary*. London: Routledge.

Ball, S. (2012b). *Global Education Inc.: New policy newtorks and the neo-liberal imaginary*. London: Routledge.

Barratt, R., & Hacking, E. (2008). A clash of worlds: Children talking about their community experience in relation to the school curriculum. In A. Reid, B. Jensen, J. Nikel, & V. Simovska (Eds.), *Participation and learning: Perspectives on education and the environment* (pp. 285–298). Dordrecht: Springer.

Benitez, M., Davidson, J., Flaxman, L., Sizer, T., & Sizer, N. (2009). *Small schools, big ideas: The essential guide to successful school transformation*. San Francisco: Wiley.

Berger, J. (2002). *The shape of a pocket*. London: Bloomsbury.

Bernstein, B. (1971). On the classification and framing of educational knowledge. In M. F. D. Young (Ed.), *Knowledge and control* (pp. 47–69). London: Collier-Macmillan.

Biesta, G. (2007). Why 'what works' won't work: Evidence-based practice and the democratic deficit in educational research. *Educational Theory, 57*(1), 1–22.

Biesta, G. (2009). Good education in an age of measurement: On the need to reconnect with the question of purpose in education. *Educational Assessment, Evaluation and Accountability (formerly: Journal of Personnel Evaluation in Education), 21*(1), 33–46.

Biesta, G. (2010a). *Good education in an age of measurement: Ethics, politics, democracy*. Boulder: Paradigm.

Biesta, G. (2010b). Learner, student, speaker: Why it matters how we call those we teach. *Educational Philosophy and Theory, 42*(5–6), 540–552.

Biesta, G. (2010c). Why 'what works' still won't work: From evidence-based education to value-based education. *Studies in Philosophy and Education, 29*(5), 491–503.

Biesta, G. (2014). Evidence based practice in education: Between science and democracy. In A. Reid, E. P. Hart, & M. Peters (Eds.), *A companion to research in education* (pp. 391–400). Dordrecht: Springer.

Black, P., & Wiliam, D. (1998). Inside the black box. *Phi Delta Kappan, 80*(2), 139–147.

Black, P., Harrison, C., Lee, C., Marshall, B., & Wiliam, D. (2004). Working inside the black box: Assessment for learning in the classroom. *Phi Delta Kappan, 86*(1), 8.

Blackmore, J. (2002a). *Is it only 'what works' that counts in new knowledge economies? Evidence based practice, educational research and teacher education in Australia*. Paper presented at the Challenging Futures. Armidale, NSW, February 2002.

Blackmore, J. (2002b). Is it only 'what works' that counts in new knowledge economies? Evidence based practice, educational research and teacher education in Australia. *Social Policy and Society, 1*(3), 257–266.

Bogdan, R., & Biklen, S. (1982). *Qualitative research for education*. Boston: Allyn and Bacon.

Boud, D. (2000). Sustainable assessment: Rethinking assessment for the learning society. *Studies in continuing education, 22*(2), 151–167.

Bourdieu, P. (2003). *Firing back: Against the tyranny of the market 2*. London: Verso.

Bourdieu, P., & Wacquant, L. (1992). *An invitation to reflexive sociology*. Chicago: University of Chicago Press.

Bragg, S. (2007). *Consulting young people: A review of the literature*. London: Arts Council England A Report for Creative Partnerships.

Brooks, R. (2013). The social construction of young people within education policy: Evidence from the UK's coalition government. *Journal of Youth Studies, 16*(3), 318–333.

Brown, I., Lysaght, P., Westbrook, R., & Robinson, R. (2007). Analysing image and text in testing visual literacy. In R. Griffin, M. Avgerinou, & J. Giesen (Eds.), *History, community & culture, celebrating tradition and transforming our future*. Loretto: International Visual Literacy Association.

Burke, C. (2007). The view of the child: Releasing "visual voices" in the design of learning environments. *Discourse: studies in the cultural politics of education, 28*(3), 359–372.

Busch, R., & Theobald, M. (2013). Evidence based practice. In D. Pendergast & S. Garvis (Eds.), *Teaching early years: Curriculum, pedagogy and assessment* (pp. 317–333). Crow's Nest: Allen and Unwin.

Butterfield, L., Borgen, W., Amundson, N., & Maglio, A. (2005). Fifty years of the critical incident technique: 1954–2004 and beyond. *Qualitative Research, 5*(4), 475–497.

Cahill, C. (2007). Doing research with young people: Participatory research and the rituals of collective work. *Children's Geographies, 5*(3), 297–312.

Cahill, C., Rios-Moore, I., & Threatts, T. (2008). Different eyes/open eyes: Community-based participatory action research. In J. Cammarota & M. Fine (Eds.), *Revolutionizing education: Youth participatory action research in motion* (pp. 89–124). New York: Routledge.

Cammarota, J., & Fine, M. (2010). *Revolutionizing education: Youth participatory action research in motion*. New York: Routledge.

Campbell, C., Proctor, H., & Sherington, G. (2009). *School choice: How parents negotiate the new school market in Australia*. Sydney: Allen & Unwin.

Campbell, E., Skovdal, M., & Campbell, C. (2013). Ethiopian students' relationship with their environment: Implications for environmental and climate adaptation programmes. *Children's Geographies, 11*(4), 436–460.

Carr, W., & Kemmis, S. (1986). *Becoming critical: Education, knowledge and action research*. London: Falmer Press.

Carr, W., & Kemmis, S. (2005). Staying critical. *Educational Action Research, 13*(3), 347–358.

Chaffee, J. (23 March 2012). Teacher: One (maddening) day working with the common core. *Washington Post*. http://www.washingtonpost.com/blogs/answer-sheet/post/teacher-one-maddening-day-working-with-the-common-core/2012/03/15/gIQA8J4WUS_blog.html. Accessed 16 Jan 2014.

Chambers, D. (1983). Stereotypic images of the scientist: The draw-a-scientist test. *Science Education, 67*(2), 255–265.

Charmaz, K. (2005). Grounded theory in the 21st century: Applications for advancing social justice studies. In N. Denzin & Y. Lincoln (Eds.), *The Sage handbook of qualitative research*. Thousand Oaks: Sage.

Cheminais, R. (2013). *Engaging pupil voice to ensure that every child matters: A practical guide*. Abingdon: Routledge.

Christensen, L., & Aldridge, J. (2012). *Critical pedagogy for early childhood and elementary educators*. Dordrecht: Springer.

Clark, A., & Moss, P. (2011). *Listening to young children: The mosaic approach*. London: National Children's Bureau.

Cochran-Smith, M., & Lytle, S. (2009a). *Inquiry as stance: Practitioner research for the next generation*. New York: Teachers College Press.

Cochran-Smith, M., & Lytle, S. (2009b). Teacher research as stance. In B. Somekh & S. Noffke (Eds.), *The Sage handbook of educational action research* (pp. 39–49). Thousand Oaks: Sage.

Collin, P., Rahilly, K., Richardson, I., & Third, A. (2011). *The benefits of social networking services: A literature review*. Melbourne: Cooperative Research Centre for Young People, Technology and Wellbeing.

Colucci, E. (2007). "Focus groups can be fun": The use of activity-oriented questions in focus group discussions. *Qualitative Health Research, 17*(10), 1422–1433.

Commissioner for Children and Young People WA. (2009). Involving children and young people: Participation guidelines. http://www.ccyp.wa.gov.au/content/Participation Guidelines.aspx. Accessed 16 Jan 2014.

Commonwealth of Australia. (2009). *Early years learning framework: Belonging, being and becoming*. Canberra: Commonwealth of Australia.

Connell, R. W. (2013). The neoliberal cascade and education: An essay on the market agenda and its consequences. *Critical Studies in Education, 54*(2), 99–112.

Cook-Sather, A. (2006). *Education is translation: A metaphor for change in learning and teaching*. Philadelphia: University of Pennsylvania Press.

Cook-Sather, A. (2007). Resisting the impositional potential of student voice work: Lessons for liberatory educational research from poststructuralist feminist critiques of critical pedagogy. *Discourse: Studies in the Cultural Politics of Education, 28*(3), 389–403.

Cook-Sather, A. (2009). Translation: An alternative framework for conceptualizing and supporting school reform efforts. *Educational theory, 59*(2), 217–231.

Cook-Sather, A., Bovill, C., & Felton, P. (2014). *Engaging students as partners in learning and teaching*. San Francisco: Jossey Bass.

Costa, A., & Kallick, B. (1995). *Assessment in the learning organisation: Shifting the paradigm*. Alexandria: ASCD.

Crebert, G., Patrick, C., Cragnolini, V., Smith, C., Worsfold, K., & Webb, F. (2011). Griffith graduate attributes ethical behaviour and social responsibility toolkit. http://www.griffith.edu.au/__data/assets/pdf_file/0009/290691/Ethical-behaviour.pdf. Accessed 14 Feb 2014.

Curtin, U. (2013). Course approval and quality manual: Consolidated policies and procedures. http://policies.curtin.edu.au/findapolicy/docs/Course Approval and Quality Manual_v2- June 2013.pdf. Accessed 23 Jan 2014.

Darling-Hammond, L. (1995). *Authentic assessment in action: Studies of schools and students at work. The series on school reform*. ERIC.

Darling-Hammond, L. (2010). *The flat world and education: How America's commitment to equity will determine our future*. New York: Teachers College Press.

Darling-Hammond, L. (2011). *The flat world and education, 2011 John Dewey memorial lecture*. Paper presented at the ASCD Annual Conference. San Francisco, CA.

Devine, D. (2002). Children's citizenship and the structuring of adult-child relations in the primary school. *Childhood, 9*(3), 303–320.

Dewey, J. (1897). My pedagogic creed. *The School Journal, LIV*(3), 77–80.

Dewey, J. (1899). *The school and society*. Chicago: University of Chicago Press.

Dewey, J. (1916). *Democracy and education*. New York: MacMillan.

Down, B., & Hogan, J. (2012). Big picture education Australia: The school and network research framework (Retrieved).

Economic and Social Research Council. (2012). *ESRC framework for research ethics*. London: Economic and Social Research Council.

Edwards, T. (1996). *The research base of effective teacher education (Universities council for the education of teachers occasional paper 5)*. London: UCET.

Eisenhart, M., & Towne, L. (2003). Contestation and change in national policy on "scientifically based" education research. *Educational Researcher, 32*(7), 31–38.

Elliott, J. (2001). Making evidence-based practice educational. *British Educational Research Journal, 27*(5), 555–574.

Ennew, J., & Plateau, D. (2004). *How to research the physical and emotional punishment of children*. Bangkok: International Save the Children Alliance, S.E. Asia & Pacific Region.

Fargas-Malet, M., McSherry, D., Larkin, E., & Robinson, C. (2010). Research with children: Methodological issues and innovative techniques. *Journal of Early Childhood Research, 8*(2), 175–192.

Federation, U. A. (2012). Student evaluation of learning and teaching policy. http://policy.federation.edu.au/corporate_governance/quality_assurance/student_evaluation/ch02.php. Accessed 23 Jan 2014.

Fielding, M. (2001). Students as radical agents of change. *Journal of Educational Change, 2*(2), 123–141.

Fielding, M. (2008a). Interrogating student voice: Pre-occupations, purposes and possibilities. *Critical Perspectives in Education* (Summer 2008).

Fielding, M. (2008b). Personalisation, education and the market. *Soundings, Spring,* 2008, 56–69.

Fielding, M. (2010). *The voice of students in an inclusive school.* Paper presented at the International Congress on Inclusive Education and XXVII National Conference of Special Education and Universities. University of Cantabria, Spain, 24–26 March.

Fielding, M. (2011a). Patterns of partnership: Student voice, intergenerational learning and democratic fellowship. In N. Mockler & J. Sachs (Eds.), *Rethinking educational practice through reflexive inquiry: Essays in honour of Susan Groundwater-Smith* (pp. 61–75). Dordrecht: Springer.

Fielding, M. (2011b). Student voice and the possibility of radical democratic education: Re-narrating forgotten histories, developing alternative futures. In G. Czerniawskii & W. Kidd (Eds.), *The student voice handbook: Bridging the academic/practitioner divide* (pp. 3–17). Bingley: Emerald Group.

Fielding, M., & Kirby, P. (2009). *Developing student-led reviews, an exploration of innovative practice in primary, special and secondary schools.* Paper presented at the New Developments in Student Voice Conference, London, Institute of Education, November.

Fielding, M., & Moss, P. (2011). *Radical education and the common school: A democratic alternative.* Abingdon: Routledge.

Fitzgerald, R., Graham, A., Smith, A., & Taylor, N. (2009). Children's participation as a struggle over recognition. In B. Percy-Smith & N. Thomas (Eds.), *A handbook of children and young people's participation* (p. 293). London: Routledge.

Fletcher, A. (2003). *Meaningful student involvement.* Washington, DC: The Freechild Project.

Flinders, U. (2012). Evaluation, monitoring and review of academic programs and teaching. http://www.flinders.edu.au/ppmanual/teaching-course-management/eval-monitoring-review-academic-programs.cfm. Accessed 23 Jan 2014.

Flutter, J., & Rudduck, J. (2004). *Consulting young people: What's in it for schools?* London: RoutledgeFalmer.

Foreman-Peck, L., & Travers, K. (2013). What is distinctive about museum pedagogy and how can museums best support learning in schools? An action research inquiry into the practice of three regional museums. *Educational Action Research, 21*(1), 28–41.

Fox, J. (2004). Empowerment and institutional change: Mapping "virtuous circles" of state-society interaction. In R. Alsop (Ed.), *Power, rights, and poverty: Concepts and connections* (pp. 68). Washington, DC: World Bank.

Fraser, S. (2004). *Doing research with children and young people.* London: Sage.

Fredricks, J., Blumenfeld, P., & Paris, A. (2004). School engagement: Potential of the concept, state of the evidence. *Review of educational research, 74*(1), 59–109.

Freire, P. (1972). *Pedagogy of the oppressed.* London: Penguin.

Freire, P. (1974). *Education for critical consciousness.* London: Sheed and Ward.

Furlong, J. (2013). *Education: An anatomy of the discipline.* Abingdon: Routledge.

Gardner, H. (1985). *Frames of mind: The theory of multiple intelligences.* New York: Basic books.

Gardner, H. (1993). *Multiple intelligences: The theory in practice: [a reader].* New York: Basic books.

Gardner, H. (1999). *Intelligence reframed: Multiple intelligences for the twenty-first century.* New York: Basic Books.

Gardner, H., & Hatch, T. (1989). Multiple intelligences go to school: Educational implications of the theory of multiple intelligences. *Educational Researcher, 18*(8), 4–10.

Garner, R. (19 March 2013). 100 academics savage education secretary Michael Gove for 'conveyor-belt curriculum' for schools. *The Guardian.*

Gewertz, C. (2011). Gates, Pearson partner on common core. [Article]. *Education Week, 30*(30), 1–20.

Gibson, R. (1985). Critical times for action research. *Cambridge Journal of Education, 15*(1), 59–64.

Goldacre, B. (2008). *Bad science*. London: Fourth Estate.

Goldacre, B. (2013a). About Dr Ben Goldacre. http://www.badscience.net/about-dr-ben-goldacre/. Accessed 7 Jan 2014.

Goldacre, B. (2013b). *Building evidence into education*. London: British Department for Education.

Goldstein, H. (1996). A response to Hargreaves on 'evidence based educational research'. http://www.ioe.ac.uk/hgpersonal/hargresp.html. Accessed 16 Jan 2014.

Gore, J. (1992). What can we do for you! What can "we" do for "you"?: Struggling over empowerment in critical and feminist pedagogy. In C. Luke & J. Gore (Eds.), *Feminisms and critical pedagogy*. New York: Routledge.

Gore, J. (1993). *The struggle for pedagogies: Critical and feminist discourses as regimes of truth*. New York: Routledge.

Gore, J., Ladwig, J., & King, B. (2004). *Professional learning, pedagogical improvement, and the circulation of power*. Paper presented at the Australian Association for Research in Education Annual Conference, Melbourne, December 2004.

Gorur, R. (2013). My school, my market. *Discourse: Studies in the Cultural Politics of Education*, 1–17.

Greig, A., Taylor, J., & MacKay, T. (2009). *Doing research with children: A practical guide* (3rd ed.). Thousand Oaks: Sage.

Griffith, U. (2012). Student experience of courses (sec) and teaching (set). http://policies.griffith.edu.au/pdf/Student Experience of Courses and Teaching.pdf. Accessed 23   Jan 2014.

Groundwater-Smith, S. (1998). Putting teacher professional judgement to work. *Educational Action Research, 6*(1), 21–37.

Groundwater-Smith, S. (2009). *Consulting young people: An untapped resource for school improvement*. Paper presented at the Sydney South West Region, NSW DET PAS Principals' Partnership Program. Sydney.

Groundwater-Smith, S., Ewing, R. & LeCornu, R. (2015). *Teaching: Challenges and dilemmas*, 5th edn. Melbourne: Cengage.

Groundwater-Smith, S., & Kelly, L. (2003). *As we see it: Improving learning in the museum*.

Groundwater-Smith, S., & Mockler, N. (2003). *Learning to listen: Listening to learn*. Sydney: University of Sydney.

Groundwater-Smith, S., & Mockler, N. (2006). Research that counts: Practitioner research and the academy. *Counterpoints on the Quality and Impact of Educational Research, Special Edition of Review of Australian Research in Education, 6*, 105–117.

Groundwater-Smith, S., & Mockler, N. (2007). Ethics in practitioner research: An issue of quality. *Research Papers in Education, 22*(2), 199–211.

Groundwater-Smith, S., & Mockler, N. (2009). *Teacher professional learning in an age of compliance: Mind the gap*. Dordrecht: Springer.

Groundwater-Smith, S., & Mockler, N. (2012). *Increasing the school leaving age: A challenge for educational policy and practice in Australia*. Paper presented at the European Council for Educational Research Conference. Cadiz, Spain.

Groundwater-Smith, S., Mitchell, J., Mockler, N., Ponte, P., & Ronnerman, K. (2013). *Facilitating practitioner research: Developing transformational partnerships*. London: Routledge.

Grundy, S. (1987). *Curriculum: Product or praxis?* London: Routledge.

Grundy, S. (1998). The curriculum and teaching. In E. Hatton (Ed.), *Understanding teaching: Curriculum and the social context of schooling*. Sydney: Harcourt Brace.

Gunter, H. (2009). The 'C' word in educational research: An appreciative response. *Critical Studies in Education, 50*(1), 93–102.

Haberman, M. (1991). The pedagogy of poverty versus good teaching. *Phi Delta Kappan, 73*(4), 290–294.

Haberman, M. (2010 [1991]). The pedagogy of poverty versus good teaching. *Phi Delta Kappan, 92*(2), 81–87.

Haberman, M. (2011). The beliefs and behaviours of star teachers. *Teachers College Record*. http://www.tcrecord.org (ID Number: 16504). Accessed 16 Jan 2014.

Habermas, J. (1974). *Theory and practice* (trans.: J. Viertel). London: Heinemann.

Habermas, J. (1976). *Legitimation crisis* (trans.: T. McCarthy). London: Heinemann.

Habermas, J. (1979). *Communication and the evolution of society* (trans.: T. McCarthy, Vol. 29). Boston: Beacon Press.

Habermas, J. (1984). *Theory of communicative action, volume 1: Reason and rationalisation of society* (trans.: T. McCarthy). London: Heinemann.

Habermas, J. (7 May 2013). Democracy, solidarity and the European crisis. *Social Europe Journal.*

Hacking, E., & Barratt, R. (2009). Children researching their urban environment: Developing a methodology. *Education 3–13: International Journal of Primary, Elementary and Early Years, 37*(4), 371–383.

Hamilton, D. (2005). Knowing practice. *Pedagogy, Culture & Society, 13*(3), 285–290.

Hammersley, M. (1997). Educational research and teaching: A response to David Hargreaves' TTA lecture. *British Educational Research Journal, 23,* 141–161.

Hargreaves, D. (1996). *Teaching as a research based profession.* London: Teacher Training Agency.

Hargreaves, D. (1997). In defence of research for evidence-based practice: A rejoinder to Martyn Hammersley. *British Educational Research Journal, 23*(4), 405–419.

Hargreaves, D. (1999). Revitalising educational research: Lessons from the past and proposals for the future. *Cambridge Journal of Education, 29*(2), 239–249.

Hargreaves, D. (2007). Teaching as a research based profession: Possibilities and prospects (teacher training agency lecture, 1996). In M. Hammersley (Ed.), *Educational research and evidence-based practice.* Milton Keynes/London: Open University Press/Sage.

Hargreaves, A. (2010). Presentism, individualism, and conservatism: The legacy of Dan Lortie's schoolteacher: A sociological study. *Curriculum Inquiry, 40*(1), 143–154.

Harris, A. (2008). Young women, late modern politics, and the participatory possibilities of online cultures. *Journal of youth studies, 11*(5), 481–495.

Hart, D. (1994). *Authentic assessment: A handbook for educators. Assessment bookshelf series.* ERIC.

Hart, R. (1992). *Children's participation: From tokenism to citizenship.* Florence: UNICEF Innocenti Research Centre.

Hart, R. (2008). Stepping back from 'the ladder': Reflections on a model of participatory work with children *Participation and learning* (pp. 19–31): Springer.

Hastadewi, Y. (2009). Participatory action research with children: Notes from the field. *Children's Geographies, 7*(4), 481–482.

Hattam, R., & Matthews, J. (2012). *Reconciliation as a resource for critical pedagogy.* Thesis, Routledge.

Hattie, J. (2008). *Visible learning: A synthesis of over 800 meta-analyses relating to achievement*: Abingdon: Routledge.

Hayes, D. (2003). Making learning an effect of schooling: Aligning curriculum, assessment and pedagogy. *Discourse: Studies in the Cultural Politics of Education, 24*(2), 225–245.

Hayes, D., Lingard, B., & Mills, M. (2000). Productive pedagogies. *Education Links, 60,* 10–13.

Hayes, D., Mills, M., Christie, P., & Lingard, B. (2006). *Teachers and schooling making a difference: Productive pedagogies, assessment and performance.* Sydney: Allen & Unwin.

Haynes, L., Service, O., Goldacre, B., & Torgerson, D. (2012). *Test, learn, adapt: Developing public policy with randomised controlled trials.* London: Cabinet Office-Behavioural Insights Team.

Hil, R. (2012). *Whackademia: An insider's account of the troubled university.* Sydney: NewSouth Publishing.

Hill, M. (2006). Children's voices on ways of having a voice children's and young people's perspectives on methods used in research and consultation. *Childhood, 13*(1), 69–89.

Hogan, A. (2013). *New policy networks: The role of edu-businesses in the production and enactment of Australian education policy.* Paper presented at the Australian Association for Research in Education Annual Conference. Adelaide, December 2013.

Hooper-Greenhill, E. (2004). *The educational role of the museum* (2nd ed.). London: Routledge.

Hooper-Greenhill, E. (2007). *Museums and education: Purpose, pedagogy, performance.* London: Routledge.

Kane, M., & Trochim, W. (2007). *Concept mapping for planning and evaluation.* Thousand Oaks: Sage.

Karseth, B., & Sivesind, K. (2011). Conceptualising curriculum knowledge within and beyond the national context. In L. Yates & M. Grumet (Eds.), *Curriculum in today's world: Configuring knowledge, identities, work and politics (world yearbook of education 2011).* Abingdon: Routledge.

Kazepides, T. (2012). Education as dialogue. *Educational Philosophy and Theory, 44*(9), 913–925.

Kelly, L., & Bartlett, A. (2009). Young people and museums. http://australianmuseum.net.au/Young-People-and-Museums. Accessed 12 Jan 2014.

Kelly, L., & Fitzgerald, P. (2011). Cooperation, collaboration, challenge: How to work with the changing nature of educational audiences in museums. In N. Mockler & J. Sachs (Eds.), *Rethinking educational practice through reflexive inquiry* (pp. 77–88). Dordrecht: Springer.

Kemmis, S. (2006). Participatory action research and the public sphere. *Educational Action Research, 14*(4), 459–476.

Kimmel, A. (2007). *Ethical issues in behavioral research: Basic and applied perspectives.* Malden: Blackwell.

L'Anson, J. (2011). Childhood and complexity orientation and children's rights, enlarging the performative dilemmas. *Education Inquiry, 2*(3), 373–384.

Ladwig, J. (2009). Working backwards towards curriculum: On the curricular implications of quality teaching. *Curriculum Journal, 20*(3), 271–286.

Ladwig, J., Smith, M., Gore, J., Amosa, W., & Griffiths, T. (2007). *Quality of pedagogy and student achievement: Multi-level replication of authentic pedagogy.* Paper presented at the presentation at the annual conference of the Australian Association for Research in Education, Fremantle.

Lanas, M., & Corbett, M. (2011). Disaggregating student resistances analyzing what students pursue with challenging agency. *Young, 19*(4), 417–434.

Lang, C., Reeve, J., & Woollard, V. (2006). *The responsive museum: Working with audiences in the twenty-first century.* Aldershot: Ashgate Publishing Ltd.

Larsen, M. (2010). Troubling the discourse of teacher centrality: A comparative perspective. *Journal of Education Policy, 25*(2), 207–231.

Lather, P. (1986). Research as praxis. *Harvard Educational Review, 56*(3), 257–277.

Lather, P. (1991). *Getting smart: Feminist research and pedagogy with/in the postmodern.* New York: Routledge.

Lather, P. (2004). Scientific research in education: A critical perspective. *British Educational Research Journal, 30*(6), 759–772.

Lather, P. (2010). *Engaging science policy: From the side of the messy.* New York: Peter Lang.

Leeson, C. (2007). Going round in circles: Key issues in the development of an effective ethical protocol for research involving young children. In A. Campbell & S. Groundwater-Smith (Eds.), *An ethical approach to practitioner research.* London: Routledge.

Lehman-Frisch, S., Authier, J., & Dufaux, F. (2012). 'Draw me your neighbourhood': A gentrified Paris neighbourhood through its children's eyes. *Children's Geographies, 10*(1), 17–34.

Lingard, B. (2010). Policy borrowing, policy learning: Testing times in Australian schooling. *Critical Studies in Education, 51*(2), 129–147.

Lingard, B. (2012). Reshaping the message systems of schooling in the UK. In D. Wyse, V. Baumfield, D. Egan, C. Gallagher, L. Hayward, M. Hulme, R. Leitch, D. Livingstone, I. Menter, & R. Lingard (Eds.), *Creating the curriculum* (p. 1). Abingdon: Routledge.

Lingard, B., & Rawolle, S. (2004). Mediatizing educational policy: The journalistic field, science policy, and cross-field effects. *Journal of Education Policy, 19*(3), 361–380.

Lingard, B., & Sellar, S. (2013). Globalization and sociology of education policy: The case of PISA. In R. Brooks, M. McCormack, & K. Bhopal (Eds.), *Contemporary debates in the sociology of education.* London: Palgrave.

Lingard, B., Hayes, D., Mills, M., & Christie, P. (2003). *Leading learning: Making hope practical in schools.* Maidenhead: Open University Press.

Lingard, B., Rawolle, S., & Taylor, S. (2005). Globalizing policy sociology in education: Working with Bourdieu. *Journal of Education Policy, 20*(6), 759–777.

Lingard, B., Mills, M., & Hayes, D. (2006). Enabling and aligning assessment for learning: Some research and policy lessons from Queensland. *International Studies in Sociology of Education, 16*(2), 83–103.

Linklater, A. (2005). Dialogic politics and the civilising process. *Review of International Studies, 31*(1), 141–154.

Lipman, P. (2004). *High stakes education: Inequality, globalization, and urban school reform.* New York: Routledge.

Livingstone, S. (2008). Learning the lessons of research on youth participation and the internet. *Journal of youth studies, 11*(5), 561–564.

Lolichen, P., Shenoy, J., Shetty, A., Nash, C., & Venkatesh, M. (2006). Children in the driver's seat. *Children's Geographies, 4*(3), 347–357.

Lortie, D. (1975). *Schoolteacher: A sociological study.* Chicago: University of Chicago Press.

Lundgren, U. P. (1983). *Between hope and happening: Text and context in curriculum.* Geelong: Deakin University.

Lundy, L. (2007). 'Voice' is not enough: Conceptualising article 12 of the united nations convention on the rights of the child. *British Educational Research Journal, 33*(6), 927–942.

Lysaght, P., Brown, I., & Westbrook, R. (2009). Integrating image and text: Where one story ends, another begins. *Current Narratives, 1*(1), 1.

Macrine, S. (2010). Critical pedagogy in uncertain times: Hope and possibilities. *Education, politics and public life.* New York: Palgrave Macmillan.

Malone, K. (2011). *Designing and dreaming a child friendly neighbourhood for brooks reach, Dapto.* Bankstown: University of Western Sydney.

Marginson, S. (1997). *Markets in education*: Sydney: Allen & Unwin.

Marginson, S. (2013). The impossibility of capitalist markets in higher education. *Journal of Education Policy, 28*(3), 353–370.

Marginson, S., & Considine, M. (2000). *The enterprise university: Power, governance and reinvention in Australia.* Cambridge: Cambridge University Press.

Marzano, R. J. (2003a). Using data: Two wrongs and a right. *Educational Leadership, 60*(5), 56–61.

Marzano, R. J. (2003b). *What works in schools: Translating research into action.* Alexandria: ASCD.

Marzano, R. J., Pickering, D. J., & Pollock, J. E. (2001). *Classroom instruction that works* (Vol. 5). Alexandria: Association for Supervision and Curriculum Development.

Mayes, E. (2013a). *Speaking for and before students: Becoming in an ethnographic study of student participation in school reform.* Paper presented at the Deleuze. Guattari. Schizoanalysis. Education. Murdoch University, Perth, 11–13 December 2013.

Mayes, E. (2013b). *Students researching teachers' practice: Lines of flight and temporary assemblage conversions in and through a students as co-researchers event.* Paper presented at the AARE Annual Conference. Adelaide, December 2013.

Mayes, E., & Groundwater-Smith, S. (2010). *Year 9 as co-researchers: 'Our gee'd up school'.* Paper presented at the Australian Association for Research in Education. Melbourne. December 2010.

Mayes, E., & Groundwater-Smith, S. (2011). *Authorised resistance in 'our gee'd up school': Students' voices in school reform.* Paper presented at the 5th Biennial Equity Conference: Schooling for futures. Darling Harbour, Sydney, 22–23 August 2011.

McCarthy, T. (1976). *Introduction to J. Habermas Legitimation crisis.* London: Heinemann.

McChesney, R. (1999). Introduction. In N. Chomsky (Ed.), *Profit over people: Neoliberalism and the global order.* New York: Seven Stories Press.

MCEETYA (2008). *Melbourne declaration on educational goals for young Australians.* Canberra: MCEETYA.

McIntyre, D., Pedder, D., & Rudduck, J. (2005). Pupil voice: Comfortable and uncomfortable learnings for teachers. *Research Papers in Education, 20*(2), 149–168.

McKenna, H., Ashton, S., & Keeney, S. (2004). Barriers to evidence based practice in primary care: A review of the literature. *International Journal of Nursing Studies, 41*(4), 369–378.

McMurray, A., & Niens, U. (2012). Building bridging social capital in a divided society: The role of participatory citizenship education. *Education, Citizenship and Social Justice, 7*(2), 207–221.

Midbjer, A., & Day, C. (2007). *Environment and children*. London: Routledge.

Miller, D. (2009). American museums as borderland. In K. Bellamy & C. Oppenheim (Eds.), *Learning to live: Museums, young people and education* (pp. 53–57). London: Institute for Public Policy Research and National Museum Directors' Conference.

Ministerial Council on Education Employment Training and Youth Affairs. (2008). *Melbourne declaration on educational goals for young Australians*. Canberra: MCEETYA.

Missal, B. (1996). *Trust in modern societies: The search for the basis of social order*. Cambridge: Polity Press.

MITRE, D. (2006). Youth as a bridge between home and school comparing student voice and parent involvement as strategies for change. *Education and Urban Society, 38*(4), 455–480.

Mockler, N. (2011a). Becoming and 'being' a teacher: Understanding teacher professional identity. In N. Mockler & J. Sachs (Eds.), *Rethinking educational practice through reflexive inquiry: Essays in honor of Susan Groundwater-Smith* (pp. 123–138). Dordrecht: Springer.

Mockler, N. (2011b). Beyond 'what works': Understanding teacher identity as a practical and political tool. *Teachers and Teaching, 17*(5), 517–528.

Mockler, N. (2013). Teacher professional learning in a neoliberal age: Audit, professionalism and identity. *Australian Journal of Teacher Education, 38*(10), 3.

Mockler, N. (2014). When 'research ethics' become 'everyday ethics': The intersection of inquiry and practice in practitioner research. *Educational Action Research, 22*(2), 146–158.

Mockler, N., & Groundwater-Smith, S. (2012). Weaving the web of professional practice: The coalition of knowledge-building schools. In B. Lingard, P. Thomson, & T. Wrigley (Eds.), *Changing schools: Making a world of difference*. London: Rutledge.

Mockler, N., & Groundwater Smith, S. (Forthcoming). Seeking for the unwelcome truths: Beyond celebration in inquiry-based teacher professional learning. *Teachers and Teaching: Theory and Practice*.

Moons, G. (2007). A sense of wonder: Pedagogies to engage students who live in poverty. *International journal of inclusive education, 11*(3), 301–315.

Munns, G., Sawyer, W., & Cole, B. (Eds.). (2013). *Exemplary teachers of students in poverty*. Abingdon: Routledge.

Nairz-Wirth, E. (2011). Early school leaving: Stigma and diversity. *Managing Diversity and Diversity Studies, 1*(11), 41–48.

Newmann, F. M., Marks, H., Louis, K., Kruse, S., & Gamoran, A. (1996). *Authentic achievement: Restructuring schools for intellectual quality*. San Francisco: Jossey-Bass.

Newton, J. (2010). A tale of two 'qualitys': Reflections on the quality revolution in higher education. *Quality in Higher Education, 16*(1), 51–53.

Noddings, N. (1988). An ethic of caring and its implications for instructional arrangements. *American Journal of Education, 96*(2), 215–230.

Noddings, N. (2003). *Caring: A feminine approach to ethics & moral education*. Berkeley and Los Angeles: University of California Press.

Noddings, N. (2010). Moral education in an age of globalization. *Educational Philosophy and Theory, 42*(4), 390–396.

NSW Department of Education and Training. (2003). *Quality teaching in NSW public schools: Discussion paper*. Sydney: NSW DET.

NSW Department of Education and Training. (2006a). *Quality teaching in NSW public schools: A classroom practice guide*. Sydney: NSW DET.

NSW Department of Education and Training. (2006b). *Quality teaching in NSW public schools: An assessment practice guide*. Sydney: NSW DET.

Nussbaum, M. (2000). *Women and human development: The capabilities approach*. Cambridge: Cambridge University Press.

O'Neill, O. (2002). *A question of trust: The 2002 Reith lectures*. Cambridge: Cambridge University Press.

Office for Human Research Protections. (2009). *Code of federal regulations, title 45, part 46: Protection of human subjects*. Washington, DC: US Department of Health and Human Services.

Ofsted. (2008). *Learning outside the classroom*. London: Ofsted.

Orner, M. (1992). Interrupting the calls for student voice in "liberatory" education: A feminist poststructuralist perspective. In C. Luke & J. Gore (Eds.), *Feminisms and critical pedagogy* (pp. 74–89). New York: Routledge.

Owen, N. (4 September 2013). Christopher Pyne warns teachers against impeding reform. *The Australian*.

Parr, G. (2010). *Inquiry-based professional learning: Speaking back to standard-based reforms*. Queensland: Post-Pressed.

Partanen, A. (29 December 2011). What Americans keep ignoring about Finland's school success. *The Atlantic*. http://www.theatlantic.com/national/archive/2011/12/what-americans-keep-ignoring-about-finlands-school-success/250564/. Accessed 16 Jan 2014.

Payne, L. (2009). Twenty years on: The implementation of the UN convention on the rights of the child in the united kingdom. *Children & Society, 23*(2), 149–155.

Perry, G. (2012). *Behind the shock machine: The untold story of the notorious Milgram psychology experiments*. Brunswick: Scribe Publications.

Polesel, J., Rice, S., & Dulfer, N. (2013). The impact of high-stakes testing on curriculum and pedagogy: A teacher perspective from Australia. *Journal of Education Policy*, 1–18. (Ahead-of-print).

Power, M. (1999). *The audit society: Rituals of verification*. Oxford: Oxford University Press.

Power, M. (2003). Evaluating the audit explosion. *Law & Policy, 25*(3), 185–202.

Ravitch, D. (2013). *Reign of error: The hoax of the privatization movement and the danger to America's public schools*. New York: Random House.

Reicher, S., & Haslam, S. A. (2006). Rethinking the psychology of tyranny: The BBC prison study. *British Journal of Social Psychology, 45*(1), 1–40.

Robinson, C., & Taylor, C. (2007). Theorizing student voice: Values and perspectives. *Improving schools, 10*(1), 5–17.

Roosevelt, T. (31 May 1916). *The weasel words of Mr Wilson: Morning speech at St Louis*.

Rowlands, J., & Rawolle, S. (2013). Neoliberalism is not a theory of everything: A Bourdieuian analysis of illusio in educational research. *Critical Studies in Education, 53*(3), 260–272

Rudduck, J. (2007). *Student voice, student engagement, and school reform International handbook of student experience in elementary and secondary school* (pp. 587–610). Dordrecht: Springer.

Rudduck, J., & Fielding, M. (2006). Student voice and the perils of popularity. *Educational Review, 58*(2), 219–231.

Sachs, J., & Mockler, N. (2012). Performance cultures of teaching: Threat or opportunity? In C. Day (Ed.), *Routledge international handbook on teacher and school development*. Abingdon: Routledge.

Sahlberg, P. (2011). *Finnish lessons*. New York: Teachers College Press.

Santos, D. (2012). The politics of storytelling: Unfolding the multiple layers of politics in (P)AR publications. *Educational Action Research, 20*(1), 113–128.

Scribner, S. (18 September 2013). Diane Ravitch: Testing and vouchers hurt our schools. Here's what works. *Salon*. http://www.salon.com/2013/09/18/diane_ravitch_testing_and_vouchers_hurt_our_schools_heres_what_works/singleton/. Accessed 16 Jan 2014.

Seiler, G. (2013). Reconstructing science curricula through student voice and choice. *Education and Urban Society, 45*(3), 362–384.

Sellar, S., & Lingard, B. (2013). Pisa and the expanding role of the OECD in global educational governance. In H.-D. Meyer & A. Benavot (Eds.), *Pisa, power, and policy: The emergence of global educational governance* (pp. 185–206). Oxford: Symposium Books.

Sen, A. (1999). The possibility of social choice. *American Economic Review, 85*(1), 1–24.

Serriere, S., & Mitra, D. (2012). Critical issues and contexts of student voice in the united states. In C. Day (Ed.), *The Routledge international handbook of teacher and school development* (pp. 223–232). Abingdon: Routledge.

Sherif, M., Harvey, O., White, B., Hood, W., & Sherif, C. (1961). *The robbers cave experiment: Intergroup conflict and cooperation.* Middletown: Wesleyan University Press.

Shier, H. (2001). Pathways to participation: Openings, opportunities and obligations. *Children & Society, 15*(2), 107–117.

Sidanius, J., & Pratto, F. (2001). *Social dominance: An intergroup theory of social hierarchy and oppression.* Cambridge: Cambridge University Press.

Sikes, P., & Gale, K. (2006). Narrative approaches to educational research. http://www.edu.plymouth.ac.uk/resined/narrative/narrativehome.htm. Accessed 24 April 2013.

Slavin, R. (2002). Evidence-based education policies: Transforming educational practice and research. *Educational researcher, 31*(7), 15–21.

Smit, B., Plomp, L., & Ponte, P. (December 2010). *Pupils and teacher as co-researchers: Conditions for equal voices.* Paper presented at the AARE Annual Conference, University of Melbourne.

Smyth, J., & McInerney, P. (2012). *From silent witnesses to active agents.* New York: Peter Lang.

Starratt, R. J. (1994). *Building an ethical school: A practical response to the moral crisis in schools.* London: RoutledgeFalmer.

Starratt, R. J. (2003). *Centering educational administration: Cultivating meaning, community, responsibility.* London: Lawrence Erlbaum Associates.

Stake, R. (1995). *The art of case study research.* Thousand Oaks: Sage.

Stake, R. (2005). Qualitative case studies. In N. Denzin & Y. Lincoln (Eds.). *The Sage handbook of qualitative research* (3rd ed.). Thousand Oaks: Sage.

State Library of NSW. (2011). Blog post: Minister opens new learning space at the state library. http://blog.sl.nsw.gov.au/media/index.cfm/2011/5/12/minister-opens-new-learning-space-at-the-state-library. Accessed 20 Feb 2014.

Stein, J., Garibay, C., & Wilson, K. (2008). Engaging immigrant audiences in museums. *Museums & Social Issues, 3*(2), 179–196.

Steiner-Khamsi, G. (2004). *The global politics of educational borrowing and lending.* New York: Teachers College Press.

Stenhouse, L. (1975). *An introduction to curriculum research and development.* London: Heinemann.

Stenhouse, L. (1981). What counts as research? *British Journal of Educational Studies, 29*(2), 103–114.

Stenhouse, L. (1983). Research as a basis for teaching. In L. Stenhouse (Ed.), *Authority, education and emancipation.* London: Heinemann.

Stiggins, R. (2004). New assessment beliefs for a new school mission. *Phi Delta Kappan, 86*(1), 22–27.

Stobart, G. (2008). *Testing times: The uses and abuses of assessment.* Abingdon: Routledge.

Stoecklin, D. (2013). Theories of action in the field of child participation: In search of explicit frameworks. *Childhood, 20*(4), 443–457.

Stoll, L. (2002). *No quick fixes: Perspectives on schools in difficulty.* Abingdon: Routledge.

Stronach, I. (2002). *Progressivism versus the audit culture: The continuing story of Summerhill and the OFSTED inspectors.* Paper presented at the European Educational Research Conference. Lisbon, September 2002.

Taber, K. (2013). *Classroom-based research and evidence-based practice: An introduction.* Thousand Oaks: Sage.

Taines, C. (2012). Educational or social reform? Students inform the debate over improving urban schools. *Education and Urban Society, 44*(3), 247–273.

Taubman, P. M. (2009). *Teaching by numbers: Deconstructing the discourse of standards and accountability in education.* New York: Routledge.

Taubman, P. (2011). Making nothing happen: Affective life under audit. In L. Yates & M. Grumet (Eds.), *Curriculum in today's world: Configuring knowledge, identities, work and politics (world yearbook of education 2011)*. Abingdon: Routledge.

Taylor, C., & Robinson, C. (2009). Student voice: Theorising power and participation. *Pedagogy, Culture & Society, 17*(2), 161–175.

Teaching, T. (2010). Ofsted and pupil contribution. http://www.teachingtimes.com/articles/pupil-contribution-community2.htm. Accessed 15 March 2013.

Terkel, S. (2008). *Touch and go: A memoir*. New York: The New Press.

Thompson, G. (2010). Acting, accidents and performativity: Challenging the hegemonic good student in secondary schools. *British Journal of Sociology of Education, 31*(4), 413–430.

Thompson, G. (2011). *Who is the good high school student?* Amhurst: Cambria Press.

Thompson, G. (2012). *Effects of NAPLAN (National Assessment Program—Literacy and Numeracy): Executive summary*. Murdoch: Murdoch University.

Thompson, G., & Cook, I. (2012a). The logics of good teaching in an audit culture: A Deleuzian analysis. *Educational Philosophy and Theory*, 1–16. (ahead-of-print).

Thompson, G., & Cook, I. (2012b). Spinning in the NAPLAN ether: 'Postscript on the control societies' and the seduction of education in Australia. *Deleuze Studies* (In Press).

Thompson, G., & Cook, I. (2014). Education policy-making and time. *Journal of Education Policy, 29*(5), 700–715.

Thomson, P., & Gunter, H. (2006). From 'consulting pupils' to 'pupils as researchers': A situated case narrative. *British Educational Research Journal, 32*(6), 839–856.

Thornberg, R. (2009). The moral construction of the good pupil embedded in school rules. *Education, citizenship and social justice, 4*(3), 245–261.

Todd, S., & Safstrom, C. (2008). Democracy, education and conflict: Re-thinking respect and the place of the ethical. *Journal of Educational Controversy*, (online Journal only). http://www.wce.wwu.edu/Resources/CEP/eJournal/v003n001/a012.shtml. Accessed 16 Jan 2014.

Tonta, Y. (2008). Libraries and museums in the flat world: Are they becoming virtual destinations? *Library Collections, Acquisitions, and Technical Services, 32*(1), 1–9.

Torrance, H., & Pryor, J. (2001). Developing formative assessment in the classroom: Using action research to explore and modify theory. *British Educational Research Journal, 27*(5), 615–631.

Tovey, J. (14 January 2014). Educators take minister to task over curriculum review. *Sydney Morning Herals*.

Tripp, D. (1993). *Critical incidents in teaching: Developing professional judgement*. London: Routledge.

Tucker, S. (2013). Considerations on the involvement of young people as co-inquirers in abuse and neglect research. *Journal of Youth Studies, 16*(2), 272–285.

Tzibazi, V. (2013). Participatory action research with young people in museums. *Museum Management and Curatorship, 28*(2), 153–171.

UNICEF. (2012). Convention on the rights of the child—Frequently asked questions. http://www.unicef.org/crc/index_30229.html. Accessed 17 April 2012.

United Nations. (1989). *Convention on the rights of the child*. Geneva: United Nations.

University of Sydney. (2001). The management and evaluation of coursework teaching. http://sydney.edu.au/policies/showdoc.aspx?recnum=PDOC2012/242&RendNum=0. Accessed 23 Jan 2014.

University of Tasmania. (2010). Student evaluation of teaching and learning policy. http://www.utas.edu.au/__data/assets/pdf_file/0009/227493/SETL-Policy.pdf. Accessed 23 Jan 2014.

University of the Sunshine Coast. (2012). Student Evaluation of Teaching and Courses (SETAC) academic policy. http://www.usc.edu.au/university/governance-and-executive/policies-and-procedures/student-evaluation-of-teaching-and-courses-setac-academic-policy. Accessed 23 Jan 2014.

University of Wollongong. (2007a). Subject evaluation questions. http://www.uow.edu.au/about/teaching/subjectsurvey/UOW033839.html. Accessed 23 Jan 2014.

University of Wollongong. (2007b). Teacher evaluation procedure. http://www.uow.edu.au/about/policy/UOW074145.html. Accessed 23 Jan 2014.

University of Wollongong. (2008). Subject evaluation guidelines. http://www.uow.edu.au/about/teaching/subjectsurvey/UOW045696.html. Accessed 23 Jan 2014.

Valenti, M. (2002). Creating the classroom of the future. *Educause Review, 37*(5), 55–62.

Vandenbroeck, M., Roets, G., & Roose, R. (2012). Why the evidence-based paradigm in early childhood education and care is anything but evident. *European Early Childhood Education Research Journal, 20*(4), 537–552.

Victoria, U. (2007). Student evaluation survey. http://wcf.vu.edu.au/governancepolicy/PDF/POA070702000.PDF. Accessed 23 Jan 2014.

Walker, R., Schratz, B., & Egg, P. (2008). Seeing beyond violence. In P. Thomson (Ed.), *Doing visual research with children and young people* (pp. 164–174). London: Routledge.

Weil, S. (2002). *Making museums matter*. Washington, DC: Smithsonian Institution Press.

Wetton, N., & McWhirter, J. (1998). Images and curriculum development in health education. In J. Prosser (Ed.), *Image-based research: A sourcebook for qualitative researchers* (pp. 263–283). London: Falmer Press.

White, R. (2007). *Youth gangs, violence and anti-social behaviour*. West Perth: Australian Research Alliance for Children and Youth.

Whitty, G., & Wisby, E. (2007). Whose voice? An exploration of the current policy interest in pupil involvement in school decision-making. *International Studies in Sociology of Education, 17*(3), 303–319.

Wiggins, G. (1990). The case for authentic assessment. *ERIC Document Reproduction Service No. ED, 328,* 611.

Wiggins, G. (1993). *Assessing student performance*. San Francisco: Jossey Bass.

Wilks, J. (2010). Child-friendly cities: A place for active citizenship in geographical and environmental education. *International Research in Geographical and Environmental Education, 19*(1), 25–38.

Wisby, E. (2011). Student voice and new models of teacher professionalism. *The Student Voice Handbook: Bridging the Academic/Practitioner Divide,* 31.

Woodhead, M. (2010). Foreword. In B. Percy-Smith & N. Thomas (Eds.), *A handbook of children and young people's participation: Perspectives from theory and practice* (pp. xix–xxii). London: Routledge.

World, B. (2011). Empowerment: Overview. http://web.worldbank.org/WBSITE/EXTERNAL/TOPICS/EXTPOVERTY/EXTEMPOWERMENT/0,,contentMDK:20272299~pagePK:210058~piPK:210062~theSitePK:486411~isCURL:Y,00.html. Accessed 1 Nov 2013.

Worts, D. (2011). Museums rising to the challenge of "Social Relevance Circa 2012". *Museums & Social Issues, 6*(2), 219–227.

Yates, L., & Grumet, M. (2011). Curriculum in today's world: Configuring knowledge, identities, work and politics. In L. Yates & M. Grumet (Eds.), *Curriculum in today's world: Configuring knowledge, identities, work and politics (world yearbook of education 2011)*. Abingdon: Routledge.

Young, L. (2002). Rethinking heritage: Cultural policy and inclusion. In R. Sandell (Ed.), *Museums, society, inequality* (pp. 203–212). Abingdon: Routledge

Index

A

Accountability, 7, 22, 26, 30, 32, 35
Action research, 66
Adams, G.L., 144
Agency, 17, 19, 40, 55, 84, 100, 105, 109, 120, 132, 155, 156
Alderson, P., 127, 154
Aldridge, J., 141
Alegounarias, T., 27
Anderson, D., 71
Apple, M.W., 142, 149, 155
Apprenticeship, 54, 112
Approaches, 8, 10, 11, 25, 27, 33, 38, 45, 48, 94, 132, 139, 143, 145, 147
Ash, D., 80
Assessment, 26, 29, 30, 34, 38, 82, 136, 139, 141, 147–150
Atkinson, E., 3, 26, 28
Audience research, 10, 70, 72, 120
Audit cultures, 8, 25
Authentic participation, 22
Authority, 3, 15, 113, 136, 152

B

Ball, S., 31, 142, 149
Barratt, R., 91
Bartlett, A., 82
Beane, J., 142
Benitez, M., 149
Berger, J., 48
Bernstein, B., 140, 142
Biesta, G., 3, 6, 18, 19, 26, 28–30, 32, 42, 54, 110
Black, P., 147
Blackmore, J., 42
Boud, D., 147
Bourdieu, P., 26, 140

Bragg, S., 91
Brooks, R., 122
Busch, R., 43
Butterfield, L., 57

C

Cahill, C., 89
Cammarota, J., 89
Campbell, C., 53
Campbell, E., 86, 87
Carr, W., 133
Celebration, 133
Chaffee, J., 28
Chambers, D., 119
Cheminais, R., 41
Christensen, L., 141
Clark, A., 113
Classroom implications of student voice work, 140
Classroom practice, 6, 10, 26, 29, 36, 37, 133, 134, 137, 139, 140, 145, 150
Cochran-Smith, M., 134
Collin, P., 121
Colucci, E., 75, 116
Community, 8, 13, 33, 48, 82, 89–91, 93, 121, 132, 143, 151, 155
Compliance, 6, 7, 10, 17, 25, 26, 32, 47, 131
Concept mapping, 114, 122
Connell, R.W., 25, 30
Considine, M., 93
Cook, I., 29, 148
Cook-Sather, A., 95
Corbett, M., 55
Costa, A., 148
Crebert, G., 154
Critical moments, 56, 59, 60, 62
Criticality, 42

© Springer International Publishing Switzerland 2015
N. Mockler, S. Groundwater-Smith, *Engaging with Student Voice in Research, Education and Community,* DOI 10.1007/978-3-319-01985-7

Printed by Printforce, the Netherlands